THE PRANKSTER AND THE CONSPIRACY

ALSO BY ADAM GORIGHTLY

The Shadow Over Santa Susana: Black Magic,
Mind Control, and "The Manson Family" Mythos

THE PRANKSTER &
THE CONSPIRACY

THE STORY OF KERRY THORNLEY AND
HOW HE MET OSWALD AND INSPIRED
THE COUNTERCULTURE

Adam Gorightly
Foreword by Robert Anton Wilson

PARAVIEW PRESS

New York

**The Prankster and the Conspiracy: The Story of Kerry
Thornley and How He Met Oswald and Inspired the
Counterculture**
Copyright © 2003 Adam Gorightly
All rights reserved. No part of this book may be
used or reproduced in any manner whatsoever without
prior written permission except in the case of brief
quotations embodied in critical articles or reviews.
For information, address Paraview, P.O. Box 416,
Old Chelsea Station, New York, NY 10113-0416,
or visit our website at www.paraview.com.

Book design by smythtype
Author photo by Andrew Taylor of Tao-Productions.com

ISBN: 1-931044-66-X
Library of Congress Catalog Card Number: 2003112931

This book is dedicated to Jim Keith and Ron Bonds

CONTENTS

The Monster in the Labyrinth

*Ye have locked yerselves up in cages of fear—and,
behold, do ye now complain that ye lack FREEDOM!
Ye have cast out yer brothers for devils and now
complain ye, lamenting, that ye've been left to fight
   alone.*

—"EPISTLE TO THE PARANOIDS," *The Gospel According to Fred*
   BY KERRY THORNLEY

Kerry Thornley wrote those words in the mid-1960s and within 10
years he had become a clinical paranoid himself, in the judgment
of almost all of his friends, including Dr. Robert Newport, a psychiatrist who had known Kerry since high school. The moral of this
seems to me: take great care which nut cases you dare to mock, for
you may become one of them.

   I do not write in any spirit of smugness or superiority. I
became somewhat paranoid myself, for a while there, or at least
experienced acute anxiety attacks. For several months I literally
could not leave my house without looking around to see if Kerry
crouched behind a bush waiting to shoot me.

   You see, he had become convinced that I worked for the CIA
and served as one of his "managers" or "brainwashers," but I
thought I worked as a freelance writer and considered myself his
friend. As his letters to me grew increasingly hostile and denunciatory, I began to fear that he might have graduated from "weirded
out" to "dangerous."

   This now seems silly to me—an overreaction—but the violence
and paranoia of the Nixon years made everybody in this country
feel a bit jumpy. A Black Panther leader in my part of Chicago

seemed to have gotten shot by the local police while sedated; the extreme Right and extreme Left both had wild conspiracy theories about everybody else; anti-war meetings, anti-segregation meetings, even pot-legalization meetings all had people making nervous jokes about who among us the government had infiltrated to report on our Thoughtcrimes. The government not only appeared irrational and out of control, but so did a large part of the population.

I finally moved to Ireland to start a new life as an expatriate, and my worries about Kerry executing me for "brainwashing" him made up only a microscopic part of my motive. The whole country seemed a bit funny in the head and I had to hide out and lie low for a while. *Silence, exile, and cunning,* as Joyce had advised.

Looking back, I feel amused and humbled. Like Kerry, I had satirized the paranoids before the sheer number of them frightened me into acting just like one of them.

I remember my last phone conversation with Kerry, during which he announced that just a week earlier I had come to Atlanta, argued with him about my alleged CIA connections, spiked his drink with LSD, and brainwashed him again. I told him that I had not left San Francisco in months, and that if he had a bad trip the previous week then somebody else gave him the acid, not me. I insisted on this as persuasively as I could.

Finally, Kerry relented—a bit. "Well, maybe you believe that," he said. "But that means your bosses have been fucking with your head and implanting false memories in you too!"

How do you argue that you haven't had your head altered? "Look," I said, "I'll put my wife Arlen on. She'll tell you I haven't left here in months."

"That won't prove anything," he said with the calm certitude of a Grand Master announcing checkmate. "They probably fixed *her* head too."

I don't remember the rest of the conversation. I felt lost in an Escher painting.

A few weeks, or a few months, before or after that conversation, the police found a young woman raped and murdered two doors from the house where Arlen and I lived. A few days before or after that atrocity I attended a meeting of the physics/consciousness research group in which the assembled Ph.D.s seriously discussed a quantum model in which the universe contains only one electron, and everything else, including this seemingly solid Earth, our own bodies, and our "minds" (if we still think we have "minds") results from the virtual interactions of virtual particles, or of probability waves.

So Arlen and I packed up and moved to a land where the weirdest critter, a six-foot-tall white rabbit, seldom roams far from the fens and farmlands.

> I'm only kidding—not.
> —Madonna, *Truth or Dare*

But let us, as the Chinese say, draw our chairs closer to the fire and examine this soberly.

All the above happened because Kerry and I, with a few others, invented a new religion, and because Kerry and I and a hell of a lot of others dared to doubt the official "lone nut" theory of the JFK assassination.

Perhaps I should say something about the religion before getting into the even murkier waters of the politics.

We called the religion Discordianism and its central catma (other, and hence lesser, religions have dogmas or absolute beliefs; Discordianism only has catmas or relative meta-beliefs) declares "All affirmations are true in some sense, false in some sense, meaningless in some sense, true and false in some sense, true and meaningless in some sense, false and meaningless in some sense, and true and false and meaningless in some sense." We owe this Divine Revelation to Gregory Hill (Malaclypse the Younger), the chief architect of Discordian atheology.

In my ministry I have added a rider promising that if you repeat this catma 666 times you will achieve Supreme Enlightenment, in some sense.

Many people consider Discordianism a complicated joke disguised as a new religion. I prefer to consider it a new religion disguised as a complicated joke.

Others consider Discordianism an American form of Zen Buddhism. I think Kerry held that view most of the time.

Whether one considers Discordianism a joke, a new religion, or Yankee Zen, it emphatically does not belong in the same arena as Aristotelian logic or criminal law, yet the life of Kerry Thornley dragged it into those precincts and I can find no way to disentangle them in discussing him. Everybody who ever looked into "the Thornley case" feels a strong need for basic either/or answers to such questions as: Guilty or innocent? Sane or insane? Victim of the CIA or victim of his own delusions?

All I can say consists of a devout wish that logic could stretch to include a maybe, or a phalanx of probabilities, between the Aristotelian yes and no, and that our law could include the Scotch "not proven" between guilty and innocent.

I think it entirely possible that Kerry went bananas on his own, due to genetics and/or traumatic early imprints and/or too damned much LSD and/or other causes unknown, with no help from the CIA at all. I also think it entirely possible that the CIA did subject Kerry—and his Marine Corps buddy Lee Harvey Oswald— to some form of *Manchurian Candidate* mind control and that his seemingly "psychotic" words and actions represented an intelligent man's attempts to break the strings of his puppet masters and find his way back to a world that made sense again.

In short, I regard all his brilliant satires and all of his "psychotic" rants as true in some sense, false in some sense, meaningless in some sense, true and false in some sense, true and meaningless in some sense, false and meaningless in some sense, and true and false and meaningless in some sense.

For instance, you will read in this book about Kerry's "delusions" concerning fascist manipulations of the CIA and/or Naval Intelligence. Pure nonsense, right?

Wrong. Let me illuminize you a bit.

Nazi worms began to infest the U.S. way back in 1945, when General Rheinhard Gehlen, Hitler's chief of Soviet Intelligence, surrendered to the U.S. Army, after first prudently burying several truckloads of "inside information" about the Soviet Union at a secret location.

Gehlen seems not only a master spy but a wizard negotiator. Within a week, he got out of his Nazi uniform and into a U.S. Army general's uniform; the U.S. intelligence services, in return, got the info about the Soviets, including access to Gehlen's agents in the Soviet government—a group of Mystical Tsarists who had infiltrated both the Red Army and the KGB.

You see, their leader and Gehlen's major "asset," General Andrei Vlassov, had a fervent belief, not just in common or garden Tsarism but especially in the Mystical Tsarism espoused in the later half of the 19th century by the anti-Semitic novelist Dostoyevsky and even more by Konstantin Pobedonostsev, an advisor to two tsars, Alexander III and Nicholas II.

Pobedonostsev, popularly called "the Grand Inquisitor" because of the vast platoons of spies, snoops, agents provocateur, and informers he unleashed upon the Russian people, combined theological obsessions with reactionary politics—always an explosive and nefarious mixture.

Mystical Tsarism deserves a whole book in itself, especially since it now rules our own country; but we must remain brief here. This holy religion, or superstition—as you will—has two major tenets: (1) The tsar is guided by God and can do no wrong, and (2) Science "is" cold and inhuman, faith "is" warm and human; therefore we should ignore reason and guide ourselves by faith in the tsar, our "Little Father," who receives his orders directly from a gaseous vertebrate of astronomical heft called "God."

I don't think any of Pobedonostsev's crew actually believed in the Tooth Fairy, though.

General Gehlen and General Vlassov formed what became the *Gehlenapparat*, the CIA's main source of info on Soviet affairs; Gehlen became the fulcrum of the CIA's "Soviet penetration" sector, working under James Jesus Angleton, chief of Counter-Intelligence, breeder of prize orchids, lover of the arts, and a devout Catholic.

Since the U.S. government based its foreign policies on CIA reports, and the CIA based its Soviet reports on Gehlen and some other former Nazis, plus a crew of Mystical Tsarists, as filtered and interpreted by a Papist intellectual, the U.S. government's ideas and actions became increasingly "weird," bizarre, and frightening, in the view of the rest of the world. The results seem very sad and very funny. In a nutshell, most of the planet thinks we've gone batshit crazy. *Tsarists and Nazis and spooks, oh my!*

As Harry Browne, Libertarian Party candidate for president in 2000, wrote in July 2003, "The whole world is now afraid of America, and America is afraid of the whole world."

Although James Jesus Angleton served as Gehlen's alleged supervisor, data indicates that the *Gehlenapparat* engaged in many activities, including kidnapping, extortion, murder, etc., about which Angleton either did not know or devoutly did not want to know.

But James J. Angleton seems to me a pathological case of some sort himself; he often hid his middle name because it revealed his half-Hispanic genes. An exceptionally intelligent and sensitive student of modern literature while at Yale, Angleton adored Ezra Pound, T.S. Eliot, I.A. Richards, e e cummings, and other superstars of Modernism; he met most of them personally. They collectively influenced Angleton's fascination with multiple perspectives, Byzantine ambiguity, and the eternal uncertainty of all inferences and "interpretations."

These modernist tendencies, which also appeared in science

and philosophy at the same time, blossomed into obsessions and, perhaps, raging madness when Angleton systematically applied them to the spy game. After all, modernism really begins with Wilde's "The Reality of Masks" and Yeats's hermetic theory that the world we know emerges from interactions of Mask, Anti-Mask, Self, and Anti-Self: which may or may not fit all of us or all the world but certainly fits the world of spooks and snoops that Angleton created.

> Records indicate that the Oswald who enlisted in the Marines was 5'11". Comrade Oswald, who went to Russia, was 5'6" while the dead version measured in at 5'9".
> —Richard Belzer, *UFOs, JFK and Elvis*

Another CIA officer, Edward Petty, described Angleton as "a lone wolf" and "a strange bird"; every other source I have found bluntly calls him "paranoid." He suspected everybody else in the CIA, and in "our" government generally, of being KGB moles, and he operated with so much modernist ambiguity and hidden trapdoors that, in Petty's words, "nobody really knows" what he was doing most of the time. In short, he became as esoteric as the poets he admired, and remade the CIA and, increasingly, our whole nation into a theater of impenetrable mystery.

A.J. Weberman, a leading Kennedy assassination buff, thinks Angleton personally organized the JFK hit, an idea also strongly hinted at by Norman Mailer's documentary novel, *Harlot's Ghost*, in which Angleton appears as "Hugh Montague." If James Jesus really arranged the JFK assassination, he had probably identified Kennedy as the top Soviet mole of all, at least to his own satisfaction.

Why not? Angleton had Tsarist agents in all sorts of nooks and crannies of the Soviet system, and he knew the KGB was smart enough and tireless enough to reciprocate by planting their own Masks and Anti-Masks in his own backyard, or maybe under his bed at night. According to Edward Jay Epstein, J.J.A.'s endless search for Soviet moles nearly destroyed the CIA itself. Certainly, everybody in "the Company" learned to distrust everybody else.

Imagine a *U.S. Caine* with not one Queeg as captain, but a whole crew of Queegs, each worrying about what the others might be plotting. Angleton created that ship of shape-shifters in the CIA and then by osmosis it spread through the government, evolving into the Tsarist occupation we now endure.

In short, the government cannot trust us, because it can never know with absolute certainty what mischief we may hatch; and every sentence we speak into a bugged phone may have as many possible meanings as Eliot's "The rose and the fire are one."

"Trust No One," the motto of *The X-Files*, seems the only safe rule in the world Angleton created.

We even have a tsar of our own now, who supervises American medicine. Allegedly, this official knows what drugs, herbs, etc., you should use for your medical problems better than your doctor knows, and our tsar knows this without doing any physical examination, blood pressure readings, other scientific tests, etc., that your doctor does, and often from a distance of 3000 miles—without even looking at you.

This makes sense *if and only if* we have a devout faith that our tsar, like the Russian tsars, receives guidance directly from "God"; the government accordingly spends more and more of our tax money financing "faith-based organizations." Without faith we might relapse into scientific or rational thinking.

> Tsarism represents an intermediate form between
> European monarchism and Asian despotism,
> being, possibly, closer to the latter of these two.
> —Leon Trotsky,
> *Russia's Social Development and Tsarism*

How much of this did I dream up the way Kerry Thornley (I still insist) imagined my own CIA activities?

For objective info on the *Gehlenapparat,* and Nazi/CIA

links, see *The Yankee and Cowboy War* by Boston University historian Carl Oglesby (Berkeley Medallion, NY, 1977). On fascist/CIA/Mafia links, excellent books include *The Strange Death of God's Banker* by Foot and della Torre (Orbis, London, 1984) and *The Calvi Affair* by Larry Gurwin of the *Financial Times* (Pan, London, 1984).

CIA/Mafia "ghost banks" and their strange links with real banks, including Chase Manhattan, are discussed amply in *In Banks We Trust* (Doubleday, NY, 1984) by Penny Lernoux.

For CIA involvement in general—and Angleton's personal involvement—in the JFK hit see ajweberman.com, probably the largest site on the Internet.

Our most recent tsar's responsibility for barbaric war crimes—as bad as any of Thornley's "fantasies"—appears well documented in "Overwhelming Force," by Seymour Hersh, *The New Yorker*, May 22, 2000.

Or you can find most of the data on Tsarist/fascist infiltrations of "our" government, in one form or another, by simply surfing the Web. Set your search engine for "Rheinhold Gehlen," "Cisalpine Bank," "Licio Gelli," and "Gladio" to start with and follow the links where they lead you. I promise you will find the journey as startling as anything in this book.

I have no certitude about how "crazy" to consider Kerry Thornley on any given day of any year, but I don't believe he ever became a simple damned fool. He understood the government of this country better than 99 percent of its citizens.

ROBERT ANTON WILSON
Santa Cruz, August 2003

Great Conspiracy Theorists Think Alike!

Back in the early 80s, I happened upon a flyer that boldly declared: "The CIA Killed JFK!" As this notion had never before entered my head, it promptly ignited a fire that, in due time, raged completely out of control. Not long after that I found myself mired knee-deep in Kennedy assassination hoopla, delving through the muck and dreck of the many conspiracy theories swirling around JFK's gaping head wound.

I was a serious student of the case at first, filled with righteous indignation over the apparent *coup d'etat* that had taken place in Dealey Plaza on November 22, 1963, when the proverbial crown was blasted from Camelot's head, spattering blood and pinkish brain matter all across the presidential Lincoln Town Car; a figurative nightmare on Elm Street forever marked by an "X" in the middle of the Dallas thoroughfare, immortalizing that infamous spot.

After awhile, though, my insatiable curiosity mutated into perverse obsession. Soon, I had gone so overboard in my preoccupation with the case that I left no stone unturned or theory unexplored, no matter how implausible or improbable. This could be termed a one-person circle jerk, leading to no ultimate conclusion, just a form of entertainment masquerading as intellectual pursuit.

One of my favorite wacky theories from this period was that of a gentleman named George C. Thomson, who garnered his obligatory fifteen minutes of fame with a brain-boggling theory which postulated that JFK didn't actually die in Dallas but went on to live in self-imposed exile, occasionally making an appearance at Truman Capote parties. As opposed to popular history, Thomson suggested that JFK didn't actually have his cranium partially catapulted across Dealey Plaza that dark November day, but in his place Officer J.D. Tippit—impersonating President Kennedy (as part of his patriotic duty)—took hot lead in the head, which rendered the aforementioned Tippit exceedingly dead. The real assassin of JFK a la Tippit (as Thomson's revisionist history went on to suggest) was none other than Vice President Johnson, who with machine gun a-blazing went rat-a-tat-tat, causing Tippit's brain to go splat all over Jackie's pillbox hat.

I eventually O.D.'d on this and other JFK assassination theories, many of them not only off the map but some soaring through deep space on a collision course for the Planet Bonkers.

And then along came Kerry Thornley at a period in my life when I was becoming just a bit jaded regarding all this JFK assassination doo-da, which—as previously stated—had became a sort of intellectual jerk-off for yours truly. Nonetheless, something seemed to draw me to Thornley's writings. There was a spirit and energy there, even if most of the time I wasn't quite sure what he was getting at, or if he was totally off his rocker.

I first became acquainted with Kerry's curious writings through such alternative sources as *FactSheet 5* and *Off The Deep End*, this during the halcyon days of the "zine revolution," which was—in essence—a precursor to the emergence of the Internet and all the weird shit (as well as vital information!) that can be found there now on a daily basis.

Like many another purveyor of the odd and arcane, Mike Gunderloy's wonderful *FactSheet 5* introduced me to this wide, weird world of self-published periodicals pushing the envelope of self-expression. Gunderloy provided an awesome service, single-handedly reviewing several hundred mags for his bi-monthly publication, this done on a shoestring budget with love, sweat, and blood. When Gunderloy finally used a calculator and figured out how much he was making, it came out to something ridiculous like 23 cents an hour. He eventually had a nervous breakdown, which brought his intrepid enterprise to an abrupt and unfortunate end.

Whatever the case, it was through *FactSheet 5* that I first became acquainted with Kerry Wendell Thornley (aka Omar Khayyam Ravenhurst aka The Right Rev. Jesses Sump aka Ho Chi Zen—not to mention the Bull Goose of Limbo!) and his regularly appearing column "Conspiracy Corner" in addition to Kerry's own self-published broadsides such as *Kultcha, Decadent Worker, Out of Order, Folk-Write* and *The Cactus Flower Gazette,* among many, many others. At the time, I didn't know quite what to make of Kerry's always-interesting rants: either the guy was tuned into things that most of us were totally unaware of—or he was nuts. Or both. (As I later came to discover, probably *both*...)

So, who the hell was this guy, anyway? And why were his curious writings suddenly turning up all over the alternative press? The more I immersed myself in the zine culture and conspiracy research network, the more ever-present Thornley's name and writings became. In time, I became an ardent admirer of the man, whom I considered to be the ultimate embodiment of a free thinker with some "out there" ideas, a true renaissance man of the fringes.

As anyone familiar with the collected rantings of Kerry Thornley can well attest, he embodied (upon occasion) the 60s spirit in the role of the archetypal Trickster/Prankster, similar to other luminaries from the period, namely Ken Kesey and his Merry Pranksters, Tim Leary, and Wavy Gravy, to name but a few. So when Kerry started making extraordinary claims about brain implants and mind-control conspiracies in the late 70s, many thought it was just a spoof or goof that Omar Khayyam Ravenhurst was riffing upon, simply another screwy vehicle with which to sow the seeds of Discordianism, the spoof religion that Kerry and longtime pal Greg Hill cooked up in a southern California bowling alley in the late 50s.

The Discordian Society—which was as much (or even more) the brainchild of Greg Hill—influenced a multitude of heads from the 60s generation who had grown jaded with organized religion, but were nonetheless looking for their own self-styled ashram in an era when spiritual truth-seeking and rebellion went hand in hand. Enter Discordianism and other irreligious movements. The type of people who could relate to the *Principia Discordia* were the same folks seeing God in a slice of bologna while blazing on a hit of Mr. Natural—and laughing their fucking heads off in the process.

In the end, regrettably, much of what Kerry said and writ has fallen by the wayside, though those who knew him will never forget him.

Kerry's vibrant memory, and a smattering of his always entertaining (though not always entirely decipherable) writings can still be unearthed on the Internet, though printed matter at this point is harder to get a hold of, particularly with the recent death of Ron Bonds of IllumiNet Press, sole publisher of Kerry's books during the 90s.

Say what you will about Kerry—crazy, paranoid, brilliant—but the fact remains that the man was a raging dynamo and one of the great leaders of counterculture thought, who produced an amazing amount of material and spread his gospel throughout the "margins of the fringe." And although Kerry's isn't a household name, he continues to influence this so-called "lunatic fringe" of artists and writers who follow the beat of their own internal drummer, however wacky or discordant it may be.

It is in this spirit that I will now bang my own somewhat cacophonous drum for the late Kerry Wendell Thornley. I encourage you all to bang along, as well.

As the saying goes: "Live like Norton!"

TIMELINE

April 17, 1938: Kerry Thornley is born in Los Angeles to Kenneth and Helen Thornley.

1956: Kerry meets Greg Hill and Bob Newport while attending California High School (CalHi) in East Whittier, California.

1957: Kerry Graduates from CalHi. That same year, Kerry and Greg Hill form the Discordian Society.

1958: Kerry attends the University of Southern California as a journalism student.

1959: Kerry enlists in the Marine Corps and meets Lee Harvey Oswald and Bud Simco. Begins work on *The Idle Warriors*. Oswald is dishonorably discharged from the Marines and defects to Russia.

1960: Kerry is discharged from the Marines and returns to Los Angeles.

1961: Kerry and Greg Hill move to New Orleans, where they meet Slim Brooks and Gary Kirstein, aka "Brother-in-law."

June 1962: Oswald returns to the U.S. from Russia.

November 1963: President John F. Kennedy is assassinated.

December 1963: Kerry moves to Alexandria, Virginia, and works as a doorman at the Shirlington House.

Spring 1964: Kerry testifies before the Warren Commission.

April 1965: *Oswald* is published by New Classics House.

December 1965: Kerry marries Cara Leach at Wayfarer's Chapel near Palos Verdes, California.

Late 1965 through early 1966: Kerry begins experimenting with psychedelics. Meets Camden Benares.

1967: Kerry helps organize and participates in the first Griffith Park Human Be-In. Begins correspondence with Robert Anton Wilson.

Late 1967: Kerry and Cara move to Tampa, Florida. Jim Garrison launches his Kennedy assassination probe.

January 1968: Kerry is served with a subpoena to testify before the New Orleans grand jury in Jim Garrison's investigation.

Later in 1968: Operation Mindfuck begins.

1969: Greg Hill creates the Joshua Norton Cabal. Kreg Thornley is born.

1970: Perjury charges against Kerry in the Garrison investigation are dropped.

Late 1971: Cara and Kerry separate.

1973: Kerry's memories of "Brother-in-law" come flooding back, and he suspects he was part of a Kennedy assassination conspiracy.

1975–1977: Kerry's paranoia intensifies. He now suspects that Robert Anton Wilson is his CIA controller and part of a clandestine assassination bureau.

1980s: Kerry lives the life of a vagabond, hitchhiking from coast to coast. Most of his time is spent in Florida or Atlanta, with occasional trips to the west coast.

1986–1987: Kerry begins circulating the *Dreadlock Recollections*, recounting his unwitting participation in a JFK assassination conspiracy.

1991: Kerry starts experiencing kidney problems.

1992: Kerry is interviewed by Oliver Stone, who is researching his forthcoming movie, *JFK*. Kerry appears on *A Current Affair*.

November 28, 1998: Kerry dies from complications related to Wegner's granulomatosis disease.

CHAPTER 1

Free-Thinking Nerd

Kerry Wendell Thornley—the hero of our story—was born on April 17, 1938, to Helen and Kenneth Thornley. Throughout the 1950s, Kerry grew up in East Whittier, then a rural southern California community, which encompassed vast orange groves within a stone's throw of the Thornley family doorstep. Nearby was the Friendly Hills development, where there were more orange groves, affording plenty of territory for kids to roam.

Often, Kerry took his younger brothers—Dick and Tom—on adventures up to Friendly Hills, where he encouraged the boys to give their own names to the some of the places they visited. So it was that "Yellow Canyon," was born, as well as "Lonely Tree," and "The Painting," which consisted of a spot overlooking the rolling panoramic hills, crisscrossed with never-ending orange groves. These orange groves (which are no more) were irrigated with concrete cylindrical devices called "weirs." Here Kerry led his younger brothers on hikes all about the groves, journeys lasting well into dusk. When night began to fall, Kerry would joke about the weirs, telling his brothers that they'd have to get back before dark, because that's when the "weir-workers" came out!

It was all great fun and high adventure, a time of innocence; an era when parents could let their children roam wild and not worry as long as they made it home by a reasonable hour. The biggest danger one would meet was an occasional rattler. Kerry instructed the boys how best to avoid stepping on a snake, what to do if they spotted one, and how to administer first aid in case of a snakebite—all stuff he had learned as a Boy Scout.

Other adventures included pre-dawn automotive quests into Friendly Hills in search of the fabled "gypsy camps" Kerry had told his brothers about. To this day, Dick Thornley has no idea whether his big brother was just putting them on about these hidden camps, or not. They never did find any gypsies.

Yet Kerry provided more than just mere entertainment for his younger brothers. As Dick recalled to this author in 2002:

> Our family was quite dysfunctional. Dad was an alcoholic. He never physically hurt us, but he was unbearably embarrassing to be around, at times. He'd get drunk on almost every special occasion, or be "sick" from having gotten drunk before it. He'd openly flirt with waitresses in family restaurants in a way that would make Chevy Chase look like James Bond. There were times we'd have to step over him to move from one room to another. Mom was too afraid of being on her own to leave Dad. Yet, she frequently talked about it. This made for a very neurotic situation for us. For me, Kerry filled a huge part of the void left by my Dad's "emotional absence." Kerry was a surrogate father figure to me for years. He was the person in the family who was most supportive of all my childish ideas. There were times in my life that I was lost, but without Kerry things would have been much, much worse for me.

In many respects—just a normal lad growing up in 1950s America—Kerry engaged in such typical activities as building model cars and airplanes, and flying box kites. Although he was never much one for sports or games, Kerry did, however, own one of the first Frisbees in existence, then called a "Flying Saucer," which he got at the Pomona County Fair. And, like many other young boys, he dreamed of one day becoming a world-traveling adventurer.

One of Helen Thornley's favorite funny stories about Kerry

occurred one day when he came out of the kitchen eating a frozen pot pie stuck on a fork. Appalled that he hadn't heated it up, Helen cried, "Kerry, what are you eating?"

"A turkey Popsicle!" he replied.

■

At California High School (CalHi) in East Whittier, Kerry made the acquaintance of Greg Hill, whom he once described in the following manner: "Elfin blue eyes combine with his squat physique to give him a Pan-like appearance of a creature from Greek mythology."

Conversely, Kerry was shaped not unlike a matchstick, with a pair of the skinniest legs known to man. And whereas Kerry was an expansive and highly energized kid, Greg was more introverted. Just the same, he and Kerry possessed similar odd interests, including a fondness for crackpots, which led to some of their first outings together to meetings of a flying saucer cult in El Monte called Understanding. As Greg later recalled: "Through our mutual general interest in wondering just what was going on out there in that gigantic world, and our many common specific interests in Humanism, anti-religionism, an enjoyment for Omar Khayyam, a curiosity for the bizarre like black magic and hypnotism, plus our common warped sense of humor, we formed a close friendship."

Another high school chum was Bill Stephens, who hung out with both Kerry and mutual pal, Bob Newport. According to Stephens: "'Nerds' would be the best way to characterize Bob and Kerry…just very strange kids…free-thinkers."

Bill also met Kerry at CalHi, when the two debated in a speech contest. Apparently, Bill's speech was rather loud, so Greg Hill approached him afterwards, saying: "Bill, your speech was outstanding!" After Bill thanked him, and gloated a bit, Greg added: "Yes, I could have heard it even if I was out *standing* in the hall."

While attending CalHi, Kerry won a number of public-speaking competitions, and became an accomplished public speaker, a skill which he continued to hone after high school.

In time, Bill and Kerry grew quite close, although they rarely agreed on much, if anything. Both were active members of the drama club, in which Kerry landed leading roles in such productions as *The Remarkable Incident at Carson Corners* and *Jenny Kissed Me*.

Dick Thornley remembers going to see Kerry in *Jenny Kissed Me*, and one scene in particular with Kerry sitting in a living room with two girls. At one point in the dialogue, Kerry tried to change the subject of their conversation, by saying: "Let's talk about something interesting...*me*, for instance!" Kerry later joked that this bit of dialogue sounded a lot like him in real life. No one disagreed.

Another CalHi friend, Sylvia Bortin, recalled a prank that occurred in drama class. Apparently the perpetrators—Kerry, Greg, and other unnamed cohorts—made a recording of what, at first, appeared to be a regular radio program, with music playing innocently from a radio positioned on the apron of the stage. In actuality, the sounds were projected from a reel-to-reel tape machine hidden backstage. Inserted into the seemingly mundane radio program, the pranksters had planted a series of interruptions, made by a newscaster, to the effect that Soviet planes were invading the U.S. and dropping bombs. As Sylvia recalled: "Somebody had told me early on that it was a joke, but some of the students didn't know and got really scared.... What made me feel bad was that one of the boys in the class was so scared that he was praying."

Oddballs though they may have been, Kerry and his cohorts—Newport, Stephens, and Hill—engaged in such normal and expected activities for youth their age, such as cruising Whittier Boulevard, and trying to be cool, which was quite a stretch for these nerdy young lads with ideas as weird and plentiful as their acne.

Among other pastimes, Kerry was a devotee of the ever-irreverent *Mad* magazine and owned every *Mad* comic book, which didn't make him a whole lot different from many other kids who had tuned into the wacky world of William Gaines.

Kerry's reading habits, though, were not entirely devoted to

Mad, and in fact ran the gamut from sci-fi novels, to books on philosophy, religion, politics, and poetry. It was Kerry who first introduced Bill Stephens to the powerful poetic works of William Blake, and the philosophy of experiencing everything to excess. "Kerry did everything to excess," Bill observed. "Of course, he didn't know when to stop." Stephens remembers Kerry as an intense character who "put a shade to everything that was really extreme.... Kerry would immerse himself in whatever it was Kerry was interested in."

Shortly after high school graduation, Stephens came out of the closet, which was quite a gutsy move given the conformist climate then present in Eisenhower's America. Kerry, in fact, was the first person to whom Bill revealed his sexual orientation, and on one occasion Bill even tried to seduce Kerry, although Kerry turned down his advances. When asked how Kerry responded to the disclosure of his homosexuality, Stephens replied: "As a good friend would: very tolerant. In the 50s, that was quite the exception."

Around this time, Kerry—as Bill Stephens recalled—became "bound and determined to lose his cherry." After getting appropriately drunk, the two visited a Tijuana brothel, where Kerry lost his virginity.

During Kerry's junior year, in the spring of 1956, he joined the Marine Corps Reserves. After attending boot camp that summer, he returned to high school for his senior year. Kerry graduated from CalHi in 1957, and in 1958 attended the University of Southern California to study journalism.

While attending USC, Kerry rented a room above a mortuary, a situation that didn't seem to bother him, although he occasionally had to walk through a room with a corpse or two in it. In fact, Kerry seemed to enjoy others' squeamish reactions to his unusual living arrangements.

Kerry pledged for Delta Sigma Phi, and—as is expected of all pledges—went through the hazing ritual known as "hell week." At the time, Delta Sigma Phi members allowed a black student to pledge, and took him all the way through hell week. Then, after making it through this humiliation, the fraternity laughingly refused to let the black student join because of his race. Kerry decided he wanted nothing further to do with fraternities, and this episode probably turned him off of college altogether.

Thereafter Kerry set about educating himself—as he later recalled—by "reading the classics, traveling, and writing."

What a long, strange trip it would be.

CHAPTER 2

A Few Good Men

In the spring of 1959, Kerry—a Marine Corps Reservist—decided to fulfill his two-year active duty and enlisted. His first stop was El Toro Marine Base, located outside Santa Ana, California, where Kerry met up with an infamous character in history, Lee Harvey Oswald, the future alleged-to-be-assassin of John F. Kennedy. The two were stationed together in Marine Air Control Squadron Nine (MACS-9), where Oswald had been reassigned after returning from overseas duty in Japan. Concurrently, Kerry had been transferred to MACS-9 from MACS-4, a sister unit located at El Toro.

Comparatively speaking, MACS-9 was a small organization located outside the main sphere of base activities, which afforded the enlisted men the opportunity to get to know one another on a more personal level than in other units. It was in this atmosphere that Kerry and Oswald struck up an acquaintance due to a mutual interest in communist theory and the writings of Karl Marx.

Later, Kerry would describe Oswald as "the outfit eight ball," earning this dubious distinction by openly subscribing to communist newspapers such as *Pravda*, and cracking jokes with an exaggerated Russian accent, answering questions with "*da*" or "*nyet*" and referring to his fellow Marines as "comrades." It was common knowledge that Oswald was studying Russian, and was fairly fluent in conversational Russian. Because of this, he acquired the nickname "Oswaldskovitch."

Previously, Oswald had been stationed as a radar technician at Atsugi Air Base in Japan, one of the CIA's largest and most critical installations, where the top-secret U-2 flights originated. Later, Kerry served at Atsugi—also as a radar technician—although he and Oswald were never stationed there at the same time.

In MACS-9, there was a relaxed general atmosphere, although by comparison the Marines just back from Japan were considered "salty," one of whom was Oswald. Most of these were short-timers who had returned from overseas duty with tales of how different the Far East was compared to stateside service.

Oswald, as it turns out, was one of the few Marines to return from Japan still with the rank of private, which was a bit out of the ordinary given the fact that most enlisted men with as much service time had been promoted to at least corporal. Apparently Oswald's lowly status was due to an incident in Japan when he got drunk one night and poured a beer over a sergeant's head, causing permanent damage to whatever promotion potential he might have had.

At El Toro, Oswald was openly rebellious, and seemed to go out of his way to get into trouble. An example of this occurred one morning during roll call when the section chief—Master Sergeant Spar—called out "Oswald!" and Oswald intentionally stepped out of rank to incur the wrath of Spar, who in turn sent Lee to clean out the latrines. Oswald portrayed himself as some sort of martyr who was being made example of by the entire Marine Corps hierarchy, and in particular such authority figures as Sergeant Spar.

As Kerry later recalled in his book *Oswald*, his first meeting with Oswald occurred in a "hurry up and wait" situation near the recreation hut when someone mentioned that Kerry was an atheist.

> "So am I," said Oswald, glancing up from his notebook. "I think the best religion is communism."
>
> "Yeah, Oswald's a Red," said one of the men, to me.
>
> "No, I'm not a communist. I just think they have the best system."
>
> "Why?" I wanted to know.
>
> "Because they have a purpose. And the com-

munist way of life is more scientific than ours.
You don't have to believe in a bunch of fairy tales
to accept it…" (p. 23-24).

Later, in testimony before the Warren Commission, Kerry stated: "You might say I was [Oswald's] best buddy, but I don't think he had any close friends. I was a close acquaintance." Of all the other enlisted men in MACS-9, Oswald spent more time in serious conversation with Kerry, it appears, than anyone else. Kerry remembered Oswald as a sad sack type with eternally scuffed boots and cap pushed down over his eyes, which he speculated was Oswald's way of shutting out the Marine world around him, a world that deeply dissatisfied him.

One of Oswald's favorite routines was to compare the Marine Corps to the society George Orwell created in *1984*. "Be careful, comrade, with Big Brother's equipment," Oswald once said, as he and Kerry unloaded government gear from a truck. In fact, it was Oswald who turned Kerry on to *1984*, which quickly became one of his favorite books.

Oswald also referred to officers as "party members"—a la *1984*—due to the special privileges they received. Later—in Kerry's Warren Commission testimony—he recalled a couple of humorous incidents involving Oswald, such as the time Sergeant Spar jumped up on the fender of a jeep and yelled out for everyone to gather around. Oswald, with a thick Russian accent, commented wryly, "Ah ha, collective farm lecture," which brought a lot of laughs from his fellow Marines.

Often, Oswald used a mock Russian accent to humorous effect, such as when he'd utter "Good morning, comrade," in ranks during muster, or when referring to the battalion formations as part of the "party function." As fellow Marine Bud Simco recalled:

We occasionally would be herded into a truck
which resembled a cattle car and driven to the

parade grounds at El Toro. When on the road
many of the enlisted men would moo like cows at
the passing motorists. It was a way of referring to
ourselves as non-entities. So when someone refers
to "Big Brother" or—as in the case of Oswald—as
comrades, it was a common sense of humor and
not the voice of a "deranged communist" or some
type of subversive.... Things like this had a way
of irritating the "military establishment" usually
personified by the Staff NCOs, and there were
always people who delighted in baiting superiors
with seemingly disrespectful remarks or an indif-
ferent "you don't scare me" type attitude. Oswald
gave me this impression.

Kerry's friendship with Oswald, such as it was, came to an
abrupt end one day when he made the tongue-in-cheek quip:
"Come the revolution, you will change all that," in response to
Oswald's persistent griping about ma, apple pie, and the American
way. Looking like a "betrayed Caesar"—as Kerry later told the
Warren Commission—Oswald shouted "Not you too, Thornley,"
and stomped away, pouting. When joking about communism,
Oswald had usually done so in the ranks, while in one-on-one conversations his interactions were quite different. Oswald made the
"Not you too, Thornley" remark in a one-on-one encounter, which
perhaps reflected his true feelings regarding his so-called communist sympathies, as it was in group settings that Oswald usually put
on his Oswaldskovitch persona.

The sum total of time Kerry and Lee spent together in MACS-
9 added up to roughly three months before Kerry was transferred
to Atsugi in June 1959, along with a few hundred other Marines
who sailed to Japan aboard the U.S.S. Breckenridge.

On board the Breckenridge, the men had a lot of spare time
and—as Bud Simco recalled—Kerry seemed always to be working

on notes (which he kept on 5 x 7 cards) of a book he'd recently started writing called *The Idle Warriors*, the theme of which revolved around the disillusionment of a young Marine as a result of overseas duty. The protagonist of Kerry's work-in-progress, Johnny Shellburn, was a composite character based on Kerry and other Marines, one of whom was Lee Oswald. Simco remembered Kerry as a "compulsive writer and just about anything out of the ordinary that would occur during the day would find its way into his notes."

Kerry arrived in Japan on the Fourth of July and was assigned to duty in MACS-1 as a radio operator. Upon arrival, there was a huge party going on the likes of which Kerry had never seen, with many a beer being hoisted at the Marines section of the base. All day and throughout the night of the fourth, there was fighting and general drunkenness as Independence Day was celebrated by a "few good men." Although this was not an everyday occurrence, it was nonetheless an eye-opening experience for Kerry, and he could tell right off that overseas duty was going to be different from what he'd experienced stateside. For example, most of the enlisted men stationed at Atsugi were under 21, and therefore couldn't drink legally back in the States. Conversely, there was no age restriction on drinking, on or off base, in Japan. This resulted in more incidents of drunken Marines running around and raising hell than would normally occur back home.

Kerry later wrote about MACS-1 in his book *Oswald*:

> For the sake of all the Marine Corps stands for, I hope MACS-1 was unique. Never did I suspect there was anything like it defending the peace, and discovering such a unit could exist was enough to give me dire reservations concerning the future of the United States…it was and had been for fourteen years the goddamnedest excuse for a military operation ever to give ulcers to a colonel.

It was magnificent! We arrived on the Fourth of
July and dragged our seabags into a barracks
littered with beer cans. A drunken Marine sat
weaving in a chair with a broken bottle. He was
cutting his own arm with it!

That night after taps there was some noise in
the barracks, and when the Duty N.C.O. called
for silence he was booed down.

At that time the men of MACS-1 had two things
about which to boast. First, they'd, believe it or
not, just won a competition in close order drill for
the entire Far East. Second, for the past three
months they'd maintained the highest venereal
disease rate on the base.

The unit had been in Japan since the end of the
war. Each month a new draft of perhaps a dozen
men or more arrived and about a dozen or so
were sent home. That way the outfit had
evidently managed to maintain its salty wartime
personality by assimilating new members in
small lots (p. 35-36).

When Kerry first entered the Marines, he considered himself
a "right winger," to the extent that he favored individualism over
servitude to the state. In other words, Kerry's "rightism" was
founded more on anarchistic than authoritarian principles.
However—during the course of his Marine service—Kerry's ideological stance gradually began to shift, as over time he drifted slowly
toward left-wing politics. A number of things attributed to this ideological change, such as the unseemly conduct of Marines on liberty
in Japan, various books he was reading at the time, the irritating living conditions in the barracks, and life in general in MACS-1.

As Kerry once explained it, the enlisted men in MACS-1 had
an extremely "high morale," but it was one with roots based in

rebellion. Kerry described it as a "people's morale," which wasn't only independent of officers and "lifers," but was totally set against the system. Since the radar defense of Japan depended on MACS-1 maintaining personnel levels at certain numbers, it made it virtually impossible for the brass to toss everybody in the brig at the same time. Therefore, the radar technicians—such as Kerry— were able to get away with a lot more than the enlisted men in other units. What this meant was that if the radar techs stuck together, they could do pretty much what they wanted, within limits, such as keeping booze in the barracks when off duty, and razzing officers foolhardy enough to enter the barracks.

An example of this was when members of Kerry's squadron would start chanting: "Hymn, hymn…." In the old Marine Corps, this was a call for the band at a parade to play the Marine's Hymn. Kerry and his fellow Marines' version of the chant ended somewhat differently than the standard version, with a "… fuck him!" Sometimes—when the brass didn't clear out after a few hymns— Kerry and his fellow rabble-rousers would shout out: "Lieutenant So-and-so walks on water!" This little chant was a call to pick up the officer, haul his ass outside the barracks, and deposit him in a pond known as "the sump." Once an officer was tossed into the sump, a riot usually resulted, as the guys would take fire extinguishers from the walls and empty their contents all over the officer as he tried to climb out. This would be followed by squirting shaving cream, unfurling toilet paper, overturning lockers and occasionally break- ing a window or two. Amazingly, no one ever got busted.

Not long after Kerry's arrival at Atsugi he learned of a "Technique of Instruction" competition on the base, with the winner receiving a trip to Washington, D.C., and up to 30 days of leave. Kerry entered the competition and won on the lower levels, earning the trip to Washington. According to Kerry, he delivered a speech in which he attempted to persuade his listeners "that behaving like storm troopers while on liberty was just as bad as signing a phony communist germ-warfare confession. Some of the men took the trouble to tell me they were really impressed with what I had to say. But later on I'd see them out in Yamato ripping up bars, insulting prostitutes, beating up drivers—the same old shit."

Kerry eventually lost at the higher levels of the competition, but due to his participation was promoted to corporal—a promotion he initially declined, but which the brass eventually forced him to accept. Kerry's slow-growing rebellion against authority continued when he rejoined his squadron. At that time, all the radar techs were made to apply for secret security clearance due to some new equipment then being installed at the operations center. As Kerry had no interest in receiving such a clearance, he listed as references certain civilian friends back in the States who he figured might be considered security risks. Surprisingly, Kerry was the first one in his squadron to get cleared.

In his outfit, Kerry was thought of as an eccentric, and—according to Bud Simco—alienated himself due to his cynical outlook on subjects others held sacrosanct. An example of this was when Kerry began referring to himself as the "Atheist chaplain," and announced his plans for a baptism in the sump at midnight simply to get a rise out of some of the guys. One man jumped at the bait, telling Kerry to "lay off my God." Kerry retorted: "Isn't your God big enough to take care of himself?" Soon after, a fight ensued.

As Simco recalled: "Kerry, possessing a thirst for knowledge, was quick to jump at a chance to debate anyone and usually on any subject. With some he gained a reputation of being argumentative, but to most he was thought of as a worthy opponent in any serious discussion. He was also noted for his keen sense of humor, one which he displayed often."

In October 1959—while at Atsugi—Kerry learned that Oswald had defected to Russia. Upon reading this news, he said: "I'll be damned. He really meant it!" To Kerry, Oswald's communist stance had always seemed a bit of a put-on, so he was surprised when Lee entered the American Embassy in Moscow, handed over his visa, and renounced his citizenship. This unprecedented event immediately influenced the direction of *The Idle Warriors*, providing Kerry with an idea for his book's ending. From that point forward, the protagonist would be re-shaped with Oswald as the main character (Johnny Shellburn) who defects to Russia due to his experiences with the Marines in the Far East.

Now—as the theme of *The Idle Warriors* became firmly fixed in Kerry's mind—Kerry started going around telling anyone who'd listen about his book-in-the-works that was going to explain why a peacetime tour of duty in the Far East "could disillusion a man with the U.S. and make him want to join the Russians."

As Kerry later wrote in his book *Oswald*:

> I am convinced that the idle warrior experience played a key role in Lee's disillusionment with the United States. If it did, Lee was not the only victim. Many men became alcoholics while serving overseas. Sympathy with Communist ideas was unusually popular. Others found an escape in indiscriminate sexual activity. A surprising number turned to masochistic pastimes such as cutting themselves with broken bottles, biting chunks out of glasses, and arm-wrestling with live cigarette butts between their arms. Others became thieves and saboteurs just for the sake of the thrills involved. Riots were common, insubordination was ordinary.
>
> As explanation for this mass disillusionment I have given consideration for several possibilities. Most prominent among them seems to be purposelessness and its two companions, disgust and boredom. Few men, if any, really understood why they were over there in the first place (p. 39).

During the winter of 1959, scuttlebutt began to circulate that

MACS-1 was going to be transferred to the States and staffed with entirely new personnel. This, in essence, was a way to dissolve the outfit. According to Kerry, MACS-1 was eventually broken up—and its men dispersed to other squadrons—because the outfit had grown so incorrigible. As this was going on, Kerry was reassigned to Marine Air Base Squadron (MABS-11), where he served as a basic training clerk, and soon after his squadron left on three-month maneuvers to the Philippines.

While on liberty in Manila, Kerry witnessed firsthand the abject poverty and starvation of a section of town called Intramuros (or the City of Walls). Due to this experience, Kerry became, for a time, a Marxist Leninist. As he later noted: "Previously I had read that roughly 60% of the people in the world were underfed, but statistics carried with them little in the way of an emotional wallop. Seeing a man who looked like a canvas-covered skeleton walking down the street with a look of utter panic and desperation in his eyes is what did it for me."

At the time, Marxism seemed to Kerry the most logical solution to the ills of the world. So when he got back to the base at Subic Bay—where his squadron was stationed—he immediately checked out *Dialectical Materialism*, the only book of Marxism available at the base library. After reading this book, Kerry officially became a "self-styled Marxist."

One famous tale from Kerry's days in MABS-11 revolved around the appearance of a fictitious Marine (named Omar Khayyam Ravenhurst) that Kerry—while performing his duties as basic training clerk—surreptitiously enrolled into the unit, complete with a partial file in administration and his own bunk and wall locker. As the fictitious records stated, Ravenhurst—a private with ten years of service—had an I.Q. of 159, and spoke 17 languages, including Upper and Lower Swahili. Ravenhurst was listed as a truck driver in motor transport—serial number 1369697, rank: private. Other conspirators in the admin office cooperated with Kerry in this hoax, as soon after there were all kinds of records on

Ravenhurst. As Kerry wrote in the introduction to the fifth edition of the *Principia Discordia*:

> When Ravenhurst, Omar K., failed to answer the role call somebody called the captain in charge of motor transport to find out where Ravenhurst was. Of course nobody in the motor pool ever heard of any such private.
>
> Motor transport called administration. No Ravenhurst on record there, either. A clerk-typist from administration, Corporal Chadwick, came by to ask me about the mysterious Marine.
>
> Upon returning to his desk, Chadwick completed an IRC card—a condensed record—which would have to do until Ravenhurst's entire file arrived from his last duty station: Marine Barracks, East British Outer Cambodia....
>
> After I was discharged I ran into Bud Simco, who remained in the same unit a short while longer than me. [He told me] "About a month after you mustered out, there was a dress rehearsal for the biggest inspection of the year.
>
> "By then Ravenhurst had a wall locker with his name on it and a bunk. Somebody even added a touch of realism by putting an old pair of size six shoes with holes in them under Ravenhurst's bunk.
>
> "There was only one other guy in that cubicle and he was pretty bent out of shape because Ravenhurst was never there in the mornings to help sweep. Once or twice he even brought it up with the top sergeant.
>
> "When the big day came, they even shut down radar center. Everybody had to stand inspection.

No exceptions.

"Colonel Fenderson and the top sergeant walked down the isle, inspecting one cubicle at a time. It was junk on the bunk," he added, indicating the most thorough inspection there is—with every piece of gear spread out neatly on the bunk. "Only one bunk with bedding on it was empty. Only one man was missing.

"They wanted to know who Ravenhurst was and, more importantly, where he was. Nobody knows, but the other guy in his cubicle reminds the top sergeant that Ravenhurst is a malingerer.

"Then they ask if anybody has ever seen this Ravenhurst. Private Monty Cantsin pipes up. Every afternoon Ravenhurst sits right there on his bunk.

"Well then, what does this Ravenhurst look like? Cantsin stretches out both arms and says, 'Oh, he's a big mountain of a man!' But just then the top sergeant bends over and picks up these little size six shoes.

"They call up motor transport. 'For the hundredth goddamned time,' the captain tells the top sergeant, 'there is nobody named Ravenhurst in motor transport.' So the brass huddle together and decide Ravenhurst must have mustered into squadron without checking in with his assigned work station—so he could just fuck off all the time. So they are ready to hang him—as soon as they find him."

A futile base-wide manhunt was conducted before Sergeant Garcia heard they were searching for Ravenhurst. Somehow—perhaps by examining the basic training files—he discovered that

Ravenhurst was a hoax earlier and now he spilled
the beans in exchange, I'm sure, for many points.

Just before Kerry's discharge, there was huge demonstration at
Atsugi following the downing of a U-2 plane over Soviet territory
piloted by Francis Gary Powers, who flew missions out of the base.
This event caused an international incident, and Powers later
placed blame for the U-2 shooting on Oswald, claiming that turncoat
Lee had shared state secrets with the Russians after his defection.

While at Atsugi, Oswald had spent many of his off-duty hours
with Japanese bar girls at a Tokyo nightclub called the Queen Bee.
During this period, Lee became acquainted with a mysterious
Eurasian woman who helped him with his Russian-language studies, as well as sharing her many charms. It was later theorized that
Oswald's girlfriends at the Queen Bee were actually Soviet spies,
who had sucked the naive lad into a web of international intrigue,
which later resulted in his subsequent defection, and the shooting
down of the U-2 plane.

■

Kerry's ideological conversion to Marxism took a noteworthy
back-flip when—voyaging back from Japan after his discharge in
August 1960—he happened upon a copy of Ayn Rand's *Atlas
Shrugged* and was turned into a "laissez-faire capitalist" overnight.
In a letter from mid-1964, Kerry related his conversion to Rand's
"Objectivism":

> What had driven me to Marxism was simply that,
> as a political philosophy, it was the only thing I
> could find without a blatantly mystical base. I
> had seen enough of U.S. Foreign Policy to know
> who was winning the Cold War, and all of Ike's
> prayers left me no more secure in the face of a

system with both coercive methods and moral (altruist) justification as its disposal. So I was about ready to look up a friend in San Francisco who belonged to the Communist Party and ask him what I could do to speed up the revolution, when I picked up *Atlas Shrugged* as a good, long book to read at sea. Well, by the time I set foot on U.S. soil again I knew I'd happened upon a genius. It took me about two years to work out and adjust to my new philosophy, but I knew it'd be worth it. It is.

CHAPTER 3

Idle Author

Kerry returned to civilian life in October 1960, and from then until February 1961 he lived with his parents in East Whittier and subsisted on his Marine discharge money. One of the first things Kerry did when he got back home was to go into business for himself, starting a lecture service.

Now an avowed capitalist—due to his recent conversion to Ayn Rand's Objectivism—Kerry figured the best way to make money was to spend money. And so, as with everything he ever did, Kerry totally immersed himself in this new enterprise, renting an answering service and purchasing an electric typewriter.

Kerry continued work on *The Idle Warriors* between delivering a lecture on the book's theme to a southern California women's club. Kerry also put on a small production of *The Idle Warriors*, a short dramatic monologue outlining the initial experiences of what it was like when an "idle warrior" first arrived in peacetime Japan. Kerry's idea was to present the monologue once for free, to selected groups, in the hopes that those in the audience would be so impressed they'd hire him to present it to their various organizations. To drum up interest, Kerry sent out free tickets to several civic organizations.

Unfortunately, the night Kerry scheduled his *Idle Warriors* monologue coincided with the first Nixon-Kennedy debate. Nevertheless, about 34 people showed up, which wasn't bad for the room Kerry had rented. Kerry kicked it all off by walking on stage and delivering the following immortal lines: "The first Marine went off to war, *parlez vous*. The second Marine went off to war, *parlez vous*. The third Marine stayed behind, kissed the girls and drank the wine, hinky dinky *parlez vous*. This story is about the third Marine..."

Among Kerry's other projects was a humor magazine, which he collaborated on with Greg Hill, titled *Apocalypse: A Trade Journal for Doom Prophets*. They put out only one issue of *Apocalypse*, but unfortunately no one found it the least bit funny. As Kerry later recalled: "Things we thought were funny, nobody else did."

One day, Kerry's old Marine pal, Bud Simco—who had recently been discharged—looked him up. This was the first time the two had seen each other since becoming civilians, and in the interim Kerry had grown a full beard. In those days, not many people sported beards of such expanse, so this attracted a lot of attention, particularly from women.

At one point, Bud had to make a trip to Houston to retrieve the family car and he invited Kerry along for company. On the bus trip, Kerry proved quite a hit with fellow passengers, due to his Lincoln-esque beard. A couple of passengers even joked with Kerry that he'd have to be careful as they headed south, because he looked so much like Honest Abe. Kerry, Simco noted, took these comments about his "beatnik" appearance with good cheer, and generally handled people well, though not always, such as an incident which occurred at the Greyhound ticket counter in Houston when Kerry discovered that he'd lost his claim ticket.

As Kerry explained his predicament to a clerk and indicated that he had personal I.D. matching the identification in his suitcase, the clerk responded that there was nothing he could do without a claim check. Kerry—who had tired of trying to reason with the clerk—climbed over the claim counter, grabbed his suitcase, and then stomped out of the terminal. The clerk—in a bit of a tizzy—started to summon the police, but Simco was able to calm down the ticket-taker by convincing him that Kerry only took his own luggage, and meant no harm to the Greyhound empire.

Kerry had a way of making things interesting.

■

Late one night, Kerry and Greg Hill were at the Thornley's house in East Whittier—laughing and carrying on—when they woke up

Kerry's parents, who told them to pipe down. Having wreaked enough havoc upon the Thornley family household, Greg and Kerry relocated to Greg's house, where they continued laughing and carrying on, and in the course of events woke up Greg's family, too. So—to not disturb Greg's family any further—they decided to wander over to downtown Whittier, where nobody could possibly be disturbed.

As Kerry and Greg walked down the main Whittier drag, the cops pulled up and told them that the next time they were caught walking around and making merriment at such odd hours they would be arrested for vagrancy. Greg replied, "I live here!" The cops shot back: "That doesn't matter: you're keeping unusual hours with no general purpose in mind!"

After the cops drove away, Kerry said, "Let's go live someplace where it's not against the law to stay up all night." Greg suggested the New Orleans French Quarter. And so it was that in early 1961, Kerry and Greg moved to New Orleans, arriving the day after Mardi Gras.

Kerry's first months in New Orleans were "harsh and sparse," as he and Greg holed up in a hovel in the slums of the Irish Channel section of town, living off day-old French bread, and scraping together just enough to make ends meet.

Kerry found Greg to be a difficult person to live with, as he was even more erratic than himself. Greg would do things like leave the iron on the ironing board overnight and burn a hole in the cover. One time he left the defroster on in the icebox and it flooded the kitchen. Soon after, Kerry moved out of their "dungeon," relocating above a place called Fred's Inn on St. Charles Street, where he returned to work on *The Idle Warriors*.

February and March were particularly lean times, and the fact that Kerry had a full beard probably contributed to the difficulty he had finding a job. Finally, in early April, he landed a position as a telephone solicitor at the Foster Awning Company, hustling awnings and aluminum sidings by day, and writing and haunting the French Quarter by dark.

Not long after arriving in New Orleans, Kerry made the acquaintance of Slim Brooks. A colorful character, Slim had worked as a seaman, lumberjack, and U.S. Marshal in Alaska, among other occupations.

True to his name, Brooks was tall and slim, sporting a Douglas Fairbanks-like moustache. He—more than anyone else—took Kerry under his wing and showed him about New Orleans, making him feel at home. Often the two sat around Slim's house, drinking cold coffee from mason jars, while Slim related his life's adventures.

It was at Slim's house that Kerry was introduced to a fellow named Gary Kirstein, who Slim referred to as his "Brother-in-law." Kerry found himself engaged with Kirstein in many lengthy discourses covering a whole host of topics, from politics and philosophy to espionage and criminal activities.

Kerry once described Kirstein in the following manner:

> Gary didn't look like a criminal at all. He dressed very straight. He wore neatly pressed slacks and short-sleeved shirts. If anything, he dressed like an off duty policeman.
>
> He was an older man—perhaps in his forties, certainly at least in his thirties. He had brown hair and was balding, was of medium build and height, smoked a pipe, and spoke in what was at times almost a whine, except his words were clipped and precise. His accent was Midwestern.
>
> One of the first things I learned about Gary was that he also hated Kennedy, but for somewhat different political reasons than mine.
>
> Gary said that he was raised in a Germanic mid-Western family and that he was a Nazi. He and Slim used to joke about this, and also about Gary's alleged skills at burglary.

Gary was keenly intelligent and had a flippant, light-hearted air about him. Therefore, even though the content of his humor was often sadistic, Gary did not seem "for real." He never sounded angry for example, but he cheerfully recounted the "little jokes" the Nazis had played on the Jews and other victims of their prejudice.

He expressed his dislike for Jews, Poles, gypsies, homosexuals, Russians, Mexicans and so on with a chuckle, usually, which left me with room to assume he wasn't really very serious about it— and that, of course, was the assumption I preferred to make, since I really liked Slim a lot and Gary was his friend.

■

In New Orleans, Kerry's main hangout was the Bourbon House restaurant, which he once described as "a central clearing house for French Quarter social life." The Bourbon House was Kerry's unofficial office, where he worked on the books and short stories that he hoped would one day make him rich and famous. Catering mainly to denizens of the French Quarter, the Bourbon House closed its doors at 2:30 a.m., so afterwards Kerry would often gravitate to other dimly lit environs.

When Kerry finished the first draft of *The Idle Warriors*, he hired a student at LSU, Joyce Talley, to type it up for him, and it was through Joyce that Kerry made the acquaintance of a LSU professor named Martin McAuliffe. One evening McAuliffe, Joyce, Kerry, and his girlfriend Jessica Luck spent several hours at the Bourbon House, discussing writing in general, and *The Idle Warriors* specifically.

Shortly thereafter, McAuliffe arranged another meeting at the Bourbon House, this time with a friend named Guy Banister, who was introduced to Kerry as "a man with a great interest in literature." Although Kerry later remembered nothing particularly monumental coming out of these conversations, Banister did seem "favorably impressed" with *The Idle Warriors*. (In 1968, Banister would become a key suspect in New Orlean's District Attorney Jim Garrison's JFK assassination probe. More on that later.)

At this point, Kerry postponed writing the final chapter of *The Idle Warriors*, as he was somewhat hesitant to take on Oswald's defection to Russia, the facts of which were only then beginning to emerge. Kerry's original idea was to place his main character (Johnny Shellburn, the Oswald composite) in Moscow at the end of the story, describing Soviet perceptions from Shellburn's point of view. Kerry had no base of experience with which to tackle this final scene. He struggled to find his way into Oswald's head.

Presented as a work-in-progress, *The Idle Warriors* was turned down by several publishers, the first rejection slip courtesy of Charles Tuttle and Sons. Kerry eventually lost hope of publishing the manuscript and turned his attention to other endeavors, such as writing poetry. Occasionally someone would recommend a certain agent or publisher and Kerry would give them a try, but to no avail.[1]

In December 1961, Gary "Brother-in-law" Kirstein took Kerry, his girlfriend Jessica Luck, and Slim for a ride in the country in a fancy black limousine. The following day, Kerry paid a visit to Kirstein's house in the nearby town of Kenner. Apparently, Kirstein was also an aspiring author, for it was on this occasion that he talked up a book he was writing called *Hitler Was A Good Guy*, which was to be a study of what the policies of members of the Third Reich would have been if they'd succeeded in their attempts to seize power from Hitler.

It was Kirstein's contention that out of the whole Third Reich, Hitler was the lesser of many evils. In fact, Kerry was paid to do research for Kirstein's Hitler book, which consisted of going to the New Orleans Public Library and transcribing the thoughts of various Nazi leaders. The most useful source Kerry found in these regards was a diary by Joseph Goebbels containing the types of quotes Kirstein wanted for his book; things that sounded far worse than anything Hitler ever uttered.

Sometime around Christmas, Slim told Kerry: "I've got a Christmas present for you: you have ridden in Carlos Marcello's car." This referred to the fancy black limo, the owner of which was now revealed to be the New Orleans mob boss. At the time, this incident held little significance to Kerry, although later it would be magnified several-fold during Jim Garrison's JFK assassination probe when Marcello would be linked to a prime suspect in the case, David Ferrie. (Gary Kirstein, it should be noted, also worked for Mafia don Papa Joe Comforto, or at least bragged as much to Kerry. Part of Kerry's motivation for meeting charismatic characters connected to the New Orleans underworld, like Kirstein, was to gather material for his book project, *The Colored Wheel*, which would depict the diverse lifestyles of the Big Easy, made up of mobsters, hustlers, writers, artists, musicians, bohemians, and the homosexual subculture.)

On another occasion, Kerry actually met David Ferrie at a party at Ferrie's house. According to Kerry, this brief meeting consisted simply of hand shaking and introductions, as well as a short and un-noteworthy conversation.

■

In January 1962, Kerry was laid off from his job at American Photocopy, and in the weeks to follow he worked at a smattering of temporary jobs, until finally landing a position as a shoe salesman at Marks-Isaacs department store, a job that he kept until mid-1962. This was also when Lee Oswald returned to the U.S. Kerry was alerted to Oswald's return by a *Los Angeles Times* article that his parents sent to him. Kerry seriously considered making a trip to Dallas to visit Oswald to gather more background material for *The Idle Warriors*.

During his stint at Marks-Isaacs, Kerry moved from his rooming house on Napoleon Avenue to a place on Barracks Street in the

French Quarter. Throughout the autumn of 1962, Kerry held a string of temp jobs, until landing a position as a waiter at the Sheraton-Charles Hotel. Shortly thereafter, he moved to a small room on the corner of Royal and Dumaine streets. Kerry occupied no less than nine different pads during his three years in New Orleans, and liked to boast that he could store everything he owned in a single war surplus footlocker.

In late 1962—in a conversation between Kerry, Slim, and Gary Kirstein—somehow the topic of assassinating President Kennedy came up, which appeared, at first, to be nothing more than a morbid intellectual exercise. To friends and associates, Kerry never minced words about his distaste for Kennedy, and he firmly believed that the world would be a better place without him around. Due to the influence of Ayn Rand, Kerry now considered himself a "capitalist revolutionary" and had no qualms whatsoever about wishing Kennedy dead.

Gary Kirstein quizzed Kerry about how he would off the president, and Kerry came up with a couple of suggestions, one of which entailed using a poison that could "blow his stomach apart," as well as another scenario involving the use of a remote control plane with a bomb in it, ostensibly blowing Kennedy to smithereens. After Kerry finished with his ideas, Gary added, "And next we'll get Martin Luther King."

Toward the end of their conversation, Kirstein said, "I think the best way to pull off a political assassination and get away with it would be to have many people involved, but kept under the illusion that they were pursuing other goals."

Kerry suggested that if one intended to pull off a conspiracy of such magnitude, they'd need "to send someone out to lead the opposition around in circles so an assassination would not be solved." Kerry had lifted this idea from *The Talent Scout* by Romain Gary, a novel about a Latin American dictator who recruits an agent provocateur to lead a revolution against himself in the prospects of infiltrating and gathering information on his enemies. Kirstein said that the problem with this idea was that whomever you would send out on such a mission would invariably switch over to the other side. Kerry interjected that if he were to take part in an assassination, he would afterwards have himself hypnotized so that he would forget his participation, words that later—like a lot of Kerry's conversations with the enigmatic "Brother-in-law"—would come back to haunt him.

As Kerry and Slim stood at the door, preparing to leave, Kirstein added: "Only one problem remains: who to frame. I figure some jailbird." When Kerry asked why, Kirstein's response was something to the effect that people who are caught for crimes are weak and don't deserve any breaks. Kerry objected to this line of reasoning, and suggested that a communist would make a better patsy.

To this suggestion, Kirstein smiled and nodded his head knowingly.

■

By the spring of 1963, Kerry decided to put *The Idle Warriors* on the shelf, and devote his time to poetry. One night he was at a French Quarter watering hole with some friends, taking turns reading poems aloud, when into the bar stumbled a somewhat intoxicated fellow named Clint Bolton, who began berating Kerry about his poetry. Kerry reacted rudely, though this didn't seem to faze Bolton, who just continued on with his harangue.

The two eventually wound up alone together in another bar "talking about Pindar by sunrise." The next morning—back at Clint's house—Kerry told his newfound friend all about *The Idle Warriors*, and Clint encouraged Kerry to forget about poetry and devote himself exclusively to his unfinished novel. When they finished their marathon rap session that morning, Clint told Kerry to "Go home and write, ya bum." This phrase was later used in the dedication of Kerry's first published book, *Oswald*.

In late October of 1963, Kerry took a job waiting tables at

Arnaud's restaurant, one of the better-known eateries in the French Quarter.

News of Kennedy's assassination broke during the lunch hour, when a waiter who'd been taking a break outside came in to report that the cops had picked up a suspect in the assassination identified as a former Marine. The waiter couldn't remember the name, but the suspect in question had defected to Russia for a couple of years before returning to America. When Kerry guessed the suspect's name, all hell broke loose among the serving staff. Someone even went so far as to ask Kerry if he'd had a hand in the assassination. "One cretinous individual," Kerry remembered, "even began gossiping, behind my back, that I was in fact Lee Harvey Oswald's brother."

In response to the news, Kerry celebrated the national tragedy in his own irreverent way, reveling while others grieved aloud. As Kerry recalled in an interview:

> I was in Arnaud's restaurant in New Orleans
> waiting tables, and when the news came through
> that Kennedy had been killed, I started singing
> "This then is Texas, Lone Star State." [Laughing] I
> was just ecstatic—I was so happy, and I hated
> him because of the Katanga Massacre. I hated
> him because he was like Wesley Mooch in *Atlas
> Shrugged*…he was trying to impose price controls,
> and all this…I thought he was going to plunge
> the whole world into starvation, you know,
> including the United States first.

Kerry's jubilance turned to horror when Oswald was shot dead two days later. Now everyone who'd been in mourning was suddenly smug about Oswald's murder, while Kerry fell into an immediate funk over the sudden shooting of poor pathetic Lee, whom he felt was a total innocent caught in the crossfire.

By this time, both the Secret Service and the FBI had been to

Arnaud's to question Kerry and middle-aged men in suits seemed always to be trailing him. Kerry, fearing that he was now a suspect, decided that the only rational thing to do was go to the local FBI office and volunteer for a lie detector test. In an article called "Oswald and I—and The FBI," Kerry recounted his interview at the FBI office:

> The man who ended up interviewing me…was an authentic police type. The kind who plays the Commissioner in movies. Greying hair. Irish mug. Hardboiled manner. Cigar. He looked bored. He put his feet up on his desk and sneered at me.
>
> I began to explain the real reason I was there, and he wanted to know if I'd had my picture taken yet. I hadn't. So we went out in the hall and they took my picture.
>
> We returned to the office and, again, I started my explanation. For I wanted my motivation clear. Oswald was once a close acquaintance, and I had sort of liked him. Besides, he would have bungled anything so complicated as a political assassination for sure. He was not the cold-blooded psychopath the pandering press was making him out to be. Although my political outlook precluded my having much sympathy for the late President, it did not dim my eagerness to see whomever had used Oswald as a tool—be he Bircher, Red, or whatever else—prosecuted to the hilt. Just as I was on the verge of volunteering my help, my friend the Commissioner interrupted to inform me that the FBI was not interested in my political opinions. They were not Thought Police, he assured, missing the whole point.
>
> I tried a few more times. I don't recall the exact

sequence, but once I was asked if Oswald was "a homo of any kind" and another time I was interrupted with a list of names. Were any of them familiar? Nope.

Another thing that happened during this interview was that a line containing what must have been half the FBI agents in New Orleans filed past the open door of the office, as if they were coming in at quitting time to punch out.

Either I wasn't such a hot suspect after all or these Feds had lousy security, risking compromise of all those men....

The Commissioner yawned. If I thought of anything more please give him a call. His name was—oddly—Kennedy.

In the days to follow, Kerry contemplated leaving New Orleans and moving to New York to be closer to the Ayn Rand crowd. The other option under consideration was a move to Alexandria, Virginia, at the behest of his childhood friend Robert McDonald, who extended Kerry an invitation to stay with him there. One afternoon, Kerry discussed these alternatives with Slim Brooks, who persuaded him to move to Alexandria on the basis that it was in closer to the nation's capital and would benefit Kerry's budding writing career, increasing the likelihood he would be called to testify about the assassination, which in turn would be good publicity for *The Idle Warriors*.

Kerry's time in New Orleans, besides being traumatic, would prove become the seminal moment of his life. Although Kerry had celebrated the news of Kennedy's death, it was nonetheless painful. Kerry's anti-Kennedy sentiments—and how they were expressed—brought him into conflict with a number of New Orleans friends and acquaintances, causing him to feel alienated. His tangled relationships and their even more tangled activities would take a life-time to unravel; each person would have their own take on what Kerry was doing, why, and for whom. What's more, Kerry caught the attention of people who had their own agendas, including New Orleans District Attorney Jim Garrison, a figure who would come to loom large in Kerry's life and psyche.

Kerry had been working only sporadically on a rewrite of *The Idle Warriors* during his last few months in New Orleans, but—with all that had gone on—it now seemed like a good time for him to buckle down and finish it. For this to happen, he knew he'd have to get away from the distractions of the French Quarter.

CHAPTER 4

Discordian Interlude

"Any theology to which I made significant contributions is going to attract plenty of screwballs."

—KERRY THORNLEY, *The New Discordian Dispensation*

From December 1963 through mid-1964, Kerry worked in Arlington as a doorman and switchboard operator at a high-rise apartment called the Shirlington House. Kerry later described his stay there as a cloistered existence, where he spent most of his off time working on *The Idle Warriors* rewrite.

While Kerry worked on *The Idle Warriors* in Alexandria, Greg Hill resurfaced in New Orleans, and the two resumed their correspondence, which was mainly concerned not with politics, but with religion. Or, rather, the spoof religion they invented while arguing in a bowling alley in 1957.

Kerry, at the time, was writing poems about how "through chaos order would at last unfold," which he read aloud to Greg amid the clattering of bowling balls and pins. Greg responded, "No, there's no such thing as order. Order is something that the human mind projects on reality—the mind shapes our perceptions and order is really a prevailing form of chaos. There is no order anywhere, it is *all* chaos…. You know, the Greeks had a deity for it."

"A deity for what?" Kerry asked.

"Chaos!" Greg replied.

The result of their bowling alley exchanges was a light-hearted and irreverent religious tract known as the *Principia Discordia, or How I Found the Goddess and What I Did to Her When I Found Her*. Much of the *Principia Discordia* was written by Greg Hill, then passed back and forth and re-written and added on to by fellow Discordian conspirators in years to follow. Over the years the anonymous authorship of the *Principia Discordia* had been rumored to be the work of everyone from Timothy Leary to Alan Watts to Richard Nixon.

Another early member of the Discordian Society was Bob Newport, whom you could refer to as the third member of a holy trinity of Discordianism co-founders. According to Newport, no specific bowling alley can claim to be the site of the birth of the Discordian movement. It evolved at several different bowling alleys. This revelation came as a devastating disappointment to your humble author, who—in the course of researching this book—had planned a grand religious pilgrimage to this envisioned holy site, where I would snap sacred photos of "The Brunswick Shrine," and perhaps even fall to my knees before this fabled Mecca of Discordianism, bowing to the Goddess Eris. But such was not to be my fate. As I discovered, the choice of a bowling alley really held no mystical significance, other than the fact that bowling alleys stayed open all night and served alcohol.

Greg Hill, who looked old for his age, usually bought the beer for the rest of the gang, which all drank thereof and through holy intoxication summoned forth the chaotic spirit of the Goddess of Confusion and Discord. So much for Hill and Thornley's contention that they were busy sipping coffee in a bowling alley when the revelation of Goddess Eris unfolded. Now, as the truth has been told by Bob Newport, the revelation of the goddess had as much to do with alcohol-induced reveries as it did caffeine-inspired visions. As related in the *Principia Discordia*:

> Suddenly the place became devoid of light. Then
> an utter silence enveloped them, and a great still-
> ness was felt. Then came a blinding flash of
> intense light, as though their very psyches had
> gone nova. Then vision returned.
>   The two were dazed and neither moved nor

spoke for several minutes. They looked around and saw that the bowlers were frozen like statues in a variety of comic positions, and that a bowling ball was steadfastly anchored to the floor only inches from the pins that it had been sent to scatter. The two looked at each other, totally unable to account for the phenomenon. The condition was one of suspension, and one noticed that the clock had stopped.

There walked into the room a chimpanzee, shaggy and grey about the muzzle, yet upright to his full five feet, and poised with natural majesty. He carried a scroll and walked to the young men.

"Gentlemen," he said, "why does Pickering's Moon go about in reverse orbit? Gentlemen, there are nipples on your chest; do you give milk? And what, pray tell, Gentlemen, is to be done about Heisenberg's Law?" He paused. "SOMEBODY HAD TO PUT ALL OF THIS CONFUSION HERE!"

And with that he revealed the scroll. It was a diagram, like a yin-yang with a pentagon on one side and an apple on the other. And then he exploded and the two lost consciousness.

They awoke to the sound of pins clattering, and found the bowlers engaged in their game and the waitress busy making coffee. It was apparent that their experience had been private...(p. 1-2 of the fourth edition).

During the course of their divinely inspired revelation, Kerry and Greg were born again into their Discordian personas of Omar Khayyam Ravenhurst (Kerry) and Malaclypse the Younger (Greg).

Over the next few years, Omar and Mal spent endless hours

researching the cryptic meanings behind the obscure symbol that appeared on the chimpanzee's parchment. On the fifth night following "the Revelation" Omar and Mal shared the same dream in which Eris appeared unto them and declared: "I am chaos. I am the substance from which your artists and scientists build rhythms. I am the spirit with which your children and clowns laugh happy in anarchy. I am alive, and I tell you that you are free." Ensuing visions revealed to Mal and Omar that the symbol—revealed unto them via the chimp's parchment—was called the Sacred Chao, and that for further information thereof they would need to consult their pineal glands.

Discordianism—for the uninitiated—is a "spoof" religion dedicated to the worship of Eris, the Greek goddess of chaos, known in Latin as Discordia, although some would contend that Discordianism is more than a mere spoof, and is, in fact, the world's first true religion. Furthermore, the Discordian movement has been described as a Non-Prophet Irreligious Disorganization which some claim is a complicated joke disguised as a new religion. Discordians themselves contend that it's actually a new religion disguised as a complicated joke.

The *Principia Discordia* is the revelation of the doctrine of Chaos and the worship of the Goddess Eris, telling the story of how humanity fell from grace due to the Original Snub. According to legend, the Original Snub came about when Zeus hosted a wedding banquet for Peleus and Thetis, but failed to invite Eris because of her reputation as a troublemaker. As payback, Eris created an apple of pure gold upon which she inscribed KALLISTI ("To the prettiest one").

The ensuing battle, over whom the apple referred to, ostensibly launched the Trojan War. This was the first war of mankind, a perfect example of chaos in action. Besides the Trojan War, the Apple of Discord subsequently unleashed other Discordian mysteries, including the Law of Fives, which suggests that all events in the universe are related to the number five, and that this relationship can always be demonstrated, given enough ingenuity on the part of the demonstrator.

The Law of Five in Discordianism is further demonstrated in the Five Commandments — but also the Five Apostles of Eris, the five ranks within Discordianism, and the five-fingered hand of Eris guiding all of humankind's chaotic movements. In this respect, it should come as no surprise that the first run of the *Principia Discordia* consisted of five copies published in 1965.

The practice of Discordianism—i.e. sowing the seeds of chaos as a means of achieving a higher state of awareness—is a perceptual game, better known in some quarters as Operation Mindfuck. In this manner, the skewing of reality can be used as a method of attaining illumination, in whatever guise it may appear. And this is just what those wacky Discordians were getting at: a spoof religion which leads to greater wisdom. (Or at least that's my take, as admittedly I've never been a card-carrying member of the Discordian Society.[2])

Like the Zen master whacking his pupil on the head and laughing at the pure idiocy of existence (which in some cases immediately produces divine visions), "peak experiences" are also known to accompany the practice of Discordianism, a practice which suggests that the absurd is just as valid as the mundane, and chaos just as valid as order.

The unstated goal of Discordianism is to liberate the practitioner from the so-called "order games" that make up our everyday routines. Among these teachings is the rejection of "dogma" for "catma." As dogma is a proposition that is either true or false, a catma can contain an infinite number of meanings, some true, others false, and some whose meaning may change at a moment's notice, the false becoming true, or the truth, suddenly a falsehood.

But alas, in time—like most major religions—division reared its ugly head within the hierarchy of the Discordian movement, and it soon grew into two somewhat opposing factions. But of course, this was according to the rule: "We Discordians must stick apart!"

On one side of this yin/yang coin was the Erisian Liberation Front (ELF) led by none other than Ho Chi Zen (another Kerry Thornley alias). ELF promoted the more anarchic and anti-authoritarian side of the Discordian movement, whereas the other faction, the Paratheo-Anametamystikhood of Eris Esoteric (POEE), led by Malaclypse the Younger, taught a more mystical doctrine. These two combating Discordianisms represent the metaphysical hodge and podge as depicted in the Sacred Chao.

More on Discordianism later.

CHAPTER 5

Star Witness

In the spring of 1964, while doing his doorman gig at the Shirlington House, and creating the Discordian Society via correspondence with Greg Hill, Kerry received a phone call from Warren Commission attorney Albert Jenner requesting that Kerry give a deposition. Kerry agreed, and was asked to bring along his writings on Oswald.

The offices of the commission were inconspicuously located in a VFW building behind the Supreme Court. Kerry arrived there one "bright spring morning" and a janitor invited him to take a seat near the open office door of J. Lee Rankin, the commission's lead attorney.

While Kerry waited, Rankin bustled in and out, conferring with other staffers. At one point, Kerry caught a glimpse of former CIA Director Allen Dulles, who shuffled by, cracking jokes with secretaries and puffing his ever-present pipe. In due time, Albert Jenner arrived, with his assistant, John Ely, and a court reporter. The four moved to a conference room where Kerry delivered his testimony. He also turned over the first two drafts of *The Idle Warriors*.

Much to Kerry's relief, Jenner didn't bring up the subject of his celebration of Kennedy's death. When Kerry returned a few days later to edit his transcript for errors, Jenner—off the record—broached the subject. "We heard about the way you reacted to the assassination, but we also asked around and found out that when you get a couple of beers in you, you mouth off a lot and like to get people riled up," he told Kerry.

While correcting his Warren Commission testimony, Kerry asked Jenner how the Secret Service had managed to track him down for questioning so soon after the assassination. To this, Jenner grinned and left the room, returning soon after with Kerry's FBI file. Jenner withdrew a half-page report, which noted that Kerry had aroused suspicion by dropping a couple of comments about Oswald at Arnaud's restaurant following the assassination and, in turn, someone had notified the Feds. Jenner then claimed he had to leave for about 15 minutes to go pick up his wife at the Supreme Court, leaving Kerry alone with his entire FBI file. Somehow, Kerry overcame the temptation to examine its contents. Later, someone in "the business" told Kerry that this was an old interrogation trick: to see if he was worried enough about his file to actually pick it up and look through it.

In total, Kerry's Warren Commission testimony consisted of 33 pages in Volume 11, and drew a picture of Oswald as an anti-social loner with communist sympathies. Although Kerry's testimony seemed innocuous enough, just a guy who'd known Oswald way back when, he'd be linked to the Kennedy assassination for the rest of his life.

■

Late in the summer of 1964, Kerry returned to New Orleans for a brief visit and to present a lecture on Objectivism at the Quorum Coffee House. Upon arrival, Kerry bumped into Slim Brooks, who told him: "There's a man who wants to see you before you leave town. A fellow whose name begins with K." Slim was referring to Brother-in-law, aka Gary Kirstein. It seemed odd to Kerry that Kirstein would make a special effort to meet, since the two had never really been close friends.

Kirstein didn't attend Kerry's lecture, but showed up afterwards, out on the back patio along with Slim. At the time, the Warren Commission Report had just been released, and Slim regarded Kerry as a celebrity of sorts, going out of his way to call people over to his table, saying, "This is Kerry Thornley—he knew Oswald." Kerry—with tongue firmly planted in cheek—would then respond: "Yeah, I masterminded the Kennedy assassination. How do you do?"

Kirstein, on this occasion, had nothing to say. He just sat in the semi-darkness with a smug grin, appearing to regard the whole spectacle with satisfaction. Kerry was a bit taken aback, as he couldn't figure out the purpose of this mysterious meeting, cast—as it was—under moonlit shadows.

Kerry thought it strange that Kirstein seemed so pleased with himself at this particular time, as his girlfriend, Ola Holcomb, had just committed suicide. Holcomb—an aspiring French Quarter writer—had been close friends with Kerry, and it was through Kerry that Ola had been introduced to Kirstein.

Ola had shot herself in the head a couple of weeks prior to Kerry's return to New Orleans, and her suicide deeply disturbed him; Ola had always appeared to be such a strong-willed woman. Years later—when Kerry reflected back upon these murky meetings with Brother-in-law—he suspected that Ola may have discovered a great many secrets about her lover, Kirstein, that, in turn, led to her undoing.

As the Quorum Coffee House meeting unfolded, Kirstein continued to sit mutely in the shadows, as Kerry, Slim, and other coffeehouse patrons made small talk, much of which revolved around the Kennedy assassination. Finally—when Slim and Gary were preparing to leave—Kerry asked Kirstein what he'd been up to. Kirstein replied that he was doing fine and enjoyed living out in the country, as there were "no neighbors to hear screaming at night." Kirstein punctuated this sinister remark with an evil glare. He followed this odd pronouncement by mumbling something about how he was going to go out and get himself a "nigger woman and beat the hell out of her." As they parted company, Kerry silently wished never to see "Brother-in-law" again.

■

After his stopover in New Orleans, Kerry visited Robert LeFevre's Freedom School in Colorado Springs, where he'd won a scholarship for a two-week course of libertarian study. LeFevre was a very important voice in the libertarian scene at the time, and due to his influence Kerry began his next important ideological change, gradually moving from, as he described it: "Ayn Rand's concept of limited government to the position that a non-violent and wholly non-governmental society was both desirable and, in time, possible." So it was that Kerry came to embrace anarchism, inspired in part by LeFevre teachings, who convinced Kerry that political violence served only to strengthen the State, and that governmental bodies were nothing but criminal protection rackets hiding themselves behind the respectability of Divine Right and constitutionalism.

As Kerry's studies of anarchism intensified, a major influence on his thinking became Max Stirner's *The Ego and His Own*. The essence of Stirner's philosophy said that if everyone was a law unto themselves, then there would be no followers, and without followers, no leaders, and without leaders there would be no State. Inspired by the words of this nineteenth century German anarchist, Kerry began making Stirneristic proclamations to libertarian friends, such as: "If I find it in my self-interest, I will lie, cheat, steal, kill, etc. I am a law unto myself. I reject not only altruism, but all systems of morality."

While living in Alexandria, Kerry subscribed to a libertarian newsletter called *The Innovator*. Although he found the discussions in *The Innovator* intellectually stimulating, he was annoyed by all of its spelling errors, and wrote a letter of complaint. In response, Kerry was offered a job as *The Innovator's* managing editor, and he accepted.

Kerry returned to southern California and began his position at *The Innovator* soon after his Freedom School visit. Kerry—who operated at a very high energy level—was renowned for changing ideas in conversation roughly every two minutes, and it could be argued that the only reason *The Innovator* had any cohesive logic was due largely to the influence of his then girlfriend, Cara Leach, who played a large and unsung role in *The Innovator's* editing chores.

According to those who knew the pair, Kerry and Cara were a bit of an odd couple: always quiet and mellow, Cara's countenance was roundish, as she was at that time somewhat overweight. Whereas Kerry—skinny as a rail—was a bundle of kinetic energy who practically vibrated with boundless intellectual energy. And so it was that Kerry provided much of the energy behind *The Innovator*, while Cara held it together and gave *The Innovator* internal focus and some semblance of sanity.

It was during this period that Kerry found himself at odds with Objectivists and other right-wing libertarians who maintained a belief in government as a "necessary evil." Kerry soon started referring to himself as an anarchist and began his self-education into the ideas of noted anarchists through history. At the same time, he discovered radical politics and began pioneering efforts among libertarian elements to cooperate politically with the New Left, instead of with conservatives, whose positions on sex, race, and unthinking patriotism, Kerry felt, limited the pursuit of individual freedom.

For several months, Kerry had been corresponding with Louise Lacey on matters related to Objectivist philosophy and the writings of Ayn Rand. At the time, Lacey worked as a secretary, and later editor, for Paul Neimark at Novel Books, a publisher of newspapers, magazines, and paperbacks. After his Freedom School visit, Kerry stopped over in Chicago to meet with Neimark and Lacey to discuss possibly writing for Neimark.

As Louise later recalled, Kerry's initial appearance left a lasting impression, if for no other reason than that he showed up wearing every article of clothing he owned, roughly six pairs of clothes, one on top of the other. Apparently the reason Kerry was dressed in this rather unusual manner was due to the fact that it was freezing cold on his bus ride into Chicago and he didn't own a suitcase.

Shortly after returning to southern California, Kerry received a letter from Neimark, who expressed an interest in publishing a nonfiction paperback written by him on Oswald. This, in turn, led to Kerry's first published book, titled—appropriately enough—

Oswald, published by New Classics House in April 1965.

Oswald, in retrospect, is a curious work, in the sense that it's an endorsement of the Warren Commission Report. This is not to say that the book, at the time, was not a sincere portrait of Oswald as seen through the lens of Kerry's perception, albeit distorted by the popular "lone nut assassin theory" as projected by the Warren Commission and the popular press.

Part of Kerry's thesis—as presented in *Oswald*—speculated on how someone who'd dabbled in left-wing politics could have evolved into a presidential assassin, a theory which deeply offended many Warren Commission critics, one of whom was David Lifton, who later went on to author one of the classic studies in the field, *Best Evidence*.

In June 1965—when Lifton happened upon a copy of *Oswald*—it aroused enough contempt in him that he tracked down Kerry to discuss the matter. As it so happened, Lifton lived near Kerry, and a meeting was arranged at Kerry's apartment in Culver City, which he was then sharing with Cara. Lifton brought along the entire 26 volumes of the Warren Report, which he proceeded to spread out all over Kerry's floor like mixed-up puzzle pieces.

Kerry described Lifton during this encounter as like a "high-pressure salesman trying to peddle a set of encyclopedias." Although Lifton's approach was a tad over the top, he nonetheless presented a convincing argument, demonstrating time and again that crucial Warren Report testimony had been ignored, and pointing out the numerous contradictions within the 26 volumes.

By the time the evening was over, Cara was in tears and Kerry had done a complete about-face from his earlier position of Oswald as a psychologically unbalanced misfit who had acted alone in the assassination.

■

On December 11, 1965, Kerry and Cara were married in a formal ceremony at Wayfarer's Chapel, a glass church overlooking the ocean near Palos Verdes, California. Its patio—situated amid live plants and running water—provided a relaxed yet spiritual setting. The only noteworthy occurrence happened when Kerry knelt to face the altar and the holes in the soles of his shoes were revealed.

In the spring of 1966—motivated by his earlier conversations with David Lifton—Kerry began speaking out against the Warren Report. These public denunciations appeared in a *Fact* magazine interview in December, and in an article Kerry wrote for *The Innovator* titled "Oswald Revisited." In addition, Kerry gave lectures at the Henry George schools in San Diego and Los Angeles, as well as an interview on KPFK public radio in L.A. on the Harry Pollard show.

In late 1966, Kerry and Cara took a trip across the country to visit Cara's parents in Pennsylvania for Christmas. As they traveled through the Midwest, news of Jim Garrison's Kennedy assassination investigation hit newspapers and flashed across TV screens. Kerry sensed an ill breeze beginning to blow.

CHAPTER 6

Sex, Drugs, and Treason

By 1967, Kerry's politics had gone through a radical shift. He—like many in the country, including Jim Garrison—saw through the Warren Report. He was deeply involved in *The Innovator*. His rallying cry was now "sex, drugs, and treason"—everything that flew in the face of the conservative agenda, an agenda that Kerry, in many respects, had previously embraced with his enthusiasm for libertarianism and free market ideas. As Kerry wrote about this period:

> When the conservatives began complaining that radical students were interested in nothing but "sex, drugs, and treason" I realized that, instinctually, they had hit the nail on the head. Sex, drugs, and treason were the three things I stood for.... Regarding sex, I became firmly convinced that unless there were trends established in our culture in the direction of uncompromising sexual honesty, tolerance for minority sexual preferences, equal treatment of the sexes, rational openness concerning VD and birth control, and saner attitudes regarding sex and child-rearing, particularly with reference to masturbation—further meaningful social change would not be possible. The basic cornerstone of the entire edifice of the authoritarian submissive/dominant personality, I came to believe, was composed of the implicit supposition that one's body does not really belong to oneself, which is contained in all sexually antagonistic attitudes, from censorship

to rape. The child who is persuaded not to masturbate will, of logical necessity, become an adult who can be conned or coerced into military behavior. Ownership of one's body is the political issue.

Regarding drugs, I gained a great deal of respect for psychedelic substances as powerful tools for restructuring portions of one's personality which could not be reached by intellectual effort alone, for expanding one's sense of identification and compassion, and for opening the narrow and dry Western ego to mystical possibilities. Zen and similar styles of meditation, along with the yoga disciplines, I came to see as methods for maintaining psychedelic levels of awareness, once the chemicals had demonstrated the nature of such modes of consciousness...

Regarding treason, I came gradually to a position of supporting nearly all factions on the radical left, except in their quarreling with each other and the dogmatic insistence of some of these groups on the insistence of political violence (or, in other cases, the immorality of violence under all circumstances). I came to this position without ever abandoning some of the more libertarian elements on the extreme right. Meanwhile, I continued to refine my own political philosophy of anarchism—not because I favored "violence and chaos" with which anarchism is nearly always falsely equated, but because of my opposition to violence and chaos, for which government military machines and bureaucratic structures are largely responsible in today's world.

During Kerry's first acid trip, he caught himself conspiring to put LSD in the Los Angeles water supply, then started laughing to himself at the lunacy of such a notion. When others wanted to know what he found so funny, Kerry explained: "And until now the one thing I could never understand about Zen masters was what made them *want* to enlighten others!"

Due to his LSD experimentation, Kerry came to feel that "the universe was infinitely more profound, and filled with many more unexpectable possibilities" than he'd previously imagined. He also encouraged his friends to partake of the divine sacrament, as chronicled in a letter to Louise Lacey from the period, instructing her to "get with the psychedelic scene soon. It is scary at first, I know, but you can overcome or shall we say ride out the fear trips if you will. And after that, one realizes the fantastic key this thing, whatever it is, provides. There is beauty in the silver singing river and the opposite of love, baby, is not hate, but fear."

In years to come, hallucinogens would become an integral part of Louise's life, as she recounted in Rebecca Klatch's *A Generation Divided*: "Smoking dope and taking acid and listening to music [made me see] the larger whole. I identified with the whole instead of just myself. LSD tends to do that to you. It's the kind of experience you don't go back from.... It's why I dropped out in the first place...I no longer wanted to be among those who were autopsying the putrid corpse of the body social. I wanted to create positive alternatives instead" (p. 154).

■

As part of Kerry's interest in sexual liberation, he joined "a sexually swinging psychedelic tribe" into mate swapping, dope smoking, and LSD-tripping. Known as the Southern California Kerista, the group was established in the early 60s by John Presmont, who thereafter took the name Brother Jud.

The Keristas were renowned for their "beautiful weekend

orgies," as Kerry fondly remembered. During this period, Kerry's income was a total of 50 bucks a week, which was derived from writing "case histories," most of them factual, for Monogram Publications—a southern California porn publisher—based on his experiences with the Keristas.

In 1966, the group's newspaper changed its name from *Kerista* to *Kerista Swinger*, presumably to generate greater appeal from a new generation of hip sexual experimenters. The *Kerista Swinger* unabashedly christened itself as the "Hippest Paper in the USA." Kerry—calling himself "Young Omar"—wrote several articles for the *Kerista Swinger*, of which the following is an excerpt:

> Kerista is a religion and the mood of Kerista is one
> of holiness. Do not, however, look for a profusion
> of rituals, dogmas, doctrines, and scriptures.
> Kerista is too sacred for that. It is more akin to the
> religions of the East and, also, the so-called pagan
> religions of the pre-Christian West. Its fount of
> being is the religious experience and that action or
> word or thought which is not infused with ecstasy
> is not Kerista. And Kerista, like those religions of
> olden times, is life-affirming.

In *Drawing Down the Moon*, Margot Adler observed that Kerry's writings on Kerista signaled the true beginnings of the neo-pagan movement in contemporary culture, which since the mid-60s has expressed itself in myriad forms, such as free-love communes, Wicca practitioners, the back-to-nature movement, psychedelic experimenters, and various other groups dedicated to spiritual discovery and sexual freedom. In *Drawing Down the Moon*, Adler cites Kerry as the first person to actually use the word "pagan" to describe past and present nature religions.

■

Kerry termed his second acid trip, taken in 1966 or so, a "horrible bummer…wherein Brahma, Vishnu, and Shiva fought it out to the tune of machine gun fire while red, white and blue hammers-and-sickles and swastikas danced around the ceiling in the dark." During the course of this trip, Kerry "perceived clearly that busting one's ass was not a commandment from Heaven, but one originated by the rich to keep the poor busy and useful."

This second acid trip provided Kerry with the realization of what it would take to make him genuinely happy: "More time, less hustle." To this end, Kerry talked to Cara, and told her he was tired of busting his butt just to make a buck, that he was no longer willing to go rushing through life "as if it were something to be gotten over with." Just the same, he agreed to keep up his end of the load; Cara, in turn, decided to take a part-time job.

Kerry's new mode of operation consisted of waking each morning and meditating until he'd figure out a way to make $10 that day—whether it was by writing, selling grass, or working odd jobs. And after this morning meditation, Kerry would then go about doing whatever he decided to do that day to make ends meet, indeed taking it "one day at a time," to use the worn cliché.

At this time, Kerry's grandparents had moved to an old folks home, and their house on 77th Street in Watts became vacant, so Kerry and Cara decided to rent it for $50 a month. A cool old house, it featured two bedrooms and a large living-dining area composed of two adjoining rooms, a glassed-in front porch, a large old-fashioned kitchen, and an enormous backyard. The dining room, with a south-facing bay window, overlooked a beautiful trellised garden. Grandpa's radio—which was four and a half feet tall and three feet wide—still stood in the corner of the dining room, but now instead of playing Amos 'n Andy and Fibber McGee and Molly, the big old box was tuned into *Radio Free Oz*, booming music by the likes of Ravi Shankar, Simon and Garfunkel, and the Beatles.

With Kerry and Cara as its occupants, the Watts house became a cozy blend of memorabilia and psychedelia. Antique window glass was decorated with pieces of translucent contact paper to give it the effect of stained glass. An ornately carved wooden mantle clock had the word "NOW" written on a round placard that covered its face.

With plenty of room for guests to roam around, Kerry's house became a psychedelic social center. One frequent visitor was Bud Simco, Kerry's buddy from the Marines. As Simco remembered in 2003:

> Kerry was charismatic and had the ability to attract diverse personalities, people who would normally not be associated with each other, except by the force of Kerry's personality. For example, there were so-called hippie types tripping under the dining room table, holding burning candles in their hands, while right-wing types were holding forth in the kitchen. One such character I recall had never been to Watts before, and showed up wearing a bullet-proof vest and armed with a .45. He seemed reasonable enough, in conversation, but he was taking no chances [having never been around hippies before]. There were people from all walks of life...including a pilot for the Flying Tiger Airlines, a student from MIT, some swingers, a fashion model, some writers, some SDS student types, and various and sundry others whom I did not know. One of my guests at one particular gathering was a former motorcycle gang member who lost his foot in a motorcycle accident, and his beautiful American Indian wife, who was at the time a co-worker of mine. He had never seen such an assorted group

of people in his life, for example, but with his tambourine, magic mushrooms, and a Donovan LP
loudly playing, asserted his presence along with
all the diverse others in one righteous happening.
The thing is, everyone was tolerant of the other,
regardless of individual inclinations and/or politics. At such an event, many people would never
even interact with other groups, in other rooms,
although many did. That was the one universal
factor re: being present at one of Kerry's gatherings, either at his home in Watts, or perhaps at one
of the original "Be-Ins" at Griffith Park.

Another frequent guest was John Overton. In the 1950s,
Overton attended Georgia State University, where he earned an
engineering degree, and—according to one source—"chased more
black tail then anybody I ever heard of." This in a state where
black/white sexual relations were punishable by imprisonment.

During the Korean War, Overton served in the Navy and
somehow finagled a tour of duty in Jamaica, spending most of his
time during the conflict hitting on beautiful black women. Overton
developed such an excellent Jamaican accent that when he returned
to the states he hosted a local black radio show in Los Angeles,
appearing as "Trinidad John."

In the mid-60s, a period of self-discovery began for Overton,
revolving around his first acid trip, which turned him into a Zen
lunatic overnight and cured him of alcoholism. Apparently, this trip
consisted of some wild satori where everything in the universe
seemingly fit together like a huge cosmic puzzle. This event transformed his life. As a result, he decided to change his name from John
Albert Overton to Camden Benares. The idea of this name change
was to bring the teachings of the East into the Western world:
"Camden" for Camden, New Jersey, and Benares after Benares,
India, the city where the Buddha delivered his first sermon.

Kerry and Camden first met through a psychotherapist at UCLA named Chung, who ran a role-playing-psychodrama-therapy group at the university theater department, which a whole cast of interesting people attended, including lots of good-looking women, who Camden would score on with frequent regularity. According to longtime pal John F. Carr, Camden possessed a manic personality that totally captivated the ladies, and when he was on the make, he'd shift into this manic phase. According to Carr, it was an awesome sight to behold: "When Camden was on a full-blown manic, man, get out of his way, 'cause he could talk at the speed of light and his eyes *blazed*...I saw him do his magic, man, I mean I've been to a couple of orgies...well, parties that turned into orgies—he'd take women and come back for seconds, and thirds and fourths—those were pretty wild days."

■

Becky Glaser was another of those adventurous souls who wandered into Kerry's wild sphere. Becky—the product of a conservative upbringing—first became politically active, through a family friend, with the John Birch Society. This same woman later sponsored Becky to attend Robert LeFevre's Freedom School in Colorado Springs, which Kerry had attended in 1964. According to Becky, the two weeks she spent at the Freedom School changed her life, as she was exposed to totally new concepts, including atheism, anarchism, and libertarian ideas. "It hadn't occurred to me that not having a government was a viable alternative...I got my mind blown all at once and no drugs!" Becky was transformed from a Bircher to a libertarian in the course of a few days.

After her Freedom School experience, Becky became involved with the paramilitary right-wing group the Minutemen. At the time, she felt that society was primed for a collapse, and thus was attracted to the survivalist mentality of the group. In due time, Becky became heavily involved in Minutemen operations, as she worked out of their national headquarters in the Ozarks and ran paramilitary training sessions. Much of her interactions with the Minutemen revolved around "cops and robbers games" which included "helping line up relationships to run machine guns." As Becky recalled: "They were some of the craziest fuckers I've ever run into in my entire life!"

At one point, the leader of the Minutemen encouraged Becky to infiltrate some left-wing organizations, and during the course of her covert infiltration of these groups, Becky discovered she enjoyed hanging out with the very same people she'd been sent to spy on. Around this time, Becky began attending Kansas University, and found herself drawn to the war protesters on campus. In due time, Becky help start a Students for a Democratic Society (SDS) chapter at the university, acting as chief secretary for the group, and in time drifted away from the far-right influence of the Minutemen.

Sometime in 1966, Becky migrated to California with a group of friends involved in the libertarian movement. While there, Becky discovered *The Innovator*, and because of this wrote Kerry a letter praising the newsletter. In turn, Kerry invited Becky to be on the staff. When Becky informed him that she hated to write, Kerry replied: "Fine, you can be the comedy editor!"

Becky found Kerry to be a breath of fresh air, in contrast to the majority of Los Angeles libertarians, who were a rather tight-assed lot, very structured and strict, anal-retentive-type Republicans. This, of course, was the polar opposite of Kerry Wendell Thornley, a human whirling dervish from whom ideas flew like bolts of lightning.

■

The less-than-astute observer might pigeonhole Kerry and his coterie of late 60s colleagues incorrectly as "hippies," which most nowadays equate with "leftists." But Kerry started his self-education on the right side of the political spectrum, influenced—in great measure—by the Objectivist philosophy of Ayn Rand, who promoted less government control and more self-reliance. It was this philosophy that brought Kerry together with the likes of Becky Glaser and Louise Lacey.

It wasn't long, though, before this libertarian contingent became influenced by radical politics, which led them away from traditional libertarian values and into the more radical anarcho-libertarianism, which is not to say that Kerry and his colleagues ever seriously considered chuckin' bombs into capitalist strongholds like that most radical of 60s anarchist cabals, the Weather Underground.

It should be understood that anarchism doesn't necessarily equate to political change achieved through violent action, although this is certainly one aggressive avenue anarchy can take. As Benjamin Tucker once explained: "An Anarchist is anyone who denies the necessity and legitimacy of government; the question of his methods of attacking it is foreign to the definition."

In contrast, Kerry's form of anarchy was all about freeing oneself from government controls and affecting change in a subversive, yet positive, manner. One form this took was all the Discordian hijinks that—at their essence—could be considered Marxism to the tune of Groucho and Harpo. Kerry's unique brand of anarchism eventually evolved into *Zenarchy!*, his philosophy which added Zen Buddhism to his already prevalent anarchist leanings, with a twist of tantric yoga thrown in.

■

In late 1966, *The Innovator* published an article titled "Postman Against the State," which dealt with the various non-governmental postal systems throughout history that had functioned more effectively than government-operated systems.

As the "Playboy Forum" was then receiving a slew of complaints from readers about snooping by the postal service, Kerry persuaded *The Innovator's* publisher to send a copy of the "Postman Against the State" issue to *Playboy*. Robert Anton Wilson—an associate editor at *Playboy*—received this issue of *The Innovator*, and in turn responded to Kerry, which initiated a longstanding correspondence.

Kerry and Bob discussed, among other things, the American Letter Mail Company operated in New England in the mid-1800s by the individualist anarchist Lysander Spooner. The American Letter Mail Company, at the time, offered cheaper postage rates than the U.S. Post Office, scheduled more deliveries per day, and made a profit to boot. Spooner was finally put out of business when Congress made it illegal to deliver a first-class letter for profit. Both Kerry and Bob agreed that the U.S. postal system was once again ripe for change, and the concept Spooner had spawned one hundred years earlier was the direction the current mail system should go.

Kerry later described his correspondence with Wilson as "one of the longest, most intense, most stimulating, rewarding, enriching, enlightening—and certainly the most unusual—of my entire life." As Wilson described in *Cosmic Trigger*:

> We began writing long letters to each other...astonished at how totally our political philosophies agreed—we were both opposed to every form of violence or coercion against individuals, whether practiced by governments or by people who claimed to be revolutionaries. We were equally disenchanted with the organized Right and the organized Left while still remaining Utopians, without a visible Utopia to believe in (p. 56).

The groundbreaking year of 1967 ushered in the memorable "Summer of Love," and with it the Griffith Park Human Be-Ins. Kerry considered the Be-Ins to be tremendously important, as these events showed thousands of people that the idea of a true revolution—fueled by "sex, drugs, and treason!"—was a real possibility.

The Human Be-Ins were the perfect set and setting for Kerry to exercise his own irreverent sense of humor, and cast his brand upon a counterculture that was growing all around him, as he grew with it. At the first Griffith Park Be-In, Kerry cut a singular swath, equipped with a sign that contained a perfectly surreal statement that seemed to say one thing while also saying something else entirely, just the sort of irreverent psychedelic koan that Kerry became famous for. The sign read: "Stamp out quicksand. Ban LSD."

In the early morning of the first Be-In, Kerry gathered rose balls from the bushes surrounding his house. Later, at the Be-In, whenever Kerry made eye contact with anyone, he'd toss them one. Some Diggers liked Kerry's rose ball idea so much that they gave him a big, fat joint of Acapulco Gold in return. Ah, life was good!

As Louise Lacey recalled in 2002 about the first Griffith Park Be-In:

> The weather was perfect. We were all stoned. A single engine plane came and circled, and I thought it was the media, keeping track of us, but then a man all in white dropped down with a parachute and the crowd roared with approval. Later I learned that an old friend of mine from Marin County was the pilot. He got that plane out fast, because it was illegal to parachute within the city limits.
>
> The Be-In was fascinating because I had never seen such a large collection of freaks. I couldn't keep from grinning. I was particularly interested because some hard assed sociologist had said that when you were on LSD you were extremely susceptible to being led. I was watching for people being led.
>
> I saw a group of people organized into a crack-the-whip game. Twenty or twenty-five people

formed and a man with a megaphone was giving them instructions. (Definitely planned.)

"Move up the hill, move down. Hang on tight. Join with more people." I couldn't tell if anyone was listening or just all having fun. The people at the end of the line were moving so fast they kept being thrown off, tumbling down the hill in the grass, laughing hysterically. Then some of the crack-the-whip people let go of the hands of the people around them and drifted off. The megaphone man yelled more loudly. "Hang on, don't let go." More people drifted away. He was screaming now. The group all dropped hands and disappeared in the crowds and the megaphone man was screaming at the top of his amplified voice, "Come back! We are playing a game here!" But the people were gone.

I didn't worry any more about what that sociologist had said.

Many groups of people were gathered as "families of friends." It was the first time I had seen this form of organization. So there were tents, and lean-to's and lots of signs pounded into the dirt, describing one thing or another to identify who the friends were. (This is where Kerry's sign fit in.) As I didn't live in L.A., I didn't recognize anyone other than Kerry's friends, who didn't stay around his sign, but it didn't matter. I "knew" the strangers as friends, and we laughed and hugged and shared doobies, and listened to music and I moved on. Nobody got hurt, everyone had a good time (except, I imagine, the man with the megaphone). As the day progressed, I gravitated back to Kerry's sign and others did, too, and we

shared what we had experienced, eventually
gathered our stuff and drove home to Kerry's. A
most successful day.

In March 1967, *The Los Angeles Free Press* ran an article about how you could get high from smoking banana skins, complete with instructions on how to prepare the stuff. Kerry—ever the adventurous spirit—decided to give this new craze a go, and in the company of co-conspirator Louise Lacey visited the local Safeway supermarket, as the two of them cleaned out the produce section of their banana supply, then brought home the banana bounty, removed the fruit, and baked the inner creamy portion of the skins on cookie sheets—just as the article had instructed—afterwards rolling the stuff up in papers in preparation for their prospective psychedelic journey.

While this cosmic concoction was baking, Louise and Kerry went around the neighborhood ringing doorbells and offering skinned bananas to all interested parties. As Louise recalled: "This was a mostly black neighborhood, who knew Kerry, at least by sight, but still they weren't interested. He explained that it was an experiment, and that no one had messed with the bananas (which were getting brown), but they thanked him and shut the door, again and again, so we gave up."

Becky Glaser remembers walking into Kerry's house and discovering that every container was filled with peeled bananas. Becky said she will always remember the wild look in Kerry's eyes when she walked in and asked him: "And what the hell are we gonna do with all these fucking bananas?"

"Well, I'm urging you all to eat them."

"And what's gonna happen if we don't eat them?"

"I'll get rid of them!"

"Yeah, but what are you going do with the peels?"

"Aha! That's the important part!"

As Dick Thornley recalled: "Kerry enthusiastically invited me and Tom over for some Mellow Yellow that night. The invitation came after they had baked it. I recall the stuff was essentially powdered charcoal by the time it came out of the oven. It was nearly impossible to light, let alone smoke."

The "Mellow Yellow" craze is now noted in history books as an urban legend that took on a life of its own, helped along by the *L.A. Free Press* article and Donovan's tune of the same name. According to the liner notes of Donovan's *Greatest Hits*, the rumor that you could get high from banana peels was started by none other than Country Joe McDonald of Country Joe and the Fish.

Whatever the origin of the Mellow Yellow mythos, Louise Lacey remembers inhaling the banana skins was anything but mellow, the harsh smoke burning her lungs. As for copping a buzz, the only one who got off on the stuff was Kerry, who after toking down on the banana-flavored reefer, proclaimed, "I'm *high*!" Leave it to Kerry to be the only person in the history of the "Mellow Yellow" hoax to actually get off on the stuff. Of course, this wasn't out of the ordinary, because—as Becky Glaser recalled—"Kerry got high off of *everything*."

As Kerry later related his frame of mind during this time:

> While I remained a free enterprise libertarian in my economics, the whole question of economics subsided in importance for me in order to make room in my consciousness for the other ideas that were flooding the cultural atmosphere of that time and place. I was absorbing philosophical influences faster than I could integrate them. All at once I was an SDS-style New Lefter, a student of Zen, a Provotarian anarchist, an Aldous Huxley, Alan Watts, and Radio Free Oz (KPFK) freak, a General Semanticist, a Timothy Leary fan, an admirer of Gary Snyder, and a Taoist, etc. I felt that at some future time I could drop out and

mull over all this input and evolve from it a more consistent personal credo.

Eventually, negative elements began to seep into Kerry's psychedelic utopian paradigm. "Paranoia strikes deep, into your heart it will creep" was a popular Buffalo Springfield song which resonated with Kerry, as every few days there would be a gory photo splashed across the front pages of mutilated or burned Vietnamese children. By this time, Kerry was vehemently opposed to the war, and wrote with chalk on sidewalks such inflammatory slogans as "Victory to the Viet Cong" and "The American eagle pisses napalm."

In early 1967, an incident occurred that Kerry later regretted, which started one day when he and Cara stopped by the Palms Post Office in L.A. to pick up *Innovator*-related correspondence. Afterwards, they passed by a restaurant where two young men and a woman hailed them, greeting Kerry and Cara as "brothers," and proclaiming that they were honest-to-goodness anarchists. Kerry informed the trio that he was also an anarchist, and he and Cara joined them for a bite to eat.

One of these anarchists was named Jonathan Leake, who referred to himself as a "theoretician" for the Resurgence Youth Movement, a group involved in recruiting outlaw motorcycle gangs for revolutionary street fighting. Before long Kerry and Leake got into a heated debate about violence as a revolutionary tactic, to which Kerry was adamantly opposed on the grounds that it involved torture. In response, Leake proclaimed: "Torture is beautiful, man," which threw Kerry for a loop, and he thought it better not to disagree with Leake any further or someday he might end up on the business end of just this sort of revolutionary mayhem.

Furthermore, Leake and his fellow anarchists told Kerry that they were carrying a trunk full of revolutionary propaganda, and that they needed a place to temporarily stash it. Leake asked Kerry and Cara if they wouldn't mind taking it home with them and keeping it till the next day, when he could come by and pick it up. Kerry warily agreed.

On the way back home, Kerry dropped off Cara at the Soaring Society, where she was then working. When he got home, he sat down on the front porch and tore into the anarchist literature. To Kerry it came across as a crude imitation of someone who believed that anarchy meant violence and chaos, a vicious parody of anarchist thought. Among other insanities, the group advocated dosing the water supplies of large cities with acid, and invading middle-class nightclubs and beating up the clientele.

Kerry smoked a joint or two (or maybe three) and proceeded to brood over the Resurgence propaganda. After acquiring a serious case of the munchies, he went into the kitchen to see what there was to eat. It was then that he noticed a man up on the telephone pole in his back alley, and he immediately had a panic attack, suspecting that this telephone-repairman-in-disguise was there to tap his phone in preparation for a prospective pot bust—although in reality the pot bust would just be a pretext for a seizure of the Resurgence literature, the ultimate goal of which was to publicize in the newspapers that Kerry was a berserk anarchist intent on subverting Western civilization. Somewhere at the core of all this marijuana-muddled paranoia, Kerry suspected that his opposition to the Warren Report was somehow at the root of this perceived harassment.

On account of these marijuana-induced revelations, Kerry came to the conclusion that Jonathan Leake was most likely an agent provocateur who was implicated in a set-up to misrepresent Kerry's anarchist ideas, after which Kerry would be kicked around in the public arena and his views on the Warren Report thoroughly discredited.

After mulling over the dilemma, Kerry decided that the only way to prevent this probable mess from blowing up was to take samples of the Resurgence propaganda to the local FBI office and alert the Feds to the existence of this subversive group. So that is exactly what he did, and before long found himself sitting in the presence of a young, clean-cut, and humorless FBI agent, who did-n't even crack a hint of a smile when Kerry informed him that his FBI file was over an inch thick. (As noted in Chapter 5, Kerry had previously seen his FBI file in the room where he corrected his Warren Commission testimony.) Kerry proceeded to lay the Resurgence literature on the FBI agent, then split for home.

When Kerry got back, he received a phone call from Jonathon Leake, who asked him what he thought of the Resurgence literature. Kerry told Leake he had only a few minor points of disagreement, and invited him over to talk about it and to pick up his material. Leake replied that that might not be immediately possible, as he and his comrades had just been picked up by the fuzz.

In June, another incident occurred that deeply disturbed Kerry: an anti-war demonstration in which protesters peacefully picketing Lyndon Johnson's visit to Century City were savagely pummeled by club-wielding cops. These casualties included chil-dren and cripples, and at least one person suffered serious brain damage. This incident was called Black Friday and left a lasting impression on Kerry. As a result of this, and other factors, Kerry began to consider dropping out and moving to the country.

Kerry began visiting the library and researching drop-out plans and drove around the outskirts of L.A. looking for a rural environment where one could live cheap and free. As Kerry described his mindset at that time:

> I felt a growing need to integrate my ideas in the
> direction of some kind of anarchistic economic
> pluralism, with a strategy based on the principles
> of Chinese Taoism, incorporating the left anar-
> chist concept of revolution which most right anar-
> chists reject in favor of social pessimism, and
> somehow finding a method of guaranteeing that
> the revolution was not strangled in its own name
> by whatever coercive authority to decentralized

participatory autonomy. I had no concrete grasp
on how to do this, but I decided to call the resulting gestalt, whenever it finally came to me,
Zenarchy. Somewhere along in there I also
decided that my nom de guerre in such efforts
would be Ho Chi Zen, as a gesture of respect to
Ho Chi Minh, and also for Zen Buddhism, the
study of which had enormously stimulated my
political creativity.

In early autumn of 1967, Kerry and Cara—unable to find anything in the rural parts of L.A. with cheap rent—decided to sell their
VW van and, with the money, fly Kerry out to Florida to hunt for
a place to live. Once there, he found an inexpensive place on a farm
in the Palm River district on the outskirts of Tampa. Kerry's long-
range plan was to learn to live off the land and eventually save up
enough money to buy a small houseboat, which would allow him
and Cara to live independently and freely among the Florida
coastal islands.

In a letter to Louise Lacey dated December 17, 1967, Kerry
talked about dropping out:

> I am on a very misanthropic trip, baby. I mean to
> tell you, people are a bunch of idiots and I'm
> tired of them. In a few months, when the warm
> weather starts, I'm dropping out totally (from the
> economic standpoint)....
>
> I've discovered the joy of foraging, and also the
> ease, and am rapidly coming to suspect these
> days that civilization is a put on. Like they fill the
> people up with propaganda about how you can't
> make it on your own.... But one person can still
> go away and not be missed. This April is the last
> time I pay taxes.

Long live Zenarchy!
Kerry
P.S. Keep hating the bastards. They deserve it.

As it turned out, Kerry and Cara never did fulfill their "back-to-nature" plan. In fact, they never got any farther in the direction of unspoiled wilderness than their cottage in the Palm River District, where they settled in late 1967. Soon afterwards, they moved to Tampa and Kerry got a couple of jobs working at a library on the weekends and washing dishes behind a redneck bar during the week.

"At least there was no smog," he later mused.

CHAPTER 7

Tales of the Jolly Green Giant

"The problem in the world today is that the hunchbrains are united."

—LOUISE LACEY, 1970

In October 1967, just as Kerry and Cara were making a new life for themselves in Florida, New Orleans District Attorney Jim Garrison (known endearingly in the press as "the Jolly Green Giant") was fundraising in Los Angeles for his JFK assassination investigation when his gargantuan path crossed David Lifton's. Garrison, aware of the fact that Lifton was friends with Kerry Thornley, at that time enlisted Lifton's help in obtaining Kerry's cooperation for his investigation. Garrison's plan was to use Kerry to indict for perjury John Renee Heindel, who—like Kerry—had served with Oswald in the Marines.

As the story goes, Kerry—while in the Marines—once overheard someone conversing with Oswald in Russian, and Garrison claimed he had reason to believe that this individual was the aforementioned Heindel, who Garrison suspected was somehow involved in the Kennedy assassination.

Garrison's plan was to call Heindel in front of the New Orleans' grand jury and ask him if he'd ever heard Oswald speak in Russian. Heindel had previously gone on record stating that he'd never heard Oswald do so, and Garrison expected that Heindel would once again testify to the same tune. Then—after Heindel's testimony was presented—Kerry Thornley would be called before the grand jury, and testify that he had, in fact, heard Oswald and Heindel speak to one another in Russian. At least, that was the convoluted scenario that Garrison envisioned unfolding. As a result of

91

this testimony—according to Garrison's imagined scenario—Heindel would summarily be indicted for perjury, which would then make spectacular headlines and propel Garrison's case to greater glory.

According to Garrison, Heindel's nickname in the Marines had been "Hidel," which was nearly identical to an alias, A.J. Hidell, that Oswald used to purchase the Italian-made Mannlicher-Carcano rifle allegedly used to kill JFK. Ultimately, Garrison envisioned a far grander plan than simply implicating Heindel as a low-level player in the assassination: it was Garrison's eventual aim to induce Heindel to provide detrimental testimony against his chief suspect, Clay Shaw.

Lifton's willingness to aid Garrison soon turned sour when he looked into the allegations against Heindel and found them lacking substance. In Lifton's opinion, Heindel probably wasn't the Marine in question who'd conversed with Oswald in Russian, and due to this discovery, Lifton refused to participate any further in Garrison's investigation. Afterwards, Lifton informed Kerry about what had transpired, and because of this, Kerry as well refused to have anything else to do with Garrison. Seeing his Heindel angle quickly unraveling, Garrison decided to turn his attentions exclusively on the hero of our story. As he no longer possessed sufficient evidence to indict Heindel, Garrison (for some reason) figured Kerry would be the next best target for a perjury indictment. Soon after, Garrison issued a press release alleging that: "In September of '63, Kerry Thornley was closely associated with Lee Oswald at a number of locations in New Orleans."

Throughout Garrison's investigation and resultant media hype, Kerry found himself in a particularly surreal setting: as a target of the underground press, of which he had been an active participant in for so many years, having written for such publications as the *L.A. Free Press* and *The Great Speckled Bird*. This irony did not go unnoticed by Robert Anton Wilson, who encountered a media blackout when trying to address Kerry's situation. As Wilson

THE PRANKSTER AND THE CONSPIRACY

explained during our July 2001 interview:

> In '67 or '68, most of the underground press was
> publishing a lot of stuff pro-Jim Garrison, and
> this included Kerry's role in the assassination.
> And I had lots of contacts in the underground
> press, so I starting sending out articles defending
> Kerry, which nobody would print, because the
> underground press was behind Garrison and the
> official corporate media was totally anti-
> Garrison—I was trying to send the message to the
> wrong place.

■

On January 9, 1968, Garrison's investigators served Kerry with a subpoena to appear before the New Orleans grand jury. On February 8, Kerry's subpoena was enforced, so—to set the record straight—he visited the New Orleans D.A.'s offices to issue a deposition. At the time, Kerry made the following statement to the *Tampa Times*: "I feel like I'm going to a mad hatter's tea party."

While on his way to Garrison's office, Kerry bumped into an old friend. As he explained it in a letter he wrote in the mid-70s:

> When I went to New Orleans in 1968 in answer to
> Garrison's subpoena, Slim [Brooks] was again the
> first person I encountered. I was walking the
> streets of the Quarter looking for familiar faces
> and Slim crossed at a corner up ahead of me, so
> that I could not possibly miss him. I yelled out to
> him and we joined company and walked along
> the street together.
>
> He said to me at one point during our
> conversation: "Look, you don't plan to mention

Brother-in-law to Jim Garrison, do you?" Since Gary [Kirstein] still did not seem at all relevant to anything that was happening, and since I certainly wasn't into stirring up Garrison's paranoia about me any further by bringing up each and every time I had bullshitted about assassinating JFK with someone, I assured Slim that I didn't plan to mention Gary—but I also wondered why he should ask. Slim said something to this effect: "Because for awhile times were really hard and Brother-in-law and I went out and did some midnight shopping, Butch-the-burglar style, and one time we got caught. But later on somebody did us a favor by stealing our police records from the files before our case got into court. So if you mention Gary to Garrison that might provoke some unwelcome memories, and some questions like what happened to the records."

… So I didn't mention Gary to Jim Garrison, but would have if I had been questioned about something that related to him. I did mention Slim, however, because Garrison was very interested in the period immediately following my arrival in New Orleans in February of 1961 [the day after Mardi Gras]. Garrison fired all kinds of names at me for identification, some of them over and over, but Gary Kirstein was not among them.

At the D.A.'s office, Kerry first met with Garrison's aide, Andrew Sciambra, who, in short order, fired off a volley of questions which Kerry found totally absurd, such as: Was he whisked away to Arlington two days after the assassination by the Secret Service?

Had NBC offered him several thousand dollars for the last chapter of *The Idle Warriors*? All of these questions portended of some high-level conspiracy on the part of the government, whom Garrison suspected was in league with such media outlets as NBC.

As for the purported NBC offer, Kerry was virtually penniless at the time of the assassination, so he certainly would have welcomed any amount of money waved his way, much less thousands of dollars, but—as Kerry explained—NBC never offered him cent one.

As for accusations that the Secret Service had "whisked him away to Arlington" this was also so much nonsense, and could easily be put to rest—Kerry informed them—by asking the Secret Service themselves. In reality, Kerry moved to Arlington 21 days after the assassination, as opposed to immediately afterwards, which Garrison had alleged. Kerry explained that his "sudden departure" bore no relation to the assassination; he'd just decided it was time to move on—although this wasn't necessarily his only reason for leaving. As noted earlier, Kerry developed a deep sense of alienation immediately following the assassination, mainly on account of his celebratory reaction to the event, which turned off many of his friends and French Quarter acquaintances.

Kerry recounted this controversial incident in a 1970 monograph titled *In The Garrison State*:

> The JFK-sanctioned, United States-financed,
> massive butchery and torture of women, children
> and other civilians in Katanga was played down
> in the American press, but Bertrand Russell was
> horrified enough to compare those atrocities to
> the crimes reviewed by the Nuremberg tribunal,
> and I was horrified enough to let my political
> opposition to John F. Kennedy turn into a deep
> personal disgust—which, combined with
> numerous other factors, both temperamental and

ideological—prompted me to take a caustic, satirical attitude toward the tears being shed over the events in Dallas....

...I goaded the Kennedy admirers and mourners among my fellow waiters at the French Quarter restaurant where I was working. I charged into the Bourbon House during my lunch break and livened things up with shouts of celebration. I spent the afternoon back at the restaurant coining witticisms and, upon learning of Oswald's involvement as a suspect, boasting of our Marine Corps acquaintance.

People kept telling me to cool it, but I wouldn't listen.

After work that night I went out and rounded up the only other person I could think of who would share my defiant mood, the politically conservative owner of a nearby Mexican restaurant. Together we strolled, singing and laughing, into the Bourbon House, where we sat at the bar entertaining a sullen and unappreciative crowd with our Presidential assassination humor.

My feelings on Oswald at this time were that he was probably innocent and would be cleared in a few days. He was the sort who provoked the suspicion of those in authority. For all of me at the snot-nosed age of twenty-five, it was the Joke of the Century.... Now, over four years later in the District Attorney's office, I was having a hell of a time keeping my sense of humor.

During the course of his Q & A session with Garrison's aides (who Kerry later referred to as "goose-stepping Garrisonites"), it soon became evident that they'd already made up their minds as to his guilt. As Kerry put it:

> Somewhere along the line I manifested my
> objection to the kind of circular reasoning, which
> prohibited giving a man an opportunity to clear
> himself on the supposition that he was guilty.
> And somewhere along the line Sciambra, who
> said he himself didn't know whether or not I was
> lying made the remark, "We are only troops
> following orders, Kerry." The moral significance
> of that statement did not hit me at the moment—I
> was too busy being bewildered at the mentality
> of the man who was giving the orders.

Kerry—who had agreed to this meeting with the understanding that he'd get a chance to discuss the case personally with Garrison—was chagrined that the Jolly Green Giant never showed, simply leaving his aides to rake Kerry over the coals. Kerry even offered to round up all his French Quarter acquaintances for a brainstorming session with the intent of retracing his movements in September 1963 on a day-to-day basis, but Garrison opted not to pursue this line of inquiry. The reason Sciambra gave for Garrison's refusal: "He thinks you are lying or holding something back—or something." Given no other option, Kerry decided to return to Tampa and wait for an indictment. As Kerry recalled:

> My wife and I spent the next few weeks in an
> utter hell. During this period I did everything I
> could to assure that I would receive a exhaustive
> investigation. I wrote three letters to Sciambra. I
> extended an invitation to the pro-Garrison
> Warren Report critics of Southern California,
> through Art Kunkin of the *Los Angeles Free Press*,

offering to throw open my life to their scrutiny. I
contacted one friend and associate after another,
urging them to cooperate completely if
approached by Garrison's office.

In a letter to Greg Hill dated February 17, Kerry wasn't
overly optimistic about his prospects:

At the moment I have every reason to believe I
may get 20 years in a Louisiana prison for: 1)
having gone to USC at the same time [alleged
spy] Gordon Novel did; 2) having written a novel
based on Oswald which re-inforced his apparent
Marxist cover; 3) having been from that point out
the victim of either the most fantastic chain of
incriminating co-incidences or the most
satanically evil plot in history…
   I was never very interested in the Kennedy
assassination until lately. But goddamn and sweet
Jesus do I want to see those bastards brought to
justice now! Not out of revenge, but just simple
self-preservation.
   As I've been telling people, I'm up to my ass in
a cheap spy novel. And right now that means I
am in over my head.

On February 21, Jim Garrison issued a press release, which
boldly proclaimed: "Kerry Thornley and Lee Oswald were both part
of a federal operation operating in New Orleans." At this time,
Garrison charged Kerry with perjury, and further stated that he was
among "a number of young men who have been identified as CIA
employees." Garrison referred to his suspects—alleged spy Gordon
Novel and Kerry Thornley, among others—as "players." Quoting
Garrison: "They get three one-hundred dollar bills in the mail every

week, with orders not to pay income tax. If there's ever a question raised, there's a phone call and that's the end of it."

The following day Kerry was picked up in Tampa on a warrant and taken into custody, where he spent several hours while Cara scraped up enough money to post bond. When he arrived in New Orleans for arraignment, Kerry pled not guilty. As he had no lawyer, this flew in the face of Garrison's contention that the CIA was protecting him, which even one of Garrison's aides, Jim Alcock, pointed out. If Kerry was such a high level CIA player, where were the CIA lawyers to get him out of this mess?

To counter Kerry's denials of involvement in a JFK assassination conspiracy, Garrison's investigators produced a witness who placed Kerry and Oswald together in New Orleans in 1963. The witness, in this instance, was Barbara Reid, a Bohemian-styled voodoo worker and scene-maker—equipped with sunglasses, beret, and cigarette holder—known endearingly in the French Quarter as "Mother Witch."

In his book *On the Trail of the Assassins*, Jim Garrison pointed out that Kerry normally wore his hair quite long during this period, but when he returned to New Orleans in September 1963—and Barbara Reid saw him at the Bourbon House—he had just got a short-cropped buzz-job, not unlike Oswald. Kerry had also shaved his beard, leading Garrison to speculate that he had adopted this new look to more resemble his old Marine buddy. To Reid, the two young men appeared to be mirror images of one another—so much so that she said to them when she saw them at the Bourbon House: "Who are you guys supposed to be? The Gold Dust Twins?"

Within weeks of the assassination, Kerry visited Barbara Reid's house on a number of occasions, usually because he was trying to track down his friend Clint Bolton, who spent a lot of time there.

During one of Kerry's visits, Barbara brought up the Bourbon House incident, and Kerry replied that it was impossible for her to have seen him and Oswald together there, because—as Kerry understood the timeline—they hadn't been in New Orleans at the same time. However, Reid produced various newspaper clippings that demonstrated that Kerry and Oswald *had* been in New Orleans at the same time, during September 1963. When Kerry asked Barbara why he didn't remember meeting Oswald, she replied: "Maybe you were drugged so you *couldn't* remember."

The next morning, over breakfast with Clint Bolton, Kerry repeated Barbara Reid's allegation that she'd seen he and Oswald together at the Bourbon House. Clint's reply was: "Dear sweet Mother Witch, whom I love dearly, and whose friendship I've enjoyed for a good many years, but whose conception of reality is entirely flexible, has been seeing notorious figures everywhere in the Quarter for as long as she's been here."

Clint brought up the time that he and Barbara had witnessed a barroom brawl at Pat O'Brien's pub, and how the following day Barbara was going around telling everyone she saw about a man getting killed there during the melee. The next day, Clint showed Barbara a story in the newspaper, reporting the disturbance at Pat O'Brien's, although nothing was reported about someone being killed. Using circular reasoning, Barbara concluded that the "murder" had been suppressed. As time went by, Kerry would hear similar tales about Barbara's imaginings, directly and indirectly. Because of this, he could no longer entertain her notion that he'd been "drugged" and/or "brainwashed" in regards to his purported Bourbon House meeting with Oswald.

By late 1967, Kerry—then in Tampa— received news from French Quarter friends that Reid was "busy being some kinda snoop for Garrison...and is den mother to aging hippies." According to Kerry's sources, Reid had gathered around her a loose-knit following dedicated to her worldview regarding a Kennedy assassination conspiracy and, in particular, Kerry's involvement therein. Kerry, in his own irreverent way, promoted this mythology during his final days in New Orleans when he went around introducing himself in the following manner: "I'm Kerry Thornley. I masterminded the assassination—how do you do?"

In time, more second-hand stories trickled back to Kerry about Barbara Reid, to the effect that she was "screening witnesses" with her psychic powers for Garrison's investigation. In fact, Reid became a de facto member of Garrison's Gestapo, as upon occasion she'd make the rounds of various French Quarter haunts in the company of a Garrison investigator, Harold Weisberg. (Kerry liked to refer to Weisberg as "Harold Half-Truth" on account of his propensity to stretch, or distort, the truth.)

Interestingly enough, Greg Hill dated Barbara Reid at one time. But wait—there's more: According to Greg, Barbara claimed she had had an affair with Garrison. As Greg noted in June of 1968: "[Barbara] told me that Garrison was an ex-lover of hers.... Like everything else she told me, I didn't know if I should believe it or not and so, like everything else she did and said, I just enjoyed the circus and didn't bother believing or disbelieving. I think she said the affair was sometime ago before Garrison became prominent."

At the very least, Garrison did—on one occasion—attend a party at Reid's bohemian/voodoo-styled pad in late January 1968, along with other members of his staff. One little-known fact is that Reid was an active member in the New Orleans chapter of the Discordian Society, and even went so far as to claim that she was the Goddess Eris incarnate!

Along the way, Reid earned a reputation as a black magic dabbler. At odd moments, she was known to pull a voodoo doll out of her purse and boast about how she'd used it to "kill Kitty," a Bourbon Street stripper whose mysterious death made headlines in the New Orleans papers. One fascinating feature of Reid's pad was a gigantic voodoo altar, which took up nearly half a room. In a privately circulated document, Greg Hill described Reid's altar:

> Barbara's altar was an impressive thing. There
> were cabinets along the walls holding jars and

vials of ointments, lotions, powders, metals and
what all; there was a lectern like thing holding a
huge very old Bible, open and I think leather
bound; several candles strategically placed; a wall
full of holy adornments like crosses, crucifixes
and pictures of saints (and I recall a large
photograph of a human skeleton—which she
claimed was taken by a friend of hers who was a
photographer from *Life,* while doing a story on
graveyard vandalism); and charts on astrology
and alchemy. Between the wall and the lectern
holding the Bible (about 5 feet) was the place for
active magic making, and here lay little dolls
representing people, and jars of magical
compounds in them, and candles burning, and
crosses standing, and personal items like a pocket
knife or a shoe or whatever, all sorts of things—
most of which would appear senseless to
someone who did not understand the symbolic
significance.

She also had a library which held many
volumes of medieval and voodoo witchcraft…

What follows is a portion of Kerry's Grand Jury testimony,
from which Garrison contended Kerry had perjured himself:

Q: Did [Reid] see you with Oswald?

A: I don't think she did because the next day I
started asking people—

Q: You don't think so?

A: I don't know whether it was Oswald. I can't

remember who was sitting there with me. I don't
think it was Oswald for two reasons. The first
thing is—if I could remember who it was then I
could say definitely, in view of the fact that—

Q: I understand those facts, but in view of the fact
that you were writing a novel about him, I should
think you would recognize him.

A: Yes, and this was Barbara's theory—

Q: Was her theory right?

A: I don't know. First of all, the next day I started
saying to people, "Barbara is sure she saw me
with Oswald in the Bourbon House." That is the
first thing. I kept asking people—

Q: Did you ask them if they saw you at the
Bourbon House with Oswald?

A: No I did not ask them...How would you know?
Barbara was there. I said, "Barbara is sure she saw
me at the Bourbon House with Oswald. I don't
know whether it is true or not, but she is sure she
saw me there and she has convinced me she saw
me." And everybody said, "Oh, Barbara Reid gets
involved with everything that happens."

Q: Is it possible that you were with Oswald at the
Bourbon House?

A: I don't think it's possible. For here is the other
reason: I remembered this thing that happened

after she turned away, and after she went back to conversing with this person at the bar—and I felt obligated to explain to this person sitting with me, "That is Barbara Reid, she is a character around here"—to somebody who did not know Barbara. "She is a witch"—or something like this. And I felt that there was a barrier to my explaining this to this person—and this could only have been one of the Cuban waiters at the Sheraton-Charles, and the only barrier would have been a language barrier. Why did I feel that this was a barrier? And on the basis of that—that is all I know—on the basis of that I am sure I was not with Oswald, but Barbara is sure I was.

Q: All right, have you finished giving me the basis for getting to what you were doing the last week in September?

A: That is the only thing…I don't know what I was doing.

Q:…Are you sure that you never saw Lee Harvey Oswald in New Orleans in 1963, for a while you seemed to be on the fence.

A: No, the only time I ever thought I did was when Barbara Reid was so sure about it and I became convinced—but I am sure I did not see Oswald and recognize him in New Orleans of 1963.

Q: You are telling me there was a point when she had convinced you that you were with Oswald?

A: Yes, she convinced me. Certainly. There was the two hours or so she was talking to me, and she said, "Kerry, what must have happened was this: You must have walked into the Bourbon House and he must have walked in, you must have seen that his face was familiar, but not recognized him out of uniform"—and all this stuff—"and he must have sat down next to you." She was so certain—so positive.

Q: Did it seem to you that was possible?

A: It seemed to be possible when she got all through, until the next day and people began to say Barbara Reid connects herself with everything that happens. Then it seemed impossible.

Q: Does it seem possible now?

A: Well, no. It doesn't seem possible to me unless I was drugged or something…

In addition to Barbara Reid, others connected Kerry to Oswald in New Orleans. In March 1968, Harold Weisberg and Andrew Sciambra interviewed an acquaintance of Kerry's named Bernard Goldsmith, who informed them that Kerry was friends with Roger Lovin, who Goldsmith claimed had been involved in the Bay of Pigs invasion. Goldsmith said that he "vaguely" remembered Lovin telling him that he had been a roommate of Lee Oswald's. Furthermore, Goldsmith recalled being in the Bourbon House on the night after the assassination, and at that time Kerry allegedly told him that he'd known Oswald in New Orleans.

During the course of Garrison's probe, his investigators came across another witness, Doris Dowell, an assistant manager at the Shirlington House, where Kerry later lived and worked, in Arlington, Virginia.

According to Dowell, Kerry told her that he and Oswald were reunited in New Orleans in 1963 at a place "in the French Quarter she probably wouldn't have approved of." Curiously enough—for several months prior to the assassination—Kerry lived only a few blocks from Oswald, and throughout this period talked often about his former Marine pal, in particular to Clint Bolton.

Garrison also claimed that Kerry was seen in the company of Marina Oswald in New Orleans, information that came courtesy of a letter received from John Schwegmann, Jr. of Schwegmann Bros. Super Markets:

> An employee of our store, Mrs. Myrtle LaSavia [LaSavia had been a neighbor of Oswald when he and Marina Oswald had lived on Magazine Street.]...says that she, her husband, and a number of people who live in that neighborhood saw Thornley at the Oswald residence a number of times—in fact they saw him there so much they did not know which was the husband, Oswald or Thornley.

Recently, Oswald researcher John Armstrong uncovered FBI documents at the National Archives which purportedly demonstrate that other neighbors of Oswald had identified photos of Kerry as a frequent visitor to Oswald's New Orleans' apartment. The problem with these witnesses, who identified Kerry by way of photographic identification, was illustrated in a series of incidents where Garrison's investigators went around showing prospective witnesses half a photograph in which Kerry appeared, informing them that the missing half was of Marina Oswald. A *Los Angeles Free Press* staffer later identified this photo as the same one that appeared in an edition of the January 1968 *Tampa Times*, showing Kerry standing outside a courtroom after his extradition hearing with his arm around wife Cara. The negative had been flopped in the print used by Garrison's investigators, but even the Jolly Green Giant's most fanatical supporters had to admit it was the same photo that appeared in *The Tampa Times*.

It has also been documented that Garrison investigator Harold Weisberg had photos of Kerry altered to make him appear more like Lee Harvey Oswald, photos which were later used to persuade witnesses to make allegations against Kerry.

At one point, Garrison dictated a memorandum titled "Time and Propinquity" which was predicated on the supposition that if people live anywhere near one another, they are therefore to be suspected of being associated. The core of Garrison's case against Kerry consisted of several "propinquities" which, in his mind, formed the basis of a conspiracy. According to Garrison's memorandum:

> While living in New Orleans, Kerry admitted meeting Clay Shaw, David Ferrie, and Guy Banister. Nevertheless, Kerry characterized these meetings as brief and uneventful.
>
> Kerry showed a copy of his *Idle Warrior* manuscript to Martin McCauliffe, a professor at LSU. McCauliffe helped found Friends of Democratic Cuba, an anti-Castro outfit which included Sergio Arcacha Smith, "who was involved with Oswald," according to Garrison.
>
> Kerry picked up unemployment checks at Julia Street, near Camp Street. Camp Street, as previously mentioned, was where Guy Banister's shadowy organization was located.
>
> Moved to Arlington soon after the assassination.
>
> At one point, Kerry lived on Dauphine Street, a couple of blocks from Clay Shaw.

Throughout the course of his probe, Garrison assembled a colorful cast of investigators, including such noteworthies as assassination researchers Mark Lane and Harold Weisberg, comic Mort Sahl, electronics whiz and purported intelligence agency spook Gordon Novel, and right-wing conspiracy buff Allen Chapman. Garrison's probable motivation for surrounding himself with such an eclectic lot—one would assume—was to generate increased media interest and place himself and his investigation at the forefront of popular consciousness. Perhaps the greatest prize in this cast of characters was Mort Sahl, who, at this time, was America's most popular political satirist.

In the mid-60s, Sahl broke the mold of what one normally considered a nightclub comedian. Early on, he distinguished himself by carrying on stage a rolled-up newspaper, which he used to discuss political and topical issues in a hip and improvisational style.

Sahl—in his routines—documented the many glaring inconsistencies of the Warren Commission Report. However, nightclub owners soon became alarmed by his position on the JFK assassination, and he was warned to stop spouting off about a "conspiracy" or he would lose work. Sahl—never one to run from a fight—continued with his criticisms of the Warren Commission Report, and his income soon sank from $400,000 to $19,000 a year. However, as the decade progressed, and dissent became a more popular and accepted form of expression because of the growing opposition to the Vietnam war—Sahl soon became accepted again by nightclub owners who wanted to cash in on those sympathies generated by the "counterculture" then filtering into the mainstream.

At the time of his involvement with Garrison's investigation, Sahl's stand-up routines often mentioned Kerry. As Robert Anton Wilson recalled during our 2001 interview: "Mort Sahl got off on this Kennedy assassination conspiracy train…and his comedy got less and less funny, and Kerry Thornley frequently appeared in Mort Sahl's monologues. And he'd just throw charges around…that Kerry lived in New Orleans at the same time as Oswald, and that

Kerry lived in Alexandria right near CIA headquarters.... Mort Sahl was more of a hassle to Kerry than Garrison was."

Sahl even persuaded Johnny Carson to invite Garrison to appear on the *Tonight Show*. Although Carson was quite critical, and tangled with Garrison during his appearance, it nonetheless gave Jolly Jim a soapbox with which he could preach his case to millions of Americans. Even *Playboy* took the bait at one point and provided Garrison exposure in its interview section.

A media superstar was born.

CHAPTER 8

Bit Players

"If they prove that you are CIA, demand back pay."

—GREG HILL, *from a letter to Kerry Thornley*
dated February 19, 1968

For those with even a cursory knowledge of the Kennedy assassination, Clay Shaw, David Ferrie, and Guy Banister should be familiar names, made popular in recent years by Oliver Stone's *JFK*, a peculiar blend of fact and fiction that once again summoned up these strange specters so thoroughly entangled in the web of JFK assassination lore.

Shaw—masterfully portrayed by Tommy Lee Jones in Stone's epic—was a wealthy New Orleans businessman fingered by Garrison as a key player in the JFK assassination. Garrison based his case on the testimony of various witnesses in New Orleans who attended meetings and parties in which the assassination was allegedly discussed in the presence of Shaw, David Ferrie, and Lee Oswald. Garrison and his staff pursued leads that purportedly demonstrated that Shaw, Ferrie, and Banister were part of an anti-Castro intelligence operation that had been functioning in New Orleans several years prior to the Kennedy assassination.

In the popular press, Shaw has been portrayed as an innocent sacrificial lamb on the bloody altar of Garrison's probe. Conversely, Garrison has been embraced by the liberal and alternative press as a heroic figure who had the *cojones* to the take on those whom he considered the true assassins of JFK: the U.S. intelligence community and military-industrial complex.

As commonly occurs in both love and war, the two sides of any given story are oft times presented as gospel (depending on the source) and never the twain shall meet. Thus is the legacy of such legendary figures as Shaw and Garrison, both heroes and villains in one and the same breath; twin enigmas wrapped in the perpetual riddle of the Kennedy assassination.

Shaw—one-time director of the New Orleans Trade Mart— was indicted by the Jolly Giant in early 1967 for "participation in the conspiracy to murder John F. Kennedy." According to Garrison, Shaw was a former high-ranking CIA official involved with Latin American and Italian CIA operations. In the New Orleans homosexual community, Shaw was reputedly known as the "Queen Bee." It was Garrison's belief that Shaw was part of a ritualistic homosexual fraternity which included among its ranks David Ferrie.

■

W. Guy Banister was another colorful character connected to the Kennedy assassination psychodrama. Banister served with Naval Intelligence during WWII, then afterwards spent 20 years with the FBI, his last position as special agent in charge of the Chicago office during the 1940s.

In 1955, Banister moved to New Orleans, where he served as assistant superintendent of the New Orleans police force until retiring in 1957 under the cloud of a scandal resulting from a pistol-whipping incident in a French Quarter bar. Banister later formed a detective agency, Guy Banister Associates, which appears in retrospect to be one of the more, shall we say, adventurous operations of its kind active in New Orleans during the early 60s.

Banister's connections with right-wing groups and Mafia operatives is well documented, not to mention the curious collection of spooks and mercenaries he surrounded himself with, such as David Ferrie, perhaps the very oddest of this whole sordid lot.

Banister's office was located at 531 Lafayette Street. Curiously enough, a side entrance to this same building could be accessed at 544 Camp Street and was headquarters for the Cuban Revolutionary

Council, a group of anti-Castro Cubans formed at the urging of the CIA. One of the CIA agents overseeing this operation was E. Howard Hunt, a name that will haunt our story until its very end. This shadowy operation—which included the CIA, Cubans, right-wingers, and the mob—had been "screened" by the FBI agent in charge of the New Orleans office, Regis Kennedy, the same agent who interviewed Kerry following the Kennedy assassination.

On several occasions, David Ferrie visited 531 Lafayette Street to receive money to bankroll anti-Castro covert operations. In these same offices, Banister was known to have stored guns and ammo for his various nefarious endeavors. An April 25, 1967, article from the *New Orleans States Item* reported that Banister had served as a munitions supplier for Bay of Pigs advance planning.

A few months after the Kennedy assassination, Banister died of an apparent heart attack, although others have suggested that his death may have resulted from foul play.

■

During the course of the Warren Commission investigation, it was established that Oswald had identified 544 Camp Street (the side entrance to Banister's office) as the address of the Fair Play for Cuba Committee (FPCC), the very same address printed on the "Hands Off Cuba" pamphlets he distributed in New Orleans. What this suggests is that Oswald was an agent provocateur, infiltrating various left-wing organizations and reporting back to his intelligence agency "handlers," one of which was, most likely, Guy Banister. As it so happens, Banister's 531 Lafayette Street office was just around the corner from the William Reilly Coffee Company, where Oswald was employed during the summer of 1963.

During this period, Army counterintelligence became curious about Oswald's New Orleans FPCC chapter, as they followed the paper trail of one H.J. Hidell, who was also using the 544 Camp Street address.

H.J. Hidell, as history instructs, was an Oswald alias. To add more fuel to this already suspect fire, after his death, Banister's widow discovered a stack of Oswald's Fair Play For Cuba leaflets in her husband's office. The FPCC emerged at the same time that the CIA began operations against Cuba, which suggests that the FPCC may have been a CIA front.

In his book *Conspiracy*, journalist Anthony Summers interviewed Delphine Roberts, who was Banister's private secretary and part-time lover. Roberts confirmed that Oswald had indeed been under the employ of Banister during the summer of 1963, and that Oswald's FPCC branch was invented by Oswald and Banister. Banister later became furious, according to Roberts, when he discovered that Oswald had mistakenly printed the 544 Camp Street address on the FPCC pamphlets.

Jim Garrison claimed that "virtually all the young men associated with Guy Banister's operation" in New Orleans carried a box key for the Lafayette Square post office, and that these keys were used for receiving mailed instructions from intelligence agency case officers, and to provide a cover story for the frequent appearance of these young men (among them, Lee Harvey Oswald) in the same building where the Office of Naval Intelligence was located.

Garrison pointed out that Kerry, too, held a box key at the Lafayette office, although this connection could be considered circumstantial, at best. In fact, Greg Hill once pointed out that "nearly every writer in the French Quarter had a box in that post office, since publisher's checks sent to home mail boxes were notoriously subject to being ripped off by desperate junkies.... As a matter of fact, Kerry changed living quarters around and needed a mailing address for manuscripts and things. That this could imply anything is ridiculous. That Garrison should infer what he does...is outrageous."

■

David Ferrie worked for Banister out of the 531 Lafayette Street office, and it was there, in all likelihood, that Ferrie associated with Lee Oswald. Further evidence demonstrates that Ferrie and Oswald first met in 1954, when Ferrie was the leader of a group of youths in a branch of the Louisiana Civil Air Patrol. Following the Kennedy assassination—when the contents of Oswald's wallet were examined—they contained David Ferrie's library card. According to witnesses interviewed by Garrison's staff, Ferrie was a close associate of Clay Shaw, and on a number of occasions Oswald was seen in the company of Shaw and Ferrie, accusations later denied by both men.

Garrison was first alerted to Ferrie's alleged role in Kennedy's murder after receiving a phone call from Banister associate Jack Martin on the day of the assassination. Martin informed Garrison that Ferrie was part of a conspiracy, acting as one of the getaway pilots, and that Ferrie had trained Oswald with a telescopic rifle as part of this assassination plot.

Immediately following Jack Martin's revelations, Garrison rushed over to Ferrie's apartment, where he found Ferrie's young roommate. From him, Garrison learned that Ferrie was then at an ice skating rink in Houston. When Ferrie returned to New Orleans, Garrison had him arrested, then notified the FBI. In turn, the FBI informed Garrison that Ferrie's plane was in New Orleans and had not been operated for several years. In addition, Garrison was told that Ferrie had been "checked out" and was not considered a suspect. Afterwards, Garrison released Ferrie from custody and dropped the matter. Five years later, when Garrison began his probe, Ferrie became a prime suspect.

Ferrie, as the record notes, had been a senior pilot for Eastern Airlines until being dismissed for purported homosexual indiscretions in the late 1950s. Around this time, he contracted a rare skin disease, which caused the hair on his body to fall off. To hide his hairlessness, Ferrie pieced together an ill-fitting mohair wig, and pasted two shards of the red mohair rug for eyebrows, creating one of the funkiest appearances to ever grace the streets of New Orleans.

Following his gig at Eastern Airlines, Ferrie worked as a private investigator and pilot for New Orleans mob boss Carlos Marcello, an avowed enemy of the Kennedy family. At the same time, Ferrie was heavily involved in the anti-Castro movement and training of troops at Lake Pontchartrain, near New Orleans, all part of a CIA-funded operation. According to Victor Marchetti—former executive assistant to the deputy director of the CIA—both Ferrie and Clay Shaw worked as contract agents for the Company in the early 60s. Marchetti's source for these allegations was ex-CIA Director Richard Helms.

Many CIA agents—rogue and otherwise—laid blame for the Bay of Pigs failure squarely on President Kennedy's shoulders due to his withdrawal of air support for the operation. In retrospect, some Kennedy assassination buffs contend that the Bay of Pigs fiasco was the proverbial straw that broke the camel's back, presumably setting in motion Kennedy's demise.

In 1961, following the Bay of Pigs, Ferrie—in the presence of a number of witnesses—began mouthing off about assassinating Kennedy. According to former CIA agent John Stockwell, it was the CIA who was actually responsible for bungling the Bay of Pigs, yet the agency condemned Kennedy for setting them up for failure when he refused to provide air support for the operation.

For quite some time, Kennedy had been simmering over the many CIA misdeeds initiated behind his back—such as the aforementioned Bay of Pigs fiasco—and just prior to his death he had reached a boiling point. Most historic is Kennedy's famous quote, which he made to a top aide, about "splintering the CIA into a thousand pieces and scattering it into the wind." JFK was not simply talking about modifying or reforming the agency, but intended to totally dismantle it and replace the CIA with a new intelligence agency headed by his brother Robert, then attorney general.

■

David Ferrie, it should be noted, was an amateur hypnotist, as well as a practitioner in strange religious rites, which included—some have suggested—"black magic" rituals. According to researcher Loren Coleman: "During Lee Harvey Oswald's last weeks in New Orleans, he attended many ritualistic parties in private homes and apartments with David Ferrie." These rituals purportedly consisted of animal sacrifice and blood guzzling, not to mention homoerotic indiscretions.

In addition, Ferrie was a high priest in the Apostolic Old Catholic Church of North America, an organization which, on the surface, appears to have been a traditional religious outfit, although late researcher Jim Keith speculated that the Apostolic Old Catholic Church may have been, in reality, a chapter of the Gnostic Catholic Church, which in turn was affiliated with occultist Aleister Crowley's infamous Ordo Templi Orientis. Garrison suspected that the Apostolic Old Catholic Church was a cover for CIA espionage.

The world of the occult and the intelligence community is one that often overlaps and intersects. The reason for this, I believe, is that the intelligence community has long been infiltrating cults and occult groups for a variety of reasons, primarily as a means of monitoring the effects of mind control, and also as a recruiting ground for "Manchurian candidates."

These conspiratorial connections are addressed in my book *The Shadow Over Santa Susana: Black Magic, Mind Control, and the "Manson Family" Mythos*, not only as it relates to the Manson Family, but as well the notorious Process Church of the Final Judgment, who many consider to be one of the most dangerous cults to have emerged from the late 60s.

In correspondence with this author from the mid-90s, Kerry Thornley noted:

[I] first encountered the Process Church in New

Orleans in Feb. '68 when I was there to testify, reluctantly, to the Grand Jury. Barbara Reid, the principal witness against me, and a friend (!) of mine, was said to be "up to her ass" in The Process, which, indeed, maintained a coffee house half a block from Barbara's apartment. I went over there with Slim [Brooks]...and saw pamphlets about *Satan On War* and *Lucifer on War* and *Jehovah on War*—which I found confusing because I thought Satan and Lucifer were both the same guy, until then, (of course—heh-heh).... A bunch of pale, thin zombies were sitting around in this place. I was telling very funny Garrison stories but nobody was laughing.

In his controversial 1987 tome, *The Ultimate Evil*, author Maury Terry fingered The Process as being the major player behind a vast Satanic underground network that dealt in pornography, drugs, and ritual murder.

Ferrie, not unlike Barbara Reid, inhabited an exceptionally strange milieu—certainly by the standards of the late 50s Eisenhower era and the subsequent innocence of the early 60s, which was forever shattered with Kennedy's assassination. Needless to say, a rabid right-wing homoerotic-hypnotist with red dyed hair and fake eyebrows was obviously quite out of place in Ozzie and Harriet's vision of America.

During his initial interview with Garrison's investigators, Kerry informed the district attorney of meeting Ferrie in New Orleans once, at a party at Ferrie's house, where he spoke briefly to the freaky redhead, although Kerry couldn't remember the exact nature of their conversation.

In February 1967, Garrison placed Ferrie in protective custody at his own request. Then, on February 22—just a day after being released from custody—Ferrie was found dead in his apartment. At this time, two suicide notes were discovered, one which was still in Ferrie's typewriter. The coroner ruled that Ferrie died from natural causes, the apparent victim of a stroke. Others suspected foul play.

■

Another curious character in Kennedy assassination lore is Gordon Novel. In 1957, when Kerry pledged Delta Sigma Phi at USC, one of his pledge brothers there was Novel, who he knew as "Gordy."

At one point during Garrison's investigation, Novel appeared at the D.A.'s office offering to help the investigation by supplying de-bugging equipment on the proviso that Garrison agree not to implicate him in his investigation due to certain admitted connections that Novel had to David Ferrie.

In short order, Novel was appointed Garrison's chief of security on account of his knowledge of electronic eavesdropping equipment. Garrison later caught Novel taking photos inside the D.A.'s office, which Novel later sold to NBC. Because of these developments, Garrison reneged on his previous agreement and subpoenaed Novel to appear before his grand jury. Before this could happen, Novel fled to Ohio. [3]

Among other allegations, Garrison fingered Novel as one of the "young men" holding a box key at the Lafayette Square post office building, where a cadre of young intelligence agents implicated in the assassination allegedly picked up their monthly CIA paychecks, in the gospel according to Garrison. Novel's wife even went so far as to testify that her husband had impersonated Oswald and fabricated evidence against him in advance of the assassination.

■

Another colorful character who caught the attention of Garrison's investigation was the Reverend Raymond Broshears, an active member of the New Orleans homosexual community and one-time roommate of David Ferrie. Also known as "Brother Ray," Broshears was active with several obscure church organizations and a number of other equally unusual groups, including the "Universal Life Church."[4]

In 1968, Broshears went public with revelations that David Ferrie had claimed to have participated in the Kennedy assassination. Broshears cooperated with Garrison's investigation, and in his interview with the D.A.'s staff, stated that (according to Ferrie) Officer J.D. Tippit was supposed to kill Oswald in the assassination's aftermath, but Oswald got wise and did it to Tippit before Tippit could do it to him. A few days later—according to "Brother Ray"—Jack Ruby murdered Oswald to preserve the secrecy of the plot.

On more than one occasion, Broshears claimed that he had accompanied Ferrie to 544 Camp Street where the red-wigged wunderkind picked up money to fund his anti-Castro activities. Broshears added that Oswald was a bisexual CIA agent who had become intimate with David Ferrie, and that Ferrie, as well, was a CIA spook. Furthermore, Broshears placed Kerry Thornley in the company of Lee Oswald, Clay Shaw, and David Ferrie in New Orleans in the fall of 1963.

In August 1968, Garrison staff member James Alcock questioned Broshears:

> Q. Do you recognize this man in the picture here?
>
> A. That is the man whom David Ferrie constantly referred to as Kerry Thornley.
>
> Q. And this person here?
>
> A. That is Kerry Thornley.

Q. Where did you meet him?

A. At Lafitte's in Exile. And I don't know what—
he always maintained that he was not a
homosexual.... David has told me numerous
times that Kerry Thornley maintains he is not a
homosexual. But I say he is and I say to the whole
world if he is not a homosexual why was he in
homosexual bars, why if he is not? And his
resemblance to Lee Harvey Oswald is rather
frightening…

CHAPTER 9

Framed In Red?

Back in August 1962, Kerry had posted a sign on a telephone pole in the French Quarter, for which he was arrested in violation of a city ordinance. Later, in 1968, when Garrison's investigators questioned the arresting officers, neither of them could remember the sign's message. Garrison suspected that the sign in question was most likely a pro-Castro Cuba placard, identical to the propaganda that Oswald dispersed during the same period. In fact, it has been alleged that Oswald recruited certain individuals to handout these pro-Castro leaflets.

On April 3, 1963, Oswald paid his landlord the rent for a full month in advance on his Neely Street apartment in Dallas. However, by April 29, Lee and his wife Marina (with infant in tow) moved to New Orleans, leaving their apartment unoccupied for several days before the landlord realized they'd left. This led Garrison to speculate that the infamous photos of Oswald—with a rifle in one hand and a copy of the communist newspaper *The Daily Worker* in the other (as well as a pistol holstered at his side)—had somehow been fabricated by Kerry Thornley and other accomplices at Oswald's empty Dallas apartment. In a second photo, Oswald once again held the rifle along with a copy of *The Militant*, another leftist magazine.

After his arrest—when these backyard rifle-wielding photos were presented as evidence of his guilt—Oswald insisted that they'd been doctored, and claimed that he knew how the photographic alterations were made. Oswald angrily charged: "That is not a picture of me; it is my face, but my face has been superimposed—the rest of the picture is not me at all, I've never seen it before…someone took a picture of my face and faked that photograph."

During the period in question—late April or early May of 1963—Kerry traveled by bus to visit his parents in California, along the way passing through Dallas, which placed him there at a very opportune time in relation to the Oswald empty-apartment scenario. Garrison—in his crusade against Kerry—pointed out that Kerry had "an unusual baby face, with rounded chin and large lower lip," both of these features presumably matching those of the rifle-wielding Oswald in the allegedly doctored photos. Garrison later noted in memoranda presented to the House Select Committee on Assassinations that Kerry's father was a photo engraver, and that Kerry quite possibly learned these same skills from him.[5]

In May 1963, Oswald began his pro-Castro activities, corresponding with the Fair Play for Cuba Committee (FPCC) in New York, the Communist Party, and the Socialist Workers Party. In most cases, Oswald usually gave false or misleading misinformation to these organizations regarding his activities. Somehow budding commie superstar Oswaldskovitch was able to scrape together enough money to print and distribute these Fair Play for Cuba leaflets, as well as membership applications for his FPCC New Orleans branch, in addition to hiring unidentified individuals to distribute these materials.

Oswald claimed that his FPCC branch had a total of 35 members, although records later revealed that the only other member (aside from Oswald) was one A.J. Hidell, an Oswald alias.

In August 1963, Oswald made contact with Carlos Bringuier—the leader of an anti-Castro Cuban group in New Orleans—expressing his desire to join Bringuier's organization. Bringuier said that Oswald came into his store at this time and "asked me for some literature against Castro, explained that he had experience in guerrilla warfare, and expressed that he was willing to help train anti-Castro Cubans in guerrilla activities." A few days later Oswald did an about-face outside the World Trade Mart in New Orleans, handing out *pro*-Castro leaflets to passersby in the street.

Bringuier—who supposedly just happened upon the scene—

angrily confronted Oswald, inciting a shoving match, which a local TV news camera crew from WSDU-TV *just happened* to capture on film. Not long after the World Trade Mart incident, WSDU's sister station, WSDU-AM, conducted a live radio debate between Oswald and Bringuier, which was "moderated" by another recurring character in Kennedy lore, Ed Butler, thought by many to be an agent provocateur engaged in a covert campaign to set up Oswald as a patsy in the assassination.

This radio debate between Oswald and Bringuier was pressed to vinyl after the JFK assassination on the recording *Self Portrait In Red*, which presented posthumous evidence that Oswald was a Marxist, and because of his political affiliations was inspired to blow the proverbial crown from Camelot's head. The organization that produced this rather heavy-handed LP was an anti-communist propaganda mill called the Information Council of the Americas (INCA). During the course of Garrison's investigation, it was discovered that INCA was headquartered out of the same building as Guy Banister's offices at 531 Lafayette.

Many assassination buffs now believe that the Oswald/Bringuier confrontation was a staged event, the ultimate design of which was to build a false history around Oswald that could be used against him at a later date. Curiously enough, Garrison's investigators later questioned a Banister operative named George Higgenbotham, who was responsible for infiltrating left-wing groups. When Higgenbotham witnessed Oswald's fight with Bringuier, he informed Banister about it, who replied: "Cool it. One of them is one of mine."

At one time, Jim Garrison had plans to indict both INCA's Ed Butler and Carlos Bringuier in his ever-widening assassination probe. In this regard, Garrison believed that the group of conspirators involved in the JFK assassination had performed two functions with Oswald in New Orleans: "babysitting" and "image-creating."

By "babysitting," Garrison was referring to those engaged in looking after Oswald and guiding his actions, such as Clay Shaw and David Ferrie. The "image-creating" part of the operation involved setting the groundwork for later misrepresenting Oswald as a communist. According to Garrison, this latter role was performed not only by Butler and Bringuier, but also by Kerry Thornley, as well. Moreover, Garrison believed that *The Idle Warriors* had been an attempt by Kerry to portray Oswald as a communist sympathizer. In the parlance of the intelligence community, this is what's known as "sheepdipping."

Whether Kerry was a party to these machinations or not, it would appear that Oswald was but a hapless patsy in a convoluted scheme, playing the role of commie agitator at the behest of his intelligence agency "handlers," often for obscure or unspecified reasons. His mission was probably stated to him by his superiors as "intelligence gathering," as all the while, unbeknownst to Oswald, he was being set up to take the rap. In other words, Oswald was a double agent who got duped. Subsequently, Jack Ruby's bullet silenced him before he could reveal how he'd been used.

In regards to Bringuier, Kerry was interviewed by Garrison's investigators about a purported meeting at Bringuier's clothing store that certain witnesses claimed Kerry had attended. Kerry, of course, denied these allegations, yet in January 1968 his former girlfriend, Jeanne Hack, described an encounter—to researcher Bill Turner—between Kerry and a man who fit Bringuier's description.

■

In the fall of 1963, John Spencer rented an apartment on Dauphine Street to Kerry and Jeanne Hack, and about two weeks before the assassination the couple split up. After their breakup—according to Spencer—Kerry changed the lock on his door, but Jeanne broke a window, entered the apartment, and stole a tape recorder, typewriter, and some other items.

Spencer, as propinquity would have it, was friends with Clay

Shaw. During Garrison's investigation, Spencer was interviewed and, in his deposition, stated that while he never saw Shaw and Thornley together[6], Kerry displayed some rather odd behavior following JFK's assassination. At that time, Kerry left a note for Spencer, stating that he'd vacated the premises, and was moving to Alexandria. In this note, Kerry said he would send his new address so that his mail could be forwarded.

Spencer was somewhat puzzled that Kerry had left so suddenly, as his rent was paid for another week or so. When he checked out Kerry's apartment, Spencer found paper—torn up into little confetti-like pieces—scattered all over the floor. It also appeared that before the paper had been shredded, it was watered down to smear the ink so that the writing was undecipherable. Spencer noted that both the Secret Service and FBI had shown up at Kerry's apartment immediately following Kennedy's assassination, and because of this Kerry had somehow been pressured to suddenly leave New Orleans. Later, Kerry described in a letter to Greg Hill what had occurred:

> When I moved out of the place after the assassination I was having a full-scale war with Jeanne, who was drawing money (it was turning out) out of our joint checking account faster than I (working 12 hours a day under enormous strain as a waiter at Arnaud's) could put it in, without telling me, and Jeanne had just come by and broken in and stolen back her things (which I was keeping as ransom until she paid back some of what she owed me) and so when I left the apartment it looked like a hurricane had struck it. And although I had been planning the move for about a week, for some reason or other I did not tell [my landlord], so I just left him a note apologizing for the mess and telling him he could keep whatever was valuable in the stuff I left

behind, as a cleaning fee. So it APPEARED as
though I had cleared out in a sudden panic.

Prior to Kerry's grand jury testimony, Garrison investigator
Andrew Sciambra told him: "If it checks out on the lie detector that
you are telling the truth about having no priori knowledge of the
Kennedy assassination, you can write *another* book: because if you
aren't lying—and I personally don't think you are—you're a victim
of the most fantastic chain of coincidences ever. This is just fantastic!" In addition to a lie detector test, Kerry agreed to take truth
serum, but Garrison never took him up on the offer.

Another time, Sciambra came flat out and said: "Maybe
you're the Second Oswald."

"I *feel* like the Second Oswald," Kerry shot back, wondering
when they were going to handcuff him and escort him through the
basement of the police building, where another proto-Ruby would
be waiting with a loaded gun.

CHAPTER 10

Lee Harvey Doppelganger

Jim Garrison suspected that Kerry was one of several Oswald doubles, a theory first introduced in *The Second Oswald* by Richard H. Popkin, who deduced that there were at least two "Oswalds" in the Texas School Book Depository (TSBD) on November 22, 1963.

As Popkin noted in his book, Oswald was observed by at least five people in the TSBD between noon and 12:30 p.m. on the day of the assassination. Two people saw Oswald on the first floor around noon; two others reported seeing him on the fifth and sixth floors at around the same time, and another individual saw him right after the assassination on the second floor. What this all amounted to— in the estimation of Popkin—was the existence of a second look-alike Oswald at the TSBD during the time leading up to, and following, Kennedy's assassination.

Some suggest that Oswald was never in the sixth-story-window sniper's perch at all, due to the fact that witnesses observed him down in the lunchroom drinking a soda at a time when he would not have been able to be upstairs and pull the Mannlicher-Carcano's trigger three times in succession within seven seconds, then race back down to appear nonchalantly with a bottle of Coke in his hand, as observed by witnesses.

Perhaps the most incriminating evidence supporting the theory that Oswald was a patsy is the Altgens photo, which shows Oswald (or a reasonable facsimile thereof) standing in the doorway of the TSBD at the same instant that Kennedy was shot. The Warren Report identified this Oswald look-alike as Bill Lovelady, although the individual in question appears to be the spitting image of Oswald and is wearing the same type of shirt that Oswald wore when he was arrested. Although this identification of Lovelady—

as the man standing in the front doorway—was taken to task by Warren Report critics, other photos snapped of that same area show Lovelady, but in a different shirt and sporting a full beard.

What assassination researchers have long suspected is that imposters were creating a false history of Oswald as a communist, the design of which was to set up him up (before the fact) as a scapegoat in the Kennedy assassination. It's my suspicion that Oswald knew he was being used in intelligence community capers, but really had no idea of the exact nature of the operation(s).

In most instances, I suspect, Oswald worked as an agent provocateur to infiltrate these communist organizations, while at the same time his handlers were building around him this false history as a communist sympathizer. Jim Garrison believed that Kerry played a major role in this alleged "sheepdipping" operation, and that the intent of his Warren Commission testimony was to demonstrate Oswald's deep-seated hatred of the U.S. system and his commitment to Marxism.

During their investigation, the Warren Commission requested CIA-taped recordings of phone calls Oswald allegedly made to the Soviet and Cuban embassies in September and October of 1963. Later, FBI agents determined that the individual on the recordings—claiming to be Oswald—was an imposter.

The Warren Commission—perhaps aware that CIA surveillance cameras were clicking non-stop at the Mexico City embassy—requested copies of all photos of Oswald taken that day. In response, the CIA released photos of someone at the embassy *claiming* to be Oswald, which only further muddied the waters, as the individual in question bore more of a resemblance to pro wrestler Killer Kuwalski than they did Lee Harvey Oswald.

But the Mexico City/Lee Harvey Oswald impersonations merely scratch the surface of some of the shady shenanigans that went on in these regards. To follow is an accounting of just a few of the many Lee Harvey Oswald impersonations.

■

One afternoon in September 1963, a young couple showed up at the Mexican consulate in New Orleans and, among other curious remarks, the young man asked, "What do you have to do to take firearms or a gun into Mexico?"—a question sure to raise suspicions among consulate workers.

Present, as well, at this curious consulate encounter was Mrs. Fenella Farrington, who was there to see about getting her family car returned from Mexico. Four days after JFK's assassination, Mrs. Farrington was contacted by an FBI agent who informed her that the scene at the New Orleans' Mexican consulate had been photographed by hidden cameras which had been activated when the young man in question had mentioned firearms. This young man, the FBI told her, had been none other than Lee Harvey Oswald.

Later, during the Garrison probe, investigator Mark Lane showed Mrs. Farrington 17 photographs, and asked her if any one of them appeared to be the young man she'd seen at the consulate. To Lane's inquiries, Farrington replied that two of the pictures she was presented with could have been the man she'd seen.

One of the pictures Farrington picked out was that of Oswald. The other photo was of Kerry Thornley. What makes this incident all the more curious is that Jim Garrison's investigator, Harold Weisberg, contracted a California artist to "touch up" several photos of Kerry to make him look more like Oswald, and it has been alleged that these photos were used to encourage witnesses to identify Kerry as the individual impersonating Oswald.

■

Another purported Oswald look-alike took place at a shooting range in Dallas between November 9 through 21, 1963, when someone calling himself Oswald was seen by several eyewitnesses taking pot shots at other peoples' targets and making an incredible nuisance of himself.

It should be noted that in the Marines, Oswald was a mediocre shot, whereas this Oswald doppelganger was an expert marksman, hitting bull's eyes with relative ease. From these actions, it would appear that this individual was going out of his way to draw attention to himself, to show that he (Oswald) was an out-of-control gun-wielding wacko with a damn good aim.

The Warren Commission, in all its wisdom, determined that the gun-wielding wacko in question was not Oswald, because the *real* Oswald was at another location when the shooting-range incident occurred. Just the same, the Warren Commission never answered—or even entertained the question—of exactly who this mysterious marksman was.

After the assassination, the shooting range witnesses were still convinced that it was Oswald who they'd seen, even though the Warren Commission concluded that this was physically impossible, unless Oswald was in two places at the same time.

■

In January 1961, two representatives claiming to be from an anti-Castro group placed an order, in the name of "Oswald," for ten trucks at a New Orleans Ford dealership.

At this time, Oswald was still in Russia, and because of this, and other obscure reasons, Jim Garrison concluded that the individual who had identified himself as "Oswald" at the Ford dealership was Kerry Thornley. It was Garrison's contention that these trucks were to be used in the Bay of Pigs operation, or some other CIA-funded anti-Cuban operation, due to the fact that this phony Oswald and his Cuban compatriots identified themselves as members of the "Friends of Democratic Cuba." Kerry—when later interviewed by Garrison investigators on this matter—denied any knowledge of the affair, although Garrison refused to believe that Kerry wasn't involved, for the simple fact that Kerry's friend, Clint

Bolton, had written publicity for the Friends of Democratic Cuba. Another fine example of circular reasoning!

■

So what are we to make of all the apparent coincidences, synchronicities, or—as Garrison liked to call them—"propinquities" surrounding Kerry in New Orleans prior to the Kennedy assassination? Out of the slew of allegations in Joe Biles' *In History's Shadow: Lee Harvey Oswald, Kerry Thornley and the Garrison Investigation*—which contend that Kerry was part of a JFK-assassination conspiracy—half can be thrown out as inaccurate, while the other half of these allegations are inconclusive in that they were never brought before a court of law.

Even if Kerry actually knew more about a New Orleans nexus of conspirators than he was willing to admit, it's still a stretch to suggest—as Garrison's supporters do—that Kerry played a prominent role in framing Oswald as a commie lone-nutter. During the course of Garrison's investigation, a handful of witnesses claimed to have either seen Kerry and Oswald together in New Orleans, or claimed that Kerry admitted contact with Oswald during that time. But one must bear in mind that Garrison's investigator Harold Weisberg was making the rounds in New Orleans with photos that had been doctored to make Kerry look like Oswald's twin brother, and thus there is reason to suspect that some witnesses may have been coerced into making statements against Kerry.

Another theory explaining these alleged Thornley/Oswald sightings was later presented by Kerry's friend Bud Simco in a memo written in 1978:

> The Oswald double may have entered the
> Bourbon House, which Kerry frequented, or one
> of the other coffee houses in the area, and
> perhaps sat at the same table as Kerry for the

purpose of being seen; possibly testing if Kerry
would react to his appearance as resembling
Oswald. Of course, this is speculation, but it is
possible Barbara Reid really did believe she saw
Thornley in the company of Oswald. Much of the
activities of this "double" have never made any
sense unless one considers there were
contingency plans pertaining to the framing of a
patsy, in this case, Oswald, and planting false
leads and evidence.

CHAPTER 11

The Roselli/Thornley Connection

"Roselli shot Kennedy once, hitting the right side of his head and blowing his brains out, with a rifle, from behind a fence in the grassy knoll area."

—BRUCE ROBERTS, *A Skeleton Key to the Gemstone Files*

It has been well documented that organized crime was in cahoots with the CIA during the post-Bautista era in Cuba. At the time, a combined CIA/Mafia alliance had been formed with the intent of bringing down the newly formed Cuban government.

Before Castro assumed control, the mob had a free hand running the Cuban casinos. This all changed with Castro's revolution and the ouster of Bautista and his mobster buddies. Subsequently, the mob—attempting to regain control of the Cuban casinos—aligned themselves with the CIA and implemented an anti-Castro campaign dubbed "Operation Mongoose" designed to poison Castro and/or blow him up with explosives shaped like seashells. Among those enrolled in this covert campaign were mob bosses Santos Trafficante and Sam Giancana, and former Al Capone gang member Johnny Roselli.

Roselli was personally involved in several botched attempts to whack Castro. One of these plans consisted of putting itching powder in Fidel's beard with the intent of causing the Cuban leader to shave it off, thus losing face with his fellow countrymen.

Other pseudo James Bond-ish schemes entailed slipping Castro a surreptitious dose of LSD prior to a speech, which would make him act irrationally, and become thereby discredit himself. Other plots along these lines included exploding cigars that would blow Fidel's head off. Needless to say, none of these plots ever came off.

Later, Roselli's testimony before the Senate Intelligence Committee proved quite damaging to the intelligence community when he revealed his association with the CIA and "Operation Mongoose." A short time afterwards, Roselli's chopped-up corpse was discovered floating in a 55-gallon drum off the Miami coast. Sam Giancana, just days before he was slated to appear before the same Senate group, in June 1975, was himself brutally murdered. Two weeks later, *The Washington Post* disclosed that Roselli had secretly informed the government that he believed some of his former Mafioso and intelligence agency associates had participated in Kennedy's assassination.

What makes this story all the more intriguing is that Kerry became acquainted with Roselli in 1965 when he worked as a switchboard operator and garage attendant—"between the exalted hours of 12 to 8 a.m."—at Glen Towers, a high-rise apartment building located in Beverly Hills. Kerry described Roselli as "by far the most colorful resident" at Glen Towers.

Glen Towers had a basement parking lot, which was wired for sound and monitored by the desk clerks. On several occasions, the desk clerks working the day shift discovered men in suits going through Roselli's car, who, when approached, always produced FBI identification.

As Roselli usually showed up in the evenings, it was Kerry who would pass the word along to him that the Feds had been caught snooping around again. One night, after another of these incidents, Roselli told Kerry: "Those people are so stupid—they don't bother me. You know who is really stupid is the CIA. They're so stupid they killed their own president—trying to get some bookie." Roselli never elaborated on what he meant by this cryptic remark. Later, Roselli took Kerry up to his apartment and showed him a small hole in the wall where he said the FBI had once planted a bug. "I stuffed Kleenex in it," Roselli told him, and then loaned Kerry a copy of *The Invisible Government*—a book about the CIA—

and indicated a specific chapter for Kerry to read that would explain the Kennedy assassination. Kerry read the chapter in question, but could find nothing specifically related to the assassination, or to "some bookie," although the chapter did contain a reference to Gordon Novel and anti-Castro training camps in Hammond, Louisiana.

The more creative of conspiracy theorists (such as can be found in *The Gemstone File* thesis) place Roselli in Dealey Plaza as member of a assassination hit team made up of Mafiosos and intelligence agency spooks. Of course, others—such as Cliff Clavin of the popular TV sitcom *Cheers*—suggest that it was actually the Beatles who shot JFK that sunny Texan day in a four-way triangulation of gunfire!

Go figure.

CHAPTER 12

Operation Mindfuck and the Bavarian Illuminati

"When your pineal gland finally lights up you will never again, as long as you live, have to relax."

—KERRY THORNLEY, from the fifth edition introduction of *Principia Discordia*

Garrison's interest in Kerry's possible involvement in the Kennedy assassination wouldn't be their only connection—just the most sinister one. Kerry's other activities, his more anarchic, Discordian ones, would also be linked to Garrison. As synchronicity would have it, an early Discordian manuscript titled *How the West Was Lost* was actually reproduced, after hours, on a mimeograph machine in Garrison's office. This clandestine copying operation occurred a couple of years before the Kennedy assassination, and was the work of Greg Hill and his friend Lane Caplinger, who worked as a typist in Garrison's office. Later, Garrison theorized that the Discordian Society was a CIA front, an idea that Kerry—ever the surrealist prankster—heartily encouraged. (Little did Garrison suspect that he was an unwitting dupe in this Discordian conspiracy, a la the covert use of his very own office mimeograph machine!)

Sometime in 1968, during the course of the Garrison investigation, Kerry discovered that one of Garrison's aides, Allan Chapman, believed that the JFK assassination had been the work of the Bavarian Illuminati, that ancient and fraternal order much ballyhooed by ring-wing conspiracy theorists (such as the John Birch Society) as a centuries-old secret society that was behind communism and damn near every other socialist-inspired ill then corrupting the world and "poisoning our precious bodily fluids."

In response to all of this Bavarian Illuminati paranoia, Kerry—in the midst of Garrison's probe—decided to mindfuck Garrison all the more by sending out spurious announcements suggesting that he (Kerry) was an agent of the Bavarian Illuminati.

These communiqués were sent under the auspices of the Discordian Society. This mindfuck eventually got Kerry interested in the history of this mysterious secret society, and the more he read about the Bavarian Illuminati, the more fascinated he became.

Eventually, Kerry and his fellow Discordian conspirators started planting stories about the Discordian Society's age-old war against the Illuminati, accusing everyone under the sun of being a member of that sinister and sneaky organization, from such politicos as Nixon, LBJ, Daley, and William Buckley to Martian invaders, and various conspiracy buffs—plus members of the Discordian Society itself—which made it all very confusing and extremely hilarious.

Robert Anton Wilson—who in due time became an authority on the history of the Bavarian Illuminati—contributed to the formation of this Illuminati/Discordian mythos, feeding his own unique perspective and arcane knowledge into this twisted loop of conspiratorial high weirdness.

On a parallel timetrack, a similar hoax had gone into effect at the campus of U.C. Berkeley where a chapter of "The Bavarian Illuminati" was formed sometime in 1967. This group sent out press releases on all sorts of weird subjects, the intent of which was to give people who wanted to believe in conspiracies something to point to, and thus become more paranoid about. Among those involved in this clandestine U.C. Berkeley Illuminati Bavarian project was none other than Kerry's friend Louise Lacey. This experiment eventually dovetailed and merged with the Discordian Society's Bavarian Illuminati mindfuck project. In the process, Louise was initiated into the Discordian Society, and became forever after known in the annals of Discordian lore as Lady L., FAB. (The Lady L.

moniker came courtesy of Kerry, named after a character from a
Roman Gary novel. The latter part of Louise's moniker came from
her friend Eldridge Cleaver, who charmed her once with "Fucking
Anarchist Bitch!")

■

Among the original of band of Discordian conspirators were Kerry,
Greg Hill, Robert Anton Wilson, Bob Shea (another editor at
Playboy), Louise Lacey, Bob Newport, Judith Abrahms, and Camden
Benares[7]—in addition to a number of other whimsical souls
engaged in the act of giving consensus reality a goose.

Discordians were located all across the country and commu-
nicated with "Groovy Packs," as Bob Newport has described
them, strange and humorous oddities sent out by mail to one and
another. Each player in the Discordian network would add their
own two bits to the mix, then pass on his or her efforts to the next
name on the mailing list, and they, in turn, would pass it on to
another.

All of this, in turn, contributed to the continual evolution of the
Principia Discordia, which was, in essence, a conceptual
hodge/podge collage created by Kerry and Greg Hill (aka
Malaclypse the Younger). Robert Anton Wilson once referred to this
process as much more than a mere parody of religion, but more
aptly an exercise in guerrilla ontology or epistemological judo. It
could also be viewed as a Marx Brothers version of Zen, otherwise
known as "Operation Mindfuck," as the Discordians liked to call it.

One of the more disruptive members from the early days of the
Discordian Society was French Quarter denizen Roger Lovin who,
at one point, was apparently excommunicated by Malaclypse the
Younger, although this didn't stop Lovin from going ahead and
forming his own Discordian Cabal, as detailed in a letter to Greg
Hill circa 1964:

As to the progress of the New Orleans Cabal: The
first Temple of Eris in New Orleans was formally
defecated on Nov. 3, 1964, at 519 Decatur St.
(which, oddly enough, is also my home address).
It occupied a converted broom closet. Admittedly,
that is rather humble quarters for such a large
and far-flung organization; but in the short space
of one month we have more than doubled our
area. This noble word was accomplished chiefly
through the untiring efforts of our noble leader,
FANG, W.K.C.: L.T.E., P.W.W., E.L.N.O.C., and
L,L.L.L.L.L. and his noble assistant, Charles
Noble. They single-handedly (one hand, three
hooks) formed K.R.U.D. (Kollectors of Revenue
Under Duress) and saw to raising the funds.

Our membership already includes two
beatniks, one wasp, a hunchbrain, and a genuine,
card carrying square who has 2.7 kids and a wife
with a cloth coat. Therefore, be of good cheer.
Today New Orleans, tomorrow the Catacombs—
with some scattered showers in the evening.

In some instances, "Operation Mindfuck" took the form of
press releases the group issued offering a non-violent anarchist
method to awake and mutate the sleeping robots of society.

One such mindfuck was known as PURSE: as acronym for
Permanent Universal Rent Strike Exchange, which encouraged
everybody to just simply stop paying rent forever and go about their
business. Another concept along these lines was PUTZ: Permanent
Universal Tax Zap, in which everyone stopped paying taxes.[8]
Other items that promoted the Discordian cause came in the form
of business cards with slogans such as "There is no enemy anywhere" or "There is no friend anywhere," each particular card going
to a particular person/mindset to jolt them awake—like a zen koan,

Discordian-style.

The guiding philosophy behind "Operation Mindfuck" was originally proposed in *The Theory of Games and Economic Behavior* by von Neumann and Morgenstern, who contended that the only strategy an opponent cannot predict is a random strategy. The principle Discordian motto in this regard came from Malaclypse the Younger when he muttered the immortal maxim: "We Discordians must stick apart" which promoted the radical decentralization of the Discordian movement, creating a built-in random factor within its ranks. In other words, nobody was ever quite sure what anybody else within the Discordian movement was doing at any given time. Thus chaos ruled.

In the early days of the Discordian Movement, Mal and Omar (Greg and Kerry) were the sole dispensers of Legion of Dynamic Discord certification, reserving the right to ordain Popes (or Episkopos) into the movement. This all changed in November 1969 when Malaclypse the Younger sent out a memo to all Discordians far and wide, proclaiming that "the way in which a person is to be an official Episkopos of the Discordian Society, is for him to declare himself as such." And so it was. Of course, the next question was: How do you know when you are ready for Discordian popehood? The answer: When you say you are!

For a normal religion, such a laissez-faire attitude would cause all sorts of mayhem, and in time lead to total, unadulterated chaos. But as Discordianism is a religion founded on total chaos, this built-in random factor of people naming themselves popes and creating their own independent Discordian cabals created just the sort of autonomy that made Discordianism flourish.

And this pleased the Goddess.

As Wilson and Shea wrote:

> To this day, neither Omar [Kerry] himself nor any other Discordian apostle knows for sure who is or is not involved in any phase of Operation

Mindfuck, or what activities they are or are not engaged in as part of that project. Thus, the outsider is immediately trapped in a double-bind: the only safe assumption is that anything a Discordian does is somehow related to OM, but since this leads directly to paranoia, this is not a "safe" assumption after all, and the "risky" hypothesis that whatever the Discordians were doing is harmless may be "safer" in the long run, perhaps. Every aspect of OM follows, or accentuates, this double-bind.

"Operation Mindfuck" got into full swing in late 1968, when Robert Anton Wilson—in cahoots with Kerry—composed a letter and answer in the Forum section of *Playboy*[9], which Wilson was then editing. This spurious correspondence put forth the theory that the wave of political assassinations then taking place in America had been orchestrated by the Bavarian Illuminati. Kerry and Wilson thus set into motion a new mythology.

In an August 1968 letter to Louise Lacey, Kerry addressed the forthcoming "Playboy Forum" hoax, and further outlined a mad-cap plan of clandestine action with the creation of Hassan-i-Sabbah X, a modern-myth-in-the-making:

Dear Louise—

The name your black writer writes under is Hassan-i-Sabbah X—this name he chose as a somewhat whimsical put-on, as Hassan i Sabbah was the Moslem heretic who founded the Assassins, after which was patterned the Roshaniya (or Illuminated Ones), after which were patterned the Alumbrados of Spain and the Illuminati of Bavaria.

Formerly, he was a student at Berkeley, where he joined the Berkeley psychedelic anarchist group, the Bavarian Illuminati, and then dropped out to become a full-time revolutionist, for the Illuminati. Previous to all of which he was a rank-and-file brother in Black Islam.

On a self-assigned mission for the Illuminati Conspiracy, he was jailed for "revolutionary activities." It is from prison that his manuscripts are smuggled via an "underground railway" to you, Lady L., whom he has asked to act as his literary agent.

Naturally you cannot reveal the country in which Hassan-i-Sabbah languishes at present nor his real name, for to do so would be to imperil these unsung heroes who transmit his work to the world, not to mention Hassan-i-Sabbah X himself.

Hassan-I-Sabbah is the only black writer we know of who is also quite explicitly a turned-on anarchist...

Later on in the letter:

… I do not know where all this will end, but we will make the bicycle scam of Amsterdam look like a game of tiddly-winks.

Of course it will first be necessary to present the Bavarian Illuminati side of things—we are a much-maligned group. We are not, for example, assassins—not PEOPLE assassins, anyhow, but EGO assassins. We pick out various targets in the power structure and, by one means or another, TURN THEM ON. And, contrary to the exaggerations of our enemies, we do NOT control ALL the TV networks—better to blame us for the assassinations than THAT! Nor have we yet secured complete control of international banking (we still need your donations out there for this project to continue).

But it is plain that we definitely ARE on the offensive these days (so much so that we can begin to come out in the open at relatively liberated places like Berkeley) and one of our membership drive slogans (as we are going to start openly selling memberships in the near future in order to raise money for various worthy causes, such as Kerry Thornley's Defense Fund— "Don't let Garrison wreck the Illuminati!") can be: GET ON THE WINNING SIDE—JOIN THE BAVARIAN ILLUMINATI!

For only five bucks, folks—or a larger donation if you can afford it—you get a Bavarian Illuminati Membership Card, which is to Illuminate the Opposition. You also get other junk and especially some ILLUMINATION STICKERS, which you paste up in heads and phone booths & which are triangular, feature the Illuminati Pyramid, and say on them either CONSPIRE or (depending on the sticker in question) ILLUMINATE. You also get an "in Gold we trust" button and a psychedelic recruiting poster—THE ILLUMINATI BUILDS CONSPIRATORS! (THE ILLUMINATI BUILDS GODS?) (BUDDHAS?)

Naturally, all illuminated people are Illuminati, and nearly all the young people are illuminated these days—but to be a Conscious Agent of the Conspiracy, you have to be a card-carrying Illuminati....

THE PRANKSTER AND THE CONSPIRACY

In conclusion, Kerry wrote:

> ...The degree of seriousness w/ which we
> Illuminati advance our claims & ideas should be
> that which will keep intelligent people saying to
> each other, "But what if it really ISN'T a put-on!"

Under the auspices of "The Bavarian Illuminati," Kerry invented a Do-It-Yourself Conspiracy Kit, which included stationary containing dubious letterheads. As Robert Anton Wilson noted, "Omar [Kerry] would send a letter to the Christian Anti-Communist Crusade on Bavarian Illuminati stationary, saying, 'We're amused you've discovered that we've taken over the Rock Music business. But you're still so naïve. We took over the business in the 1800s. Beethoven was our first convert.'"

As Wilson noted in *Cosmic Trigger*, these Illuminati/Discordian hijinks set in motion a new mythology:

> The Discordian revelations seem to have pressed
> a magick button. New exposes of the Illuminati
> began to appear everywhere, in journals ranging
> from the extreme Right to the ultra-Left. Some of
> this was definitely not coming from us
> Discordians. In fact, one article in the Los Angeles
> Free Press in 1969 consisted of a taped interview
> with a black phone-caller who claimed to
> represent the "Black Mass," an Afro-Discordian
> conspiracy we had never heard of. He took credit,
> on behalf of the Black Mass and the Discordians,
> for all the bombings elsewhere attributed to the
> Weather Underground.
>
> Other articles claimed the Illuminati definitely
> were a Jesuit conspiracy, a Zionist conspiracy, a
> banker's conspiracy, etc., and accused such

worthies as FDR, J. Edgar Hoover, Lenin, Aleister
Crowley, Jefferson and even Charlemagne of
being members of it, whatever it was (p. 64).

The current-day existence of the Bavarian Illuminati is not an easy thing to prove, although fringe Christians and right-wing extremists would have us believe that those Bavarian bad-guys have been behind nearly every crucial development in the history of humankind over the past few hundred years, from the French and American revolutions to the forthcoming New World Order/One World Government takeover—not to mention the Kennedy assassination and water fluoridation!

According to certain legends, the Illuminati was purged in 1785 by the Bavarian government on the grounds that it had attempted to overthrow Europe's ruling class. Other legends suggest that the Illuminati were merely driven underground at this juncture, meanwhile continuing their multifarious activities under a maze of guises—including such contemporary incarnations as the Bilderbergers, the United Nations, and the Council of Foreign Relations—and exist unto this day as a many-armed octopus pulling the levers behind the scenes of world events.

Other researchers contend that the Illuminati is simply an off-shoot of Freemasonry, this due to the fact that the original Order of the Illuminati was formed within Masonic lodges in Germany by one Adam Weishaupt. Robert Anton Wilson (hereafter referred to in this book as Bob Wilson) spent many years attempting to unravel this mystery. According to Wilson: "Since Masonry itself is a secret society, the Illuminati was a secret society within a secret society, a mystery inside a mystery, so to say."

In a recent interview, Wilson remembered: "I appointed myself the head of the Illuminati, which led to a lot of interesting correspondences with other heads of the Illuminati in various parts of the world. One of them threatened to sue me. I told him to resubmit his letter in FORTRAN, because my computer wouldn't accept it in English and I never heard from him again. I think that confused him."

And so it was that the Discordian Movement—in the capable hands of Thornley, Hill, Wilson, et al.—created their own mythology in the form of the resurrection of the Ancient Illuminated Seers of Bavaria (AISB), a sort of sociological experiment to observe how conspiracy theories are born and bred, then, in time, work themselves into the cosmologies of the paranoid and enlightened alike.

This Bavarian Illuminati resurrection was only one aspect of Operation Mindfuck. Collecting rubber stamps was another. One day, Bob Wilson appropriated a rubber stamp while visiting a public-health clinic, which said SEE MENTAL HEALTH RECORDS. Afterwards, any mail Wilson received that he considered insulting— especially that which originated from a government office—he stamped with the above message and sent back, otherwise untouched. Another glorious example of Operation Mindfuck!

Greg Hill, as well, was a rubber stamp enthusiast, as Kerry observed in the fifth edition introduction to the *Principia Discordia*:

> You will also notice an unusual number of unusual rubber stampings scattered about among the following pages. That was Greg showing off his rubber stamp collection. Few hobbies are as psychologically gratifying—especially when some bureaucrat is making you wait, with his or her back to you for a moment—as collecting rubber stamps. This is also an exciting way to recoup some of your tax losses. But you must abide by the laws of the Rubber Stamp Congress. All Discordians are permitted to collect rubber stamps *provided* they don't mention the Discordian Society if they are caught. Just point out to them that among people of all faiths stamp collecting is a popular hobby. And tell them your

religious preference is none of their business. Tell them that collecting stamps in the name of your nameless religion is your Constitutional right and then, to make your point, take the Fifth Amendment. They will find themselves in a legalistic quandary.

■

Sometime in 1969, Malaclypse the Younger (Greg Hill) started what has become known in Discordian lore as the Joshua Norton Cabal. Norton—who lived in San Francisco in the late 1880s—declared himself emperor of the world, as well as protector of Mexico, as he wandered the streets of old San Fran dressed in pseudo-regal attire and accompanied by his two mangy dogs.

Although a pauper, Norton was allowed to dine in the finest restaurants and was treated as royalty throughout the city. Considered by many to be a kook, Norton issued his own currency, much of which was accepted in bars and other establishments. A popular Discordian mantra, courtesy of Malaclypse the Younger, went:

> Everybody understands Mickey Mouse. Few
> understand Herman Hesse. Only a handful
> understood Albert Einstein. And nobody
> understood Emperor Norton.

Norton, among other accolades, was recognized as an Illuminated Being by the Ancient and Accepted Freemasons, who granted him a 33rd degree in the order, the highest rank achievable. When Norton died, ten thousand San Franciscans attended his funeral, and he was buried in the Masonic cemetery, courtesy of his Freemason brethren.

In the fifth edition introduction of the *Principia Discordia*, Kerry wrote the following about Emperor Norton:

His Royal Decrees were printed free of charge in the newspapers, the currency He issued was accepted in the saloons, local shopkeepers paid the modest taxes He occasionally demanded and on at least one occasion a tailor furnished Him with a new set of Royal finery.

Although a madman, Norton wrote letters to Abraham Lincoln and Queen Victoria which they took seriously.

One night a gang of vigilantes gathered for a pogrom against San Francisco's Chinatown. All that stood in their way was the solitary figure of Norton. A sane man would not have been there in the first place. A rational man would have tried to reason with them. A moralist would have scolded them. A man as daft as Norton usually seemed would have loudly ordered them to cease and desist in the name of His Royal Imperial authority. All such tacks would probably have been futile, and Norton resorted to none of them.

He simply bowed His head in silent prayer.

The vigilantes dispersed.

Discordians believe everybody should live like Norton.

So write your legislative representatives demanding harsh laws with teeth in them requiring people of all faiths—especially Christians and especially on Sunday—to live as Joshua A. Norton did.

Soon after the formation of the Joshua Norton Cabal other Discordian cabals began popping up like so many mind-bending mushrooms in a fertile spring meadow fed by cosmic bulldada. Goddess only knows how many of these daffy Discordian cabals exist today, as a brief perusal of the Internet will most certainly illustrate. Many of these Discordian cabals have members in other cabals, so there is a lot of overlap within the ranks of the movement, as there likewise was in the early days of the scene.

As Greg Hill once described those heady times:

> The 1969 Discordian Society was an exchange
> between independent artists of various kinds.
> Norton Cabal was just me and my characters and
> I used the other cabals as sort of a laboratory. In
> return other Discordians would bounce their stuff
> off of me. We would toss in ideas and anybody
> could take anything out. It was a concept stew.
> *Principia* was my product from my perspective.
> Thornley, and Wilson and Shea, had other
> perspectives, which had substantial influence on
> me. It was mutual, but without the exchange each
> would have done something similar anyway. The
> exchanging of ideas and techniques broadened
> and encouraged all of us.

Another favorite mindfuck of the Discordian Society was Project Jake, originally instigated by the legendary Discordian Harold Lord Randomfactor. As Shea and Wilson described in *Illuminatus*:

> Once or twice a year, a public servant who has
> distinguished himself by more than common
> imbecility is selected as target for a Jake and all
> Discordian Cabals are alerted—including the
> various branches of the Erisian Liberation Front,
> the Twelve Famous Buddha Minds, the St. Gulik
> Iconistary, the Earl of Nines, the Tactile Temple of
> Eris Erotic, the Brotherhood of the Lust of Christ,

Green and Pleasant Enterprises, Society for Moral
Understanding and Training, the In-Sect, the
Golden Apple Panthers, the Paratheo-
Anametamystikhood of Eris Esoteric, Sam's Café,
the Seattle Group, the Stone Dragon Cabal, the
Universal Erisian Church, and the Young
Americans for Real Freedom. On Jake Day, the
public servant being honored receives mail from
all of these, on their official letterheads (which are
somewhat weird, it must be granted), asking for
help in some complicated political matter that
passes our rational understanding. The official so
honored can conclude either that he is the target
of a conspiracy composed entirely of lunatics, or
that the general public is much more imaginative
and less stodgy than he had previously assumed
(p. 232-233).

The John Dillinger Died For You Society was another milestone
in the annals of Discordian mindfucks, initially engineered by
Mordecai the Foul—under the auspices of the Chicago Cabal
Discordian Society—its secret headquarters situated somewhere in
Bob Wilson's head. Wilson and gang expounded upon the Dillinger
legend, thus creating a whole mythology around the notorious bank
robber that was later expanded upon in *Illuminatus*, which featured
John Dillinger as a major character.[10]

Another mindfuck that the Discordian bunch was quick to
pick up on was the 23 Enigma, which was first introduced into the
popular lexicon of contemporary weirdness by William Burroughs,
author of such mind-bending novels as *Naked Lunch*, *The Nova
Express*, and countless other classics.

It was in the early 60s in Tangier that Burroughs made the
acquaintance of a certain Captain Clark who ran a ferry from
Tangier to Spain. Clark, one day, happened to mention to Burroughs

that he'd been running the ferry for 23 years without an accident.

As fickle fate would have it, that very day the ferry sunk, killing Captain Clark and everyone else on board. That evening, as Burroughs was musing over the incident, he turned on the radio, and the first newscast told about the crash of an Eastern Airlines plane on the New York-Miami route. The pilot of the flight was another *Captain Clark* and the flight was listed as *Flight 23!*

Burroughs—fascinated by this 23 phenomenon—began keeping records of odd coincidences, and to his astonishment the ubiquitous number 23 began appearing in a lot of them. Soon others, such as Bob Wilson, began looking into the phenomenon, and noticed that the number 23 continually turned up in odd places. This, in time, wove itself into the Discordian mythos, which embraced the number 23 with as much passion as it had previously embraced the Law of Fives. For instance, Bob Wilson's first meeting with Greg Hill occurred on April 23, and while they were discussing this anomaly, a glazier who was repairing a broken window in Bob's apartment presented his bill. The bill was numbered 05675 (5+6+7+5=23) and the price was \$7.88 (7+8+8=23). In commemoration of this "triple whammy," Shea and Wilson rearranged the chronology of *Illuminatus* to begin on April 23.

On a related note, the Discordians—somewhere along the line—decided that they needed their own mystery sign, like the Masons and other secret societies. And so it was that they lifted the V-for-victory sign made popular by Winston Churchill during WWII. Of course, to those daffy Discordians, this sign had its own special meaning: V, being the Roman numeral for five, illustrates the Law of Fives. The way the sign was made, with two fingers up and three bent down, exemplified the hidden 23 encoded in the Law of Fives. As Bob Wilson noted in *Cosmic Trigger*:

> The fact that this sign is also used by Catholic
> priests in blessing and by Satanists in invoking
> the devil illustrates the essential ambiguity of all

symbolism, or the Cosmic Giggle Factor....
Between the first edition of the *Principia Discordia*,
run off on Jim Garrison's Xerox machine in 1963,
and the fourth edition, published by Rip-Off
Press in Berkeley in 1969, only 3,125 copies of that
basic Discordian text were ever distributed.
Nonetheless, the V sign, somehow, got accepted
by the whole counter-culture, especially circa
1966-70. One saw hundreds of thousands of
protesters using it at the Pentagon demonstration
in October 1967 and again at the Democratic
convention in 1968. The odd part was that
virtually nobody using it was aware that we
Discordians had revived it.

In due time, all of these various Discordian mindfucks led to the writing of the aforementioned *Illuminatus* trilogy by Wilson and fellow Discordian Bob Shea, Part 1 of which was dedicated to the dynamic duo of Kerry Thornley and Greg Hill. The *Illuminatus* trilogy—in addition to using several quotations lifted directly from the *Principia Discordia*—can best be described as a science fiction/occult/conspiracy novel constructed in a Discordian mind-fuck framework which incorporated many of the themes, concepts, weird ideas, and humorous hoaxes that Thornley, Wilson, Hill, et al. had perpetuated throughout the late 60s and early 70s.

Greg Hill once described *Illuminatus* as "a rare example of extended and sustained Discordian art, and also makes an exemplary textbook of Discordian theory and practice. All you have to remember is that different Discordians define the Society differently, so the Truth of Goddess according to Shea and Wilson may have little or nothing to do with the Truth of Goddess according to other Discordians. That's an old tradition of ours."

Illuminatus—which has also been described as "the longest shaggy dog story in literary history" and "a fairytale for paranoids"—is a mind-cracking romp which parodies damn near every conspiracy theory ever conceived against a surreal backdrop of the 60s counterculture littered with crackpots, occultists, and psychedelic supermen weaving in and out of an ever-changing sea of shifting realities. In other words, *Illuminatus* defies description, a book that leaves the reader questioning the very meaning of reality, and wondering if the reality s/he was witnessing a moment before is actually the same one they are witnessing at present. *Illuminatus* did, indeed, carry on the tradition of Operation Mindfuck, and continues to warp heads to this very day. (Exhibit A, your present author!)

Eventually, though, Operation Mindfuck started to run amok, as Wilson noted in *Cosmic Trigger:* "We were all having a lot of fun with Discordianism. None of us were aware, yet, that Operation Mindfuck could get out of hand."

CHAPTER 13

Zenarchy and Other High Adventures

"Among Zen Buddhists it is said, 'When you meet another bodhisattva on the road, greet him with neither words nor silence.' That leaves you with a vast selection of barnyard noises from which to choose."

—KERRY THORNLEY

With Operation Mindfuck in motion, and Garrison's investigation playing out, Kerry and Cara made a life for themselves in Florida. In July 1969, Kerry was working full time as a cook in a pancake house in Tampa, entertaining designs of starting his own private elementary school to be called the Sacred Mind Ashram, which he envisioned as a "hip school for little kids...with night classes for adults in such subjects as Basic Mindblowing, Intermediate Mindblowing, and Advanced Mindblowing—not to mention yoga and all the old standbys."

On February 1, 1970, Kerry received notice from his bonding agent, informing him that he was slated to go to trial in New Orleans on February 16, which came as a bit of a surprise, as Kerry was been under the impression that Garrison had dropped the perjury charges against him following Clay Shaw's acquittal in late 1969.[11]

On February 16, Kerry's lawyer—Ed Baldwin—filed a motion to quash on grounds of lack of materiality and a second motion to quash on grounds of deprivation of right to counsel. As it was, the prosecution wasn't prepared to address these motions and a continuance was granted until March 17. During this time, a "Kerry Thornley Defense Fund" was put into motion, orchestrated by

Louise Lacey and Greg Hill. However, this was short-lived, due to the fact that Kerry was never brought to trial. Ultimately, charges against him were dropped by Garrison's successor, Harry Connick, Sr.

In a manuscript titled *Star Witness Story*, Kerry later recalled his one and only Jim Garrison encounter:

> The only time I saw him was across the grand jury table during an agonizing, hectic morning of seemingly irrelevant questions. But the vibes he put out were unmistakably genuine. The embattled District Attorney really wanted to know who killed JFK; our only problem was that he thought I had the answer.
>
> He didn't seem crazy, either. At the time of my grand jury appearance I felt like I must be the nutty one. His Assistant D.A.'s had laid so many reasons on me for thinking that I was part of the conspiracy that I began very seriously questioning the validity of my own consciousness. I wondered if I was not some kind of Manchurian Candidate or if I had not been drugged or hypnotized to forget my role in the assassination. Fortunately for my sanity, very few "coincidences" withstood the test of independent research.

■

Another project Kerry was passionately involved in was *Zenarchy*, a "sporadical religious literary bulletin of political necrophilia." *Zenarchy* dispatches were sent out to underground newspapers of the period, and for a while appeared under the pen name of Blake Allen Green (BAG). Much of this material later made it into Kerry's book, *Zenarchy*, published by IllumiNet Press in 1991. In one early issue of *Zenarchy*, Kerry described his concept this way:

> ZEN is Meditation.

> ARCHY is Social Order.

> ZENARCHY is the Social Order which springs from Meditation.

> As a doctrine, it holds Universal Enlightenment a prerequisite to abolition of the State.

> After which the State will inevitably vanish.

> Or—that failing—nobody will give a damn.

Along with his *Zenarchy* writings, Kerry and Cara worked together on *I Tao: A Manual For Yin Revolution*, a book project about social conditioning and how to break free from the chains imposed upon the individual by the state, and in the process eventually liberate the human spirit.

As always Kerry kept up his incredible network of contacts, among them Louise Lacey who, in the spring of 1969, turned him on to Castaneda's *The Teachings of Don Juan: A Yaqui Way of Knowledge*. Kerry commented that: "Don Juan was quite a head fucker—just what I needed: one more good lay. Greg Hill (Malaclypse The Younger, Co-Founder of the Discordian Society) was here visiting and he, being a rationalistic cynical sort, read it, too, and it <u>really</u> fucked his mind. Took it with him up to Chicago to lay on Rob't Anton Wilson (Mord—in the Illuminati). Just his sort of book."

And if Don Juan wasn't enough, an even greater and more mind-expanding experience entered Kerry's life during this period, the birth of his son Kreg, thereafter known as Kregor, the golden apple of Kerry's eye in the pyramid. In a letter from the time, Cara wrote: "Kerry is beautiful with him—perhaps more 'purely joyous' than anyone I've seen."

Kerry, Cara, and Kregor relocated several times during 1969 through 1971. In Tampa, they rented a cottage on Marlin Street near the Yacht Club, where Kerry made ends meet washing dishes in a Zen-like frame of mind. To get about town, his mode of travel was a used $8 bike he picked up from Goodwill.

During this period, Greg Hill and Bud Simco paid a visit to Kerry in Tampa. According to Simco:

> The only real time we had to visit was while [Kerry] was at work. So Greg and I went with him and washed dishes at the Yacht Club for free—just to hang out in the kitchen to visit with Kerry...and it was a lot of fun—we did that for a day or two. And the management, they were really amazed that people would do that—these three guys back there washing dishes, two of them for free—all of them, by all appearances, over qualified to be washing dishes.... And they couldn't figure out why Kerry was back there washing dishes because he was obviously a very intelligent person, and they knew he was a writer—basically that's what [Kerry] said: "I just want to write—I just want to cover the basic minimum daily requirements, and be left alone to write."

Kerry put out a newsletter called the *Liberated Yoga Network* (LYN). In one issue of LYN, he listed the principles of liberated yoga, which included "advocation of sexual freedom; condemnation of sexism; support for erotic mysticism."

Part of Kerry's envisioned Utopia was a world free of sexual hangups, which included advocacy for pedophilia. I had assumed this stance was merely idealistic until Grace Caplinger shared the following E-mail correspondence in 2003:

> There was an incident in Atlanta, when Kerry and Cara and Kreg were living across the street from me and my family. He took my daughter Marion, when she was seven or eight, into a room at the home of a family, close friends of mine, who lived around the corner. He closed the door and began trying to fondle Marion. This was stopped by my friend, Jane, coming to the door and demanding that it be opened. She told me about it, as did Marion at the time, and I know now that I did not deal with this properly. Part of me was simply unable to understand the gravity, even the total reality of it. But it did happen.

It appears that this was an isolated incident, as during the course of my research no other episodes of this nature surfaced. Louise Lacey shared the following:

> I think Kerry was an omnivore sexually…he would have fucked a rhinoceros if he had the opportunity. (Perhaps he did. I don't know.) I do know he had a lot of sexually transmitted diseases over the years, and I am glad I never slept with him…. He was an idealist…. What it came down to was he thought that everyone was sexual, at any age, and someone (Kerry?) should be accommodating all of them. I tried to tell him that kids were different, but he thought I was conservative about sex.

■

The Thornleys moved to Marietta, Georgia, in 1971, living on the edge of the suburbs in a good-sized middle-class house, which, as Kerry noted, was "very quiet whenever Kreg was asleep." Kerry would rise at a quarter to six each day and catch a bus for work in Atlanta. As Kerry wrote in a letter of the time, "This is my opportunity to meditate. I have decided that posture, chants, breathing, beads and such are all in the class of purely secondary aids to fall back on if need be— but that anyone can meditate under almost any conditions." In another letter, Kerry described this period in the following serene manner: "Kregor and Cara are just beautiful these days. A small child can really help you patch up the holes in your buckets."

Along with raising a budding young Infantus Illuminatus, Kerry and Cara were also teaching yoga during a Friday-night class in their living room, which had been converted into a self-styled ashram. Classes included hatha yoga, raja yoga and "trippy raps after the manner of Stephen Gaskin." Like Gaskin's group, Kerry was looking to "cultivate sex-positive attitudes on the theory that they are part of the mystical life. This will be more than the groovy sexual freedom of the Keristas, though I hope it will include that. But the main idea will be to establish an atmosphere of complete openness on erotic hang-ups and fantasies." Kerry described the first class as "a big success. A dozen people were there, and we all got very high on Hatha Yoga led by Cara, meditation, OM chanting, a stoned sermon by Omar [Kerry], and a general rap session."

Kerry attempted to merge this project into the curriculum of the Free University of Emory, but for whatever reasons, this never panned out. He had a lot of plans along these lines, which included a free school for hip children where they could be taught yoga, read Zen stories, and do meditation instead of taking naps.

In late 1971, Kerry and Cara separated, albeit on good terms, with Kregor staying with his mom. As Kerry explained the situation in a letter from this period:

> I need to own less. Have more time to myself.
> Have a room or apartment or house that is not
> mine, but is a temple to the Lord. This is not why
> we are separating, but it will be one of the things
> I've been needing for a long time. I cannot do the
> middle class thing—I can do the work, I can
> handle the indoctrination, but I cannot live in the
> comfortable concentration camp.

At loose ends, Kerry decided to enroll at Georgia State, where he held down a job at the university library, cleaning films and thinking "about things and sometimes chant to my little machine with its humming prayer wheels.... Libraries are good temples in which to work."

Along with meditation, Kerry continued to experiment sexually: "I've been coming out strong as an exhibitionist in past months. You can't imagine what a difference it has made in the way I feel/respond. Jacked off on Cara's living room floor one day while two female friends, who'd been invited, watched. Done a few numbers for a gay friend with Eve, the lady I now live with, present also. Certainly among the most satisfying sexual experiences of my entire life."

■

By the early 70s, fellow Discordians Bob Newport and Greg Hill had relocated to the Russian River area of California, and started a movie theater in the town of Monte Rio.

Housed in an old converted military Quonset hut, Cinema Rio had five hundred seats, as well as a vast population of rats until a 22-pound Siamese cat named Eldritch became a Cinema Rio regular. "And," as Bob Newport recalled, "that was the last of the rats, the night Eldritch walked into the theater. We brought him in, put him down in the lobby, his ears went up, and he was gone like a flash—and from that night on there was no rats!"

Cinema Rio was unique in the sense that it was a community effort, a theater by and for the local residents. In this spirit, local artists were enlisted to help decorate the digs, which included a beautiful marquee outside that displayed a cartoonish Mayan motif. The inside of the theater was originally a dull pink, so—to give it some pizzazz—columns and figures, swirling and twirling about, were painted on the walls, giving the place the funky feel of an old-time theater reborn with a psychedelic sensibility.

Greg and Bob ran Cinema Rio on a shoestring, with Greg putting the programming together, in addition to designing the posters and advertisement blurbs. As part of their community outreach, once a month programming meetings were held where the locals could contribute suggestions for films. Thus a concerted effort was made to involve the community, which meant employing it, as well. In fact, Greg and Bob ended up employing way too many locals to ever turn a profit.

Eventually, Greg and Bob decided to expand their vision. Right next to Cinema Rio was a huge old abandoned redwood dance hall. When it came up for sale, Greg and Bob decided they would start a community center there. After acquiring the building, they put in a restaurant and a health clinic, ran a community newspaper, and had weekend gatherings, including concerts on the beach, where they fed the homeless.

While all of this was going on, the intrepid Dr. Newport was somehow able to operate a psychiatry practice out of his house in nearby Guerneville, often getting paid for his services in baskets of garden vegetables or apples. Bob's "office"—it turns out—was in a tree house on his property, located in the center of a circle of redwoods. The entire property consisted of an acre and a half, with several cabins scattered throughout the redwoods. It was a diverse operation, including a school in his garage, which twenty or so kids attended. Dr. Bob was also heavily involved with the psych department at nearby Sonoma State, as on his property various group sessions were ran, such as encounter groups and primal groups. In the process, a fun time was had by all. Bob Wilson—who had relocated just north of Guerneville, in Rio Nido—was also a frequent visitor to this scene.

Meanwhile, Camden Benares had his own scene at Camp Meeker, a tiny crossroads a few miles south of Monte Rio, where he served as Head Postmaster. The post office itself was located in a quaint old railroad car, patriotically painted red, white, and blue.

Camp Meeker consisted of a bunch of summer cabins that in recent years had been overrun by hippies. Kerry—after attending Georgia State for a semester—joined Camden in a lifestyle there dedicated to sexual freedom and Zenarchy.

At the time, Camden was married to his second wife, Melissa, and mate swapping was common at Camp Meeker, as both Camden and Kerry had been into swinging since the days of Kerista. In fact, Kerry and Melissa were an item for awhile, and Kerry referred to her as "his ambassador to the world." Another member of the party was a six-foot-two lady named Jerry.

Camden, it should be noted, was one of the original exponents of the Sexual Freedom League (SFL). Both he and Kerry saw the SFL as a revolution that was going to take over the planet and illuminate the masses. Of course, sex had always been a major component of Camden's consciousness, being—as he was—the consummate woman chaser, not to mention an avowed pornography devotee. In fact, Camden made extra cash in his spare time freelancing porn. Some of his exposes appeared in *The San Francisco Ball*. Camden would often go out and have all kinds of wild sexcapades, then afterwards write about these adventures in *The Ball*.

Kerry was also a frequent contributor to *The Ball*, chronicling his opinions in a column called "Erotic Minority Liberation." In a 13-part series he defended nearly every taboo, among these exhi-

bitionists, voyeurs, fetishists, pedophiles, transvestites, nympho-
maniacs, obscene phone callers, animal lovers, and sadomasochists.

For added kicks, Camden sent out sporadic dispatches to his
Discordian friends under the title of *The Camp Meeker Truth and Foma
Forum*. He was also working on a book project, *Zen Without Zen
Masters*, which was later published in the late 70s and, like
Illuminatus, was dedicated to the dynamic duo of Thornley and Hill.

■

Cinema Rio and the Monte Rio Community Center eventually
folded in the spring of 1973, largely because Newport and Hill were
over extended financially. But there were other factors, as well,
which caused the scene to run its course, namely the dissolution of
Greg's marriage to his wife, Jeanetta.

Clinically speaking, Greg suffered from chronic depression
and never really got over his breakup with Jeanetta. Instead, he
smoked and drank to medicate the pain, and never dealt with his
failed marriage. As Bob Newport recalled:

> It would have been a miracle if the marriage had
> survived. Life at the River was incredibly
> difficult. I mean it was wild, it was high and it
> was fun, it was creative…and there was no
> money. Which meant that just trying to scrimp by
> with a living was hard to do, and it was hard for
> everybody. It was hard for me, too. I mean I had a
> little income because I had a little practice going.
> But the theater made no money—that cost us
> money. All these other activities we had going—
> none of them made money…. So things were
> incredibly stressful. And when the marriage
> broke up, Greg became very depressed. And
> basically about that time, my mentor who lived

next store to me, who had been a very interesting
old man, who had dropped out as a President of
Union Bank, and had come to the River, and had
a very interesting Libertarian philosophy…ah,
anyhow, he died, Jeanetta left, and pretty much
everything collapsed. And Greg became
incredibly depressed. And he went off to New
York…and got a job with a bank doing clerical
work, which is about as bleak an outcome as you
can imagine. So he drank and that became his
way of dealing with things.

CHAPTER 14

Dreadlock Recollections

"Is it not possible that Kerry's involvement with the JFK assassination is simply synchronicity—that the many meaningful connections are part of a synchronous pattern rather than evidence that he has unwittingly been involved in a conspiracy?"

—Bob Shea, from a letter to Greg Hill,
   dated November 22, 1975

In the summer of 1973, Kerry visited Greg Hill in New York City, where the two took in a folk concert in Washington Square. At this concert, Kerry came across a copy of the *Yipster Times* which forever after changed his life and reawakened long-forgotten ghosts.

The *Yipster Times* contained material which was afterwards expanded upon and published in a book by A.J. Weberman and Michael Canfield called *Coup d'Etat in America*, an acronym for the CIA and an allusion to "Company" complicity in the JFK assassination.

The thesis of *Coup d'Etat in America* suggested that Watergate conspirator and longtime CIA spook E. (Everett) Howard Hunt was one of the three mystery tramps renowned in Kennedy assassination lore, and it was the photographic evidence presented therein that led Kerry to believe that Hunt was, in fact, the shadowy character he'd met a full decade before—Gary Kirstein, aka Brother-in-law. Furthermore, Kerry came to believe that he'd been hypno-programmed as a substitute fall guy in the Kennedy assassination (in the event that the Oswald set-up went awry) and that E. Howard Hunt (in the guise of Brother-in-law) was one of Kerry's "handlers."

For those not in the know, the "three mystery tramps"—as they have been dubbed—were photographed in the vicinity of the grassy knoll not long after Kennedy got a chunk of his cranium cat-apulted across Elm Street and into the history books. These three tramps were picked up by the Dallas police and then released without any record of arrest. Weberman and Canfield put forth the theory that the three tramps were involved in the Kennedy assassination, and to bolster their theory the authors presented a series of photographic overlays that compared the profiles of certain notorious individuals to those of the tramps.

Fingered by the authors as one of the tramps was CIA contract agent Frank Sturgis, who was involved with E. Howard Hunt in the Bay of Pigs fiasco, as well as being a party to the infamous Watergate break-in, which some say Hunt "masterminded."

Soon after the publication of *Coup d'Etat in America*, Hunt sued the authors for several million in damages, claiming he was in Washington, D.C., at CIA headquarters, on the day of the assassination. This alibi, however, was subsequently discredited. Soon after, Hunt changed his tune, alleging that on the day of the assassination he'd been on leave, performing husbandly household errands, which included a shopping trip to a grocery store in the Chinatown section of D.C.

Canfield and Weberman investigated Hunt's new alibi and discovered that the Chinatown store Hunt claimed to have visited never existed. As a result, Hunt offered to drop his lawsuit for a token settlement of $1, but Canfield and Weberman were having no part of the deal, and refused to settle.

Later, in 1978, a *Sunday News Journal* article cited anonymous sources in the CIA regarding a secret agency memo, dated 1966, which placed Hunt in Dallas on the day of the assassination. Those CIA sources who had provided the memo told the *Sunday News Journal* that Hunt's story about shopping in downtown Washington on the day of the assassination was a cover story concocted as a result of this memo, and that Hunt's wife, Dorothy, could not be questioned about this due to her death in a mysterious plane crash in Chicago in 1972. It was rumored at the time of her demise that Mrs. Hunt was about to leave her husband and had plans to testify against him.

During E. Howard Hunt's tenure with the CIA, he was involved in a whole host of nefarious endeavors, which included the overthrow of the Guatemalan government in the 1950s, as well as covert operations in Cuba, including the Bay of Pigs operation, in which he played a pivotal role. On account of the Bay of Pigs disaster Hunt hated JFK and blamed him for its failure.

It has been further alleged that Hunt was a member of an assassination squad, headed by Col. Boris Pash, that was created to eliminate suspected double agents and low-ranking foreign intelligence officers. It has been further alleged that Hunt, in cahoots with G. Gordon Liddy, was part of a plot to assassinate whistle-blowing columnist Jack Anderson. If that weren't enough, Hunt also served as a top official at the CIA station in Mexico City during Oswald's visit there in September 1963 and, according to Hunt's autobiography, was stationed at Atsugi Air Base at the same time as Kerry Thornley. Curiouser and curiouser…

A letter in Oswald's handwriting surfaced after the Kennedy assassination, dated November 10, 1963, and addressed to a certain "Mr. Hunt," in which he asked for a job with Hunt's organization. Some have speculated that the addressee of this mysterious letter was Texas oil millionaire H.L. Hunt, while others have suspected more sinister implications: namely, that this mysterious letter was intended for E. Howard Hunt.

A true renaissance rogue, Hunt was described by the *New York Post* thusly: "author of 44 mystery thrillers, a man with a spooky fondness for masks and wigs, aliases, surgical gloves and surveillance devices, Hunt stands out as the conspirator you'd most like to interview…a man with a keen, restless mind, a clever rogue with a deep cynicism about human nature and a casual view of death." Many, if not all, of these characteristics seem to fit Kerry's Brother-in-law to a T. Kerry believed that Brother-in-law was in disguise, perhaps even wearing a wig. As well, Kerry's "Brother-in-law" possessed a keen mind and a casual view of death, not unlike Hunt.

As Kerry's Brother-in-law memories came flooding back, the conversations he'd shared with Gary Kirstein/Brother-in-law so many years before began to take on greater significance. One of the oddest things that Brother-in-law had brought up during their initial conversations were instances of "freak radio reception," such as the case of a woman in Des Moines who had picked up a radio broadcast through her hair curlers. In the same manner, other people had discovered that their tooth fillings were sensitive to radio waves. "Things like that happen," Brother-in-law told Kerry.

"Yes," Kerry answered. "I think maybe once or twice it happened to me. A few months ago, when I was lying across from Lafayette Square in a little room over Fred's Inn, I seemed to hear radio programs as I was drifting into sleep during my afternoon naps—with station breaks, news, commercials, weather reports and music. When I woke up afterwards, though, I couldn't remember the call letters of the station." Kirstein laughed and nodded, as if to indicate that he had foreknowledge about the event, which Kerry found rather peculiar. Kerry neglected to mention that—while serving in the Marines—he had often experienced audio hallucinations before falling to sleep. At the time, he wrote off these episodes as nothing more than a peculiar category of dream. Kerry didn't consider his "freak radio reception" experiences any differently. But now, over ten years later, these memories were starting to worry him.

■

In August 1973, Kerry wrote an article for the underground paper *The Great Speckled Bird* titled "Did the Plumbers Plug JFK Too?" which drew parallels between the Watergate break-in and the Kennedy assassination. Soon after this article appeared, Kerry received a couple of curious phone calls, the first of which was a male voice imitating the sounds of a speeded-up tape recorder. Ten years before, Kerry and his French Quarter pal Roger Lovin used to speak to each other (goofingly so) at the Bourbon House in noises identical to this strange telephone call.

Upon receiving the first of these two curious phone calls, Kerry replied with a word or two of bewilderment, and the mysterious sped-up caller hung up. A few seconds later, the phone rang again, and this time a male voice said very distinctly: "Kerry, do you know who this is?" Kerry answered no, and the voice on the other end of the line said: "Good!" and then hung up.

To Kerry, the caller sounded strikingly similar to how he remembered Gary Kirstein, so much so that he decided he couldn't keep his suspicions to himself any longer, although it took Kerry another year (February 1975) to finally start compiling notes on his Brother-in-law/Kennedy assassination-associated memories. During this period, a revived interest in the JFK assassination caused many in the media and political circles to begin calling for a congressional probe of those tragic events of November 1963. With this revived interest, Kerry began receiving calls from various media outlets, such as CBS and *Reader's Digest*. At this time, he avoided issuing statements to the media, so that he would not "divulge anything sensational" until he had the opportunity to testify under oath. Behind the scenes, though, Kerry continued to work on his Kennedy assassination notes, excavating disturbing memories, which—more by more—started taking on greater significance.

One morning, while at the campus of Georgia State—where he was then employed as a part-time student assistant—Kerry received a phone call from an ACLU lawyer, Reber Boult, whom he hoped would represent him for his prospective appearance before a congressional committee. Boult asked Kerry if he'd been following the headlines in the Atlanta papers regarding the investigation by City Commissioner of Public Safety Reginald Eaves into the assassination of Martin Luther King, Jr. When Kerry admitted his ignorance of Eaves' investigation, Boult suggested he might want to look into it, as the principal witness in the case seemed to be talking about a lot of the same people (with connections to Carlos Marcello) that Kerry had alluded to in previous conversations with Boult.

That same afternoon, Kerry picked up an Atlanta newspaper and read the article in question, which concerned a young man, Robert Byron Watson, who had supplied information to the police about a narcotics ring. Watson insisted that just prior to Martin Luther King's assassination, he had heard one of the drug ring leaders say: "I'm going to shoot that damned nigger [King] in the head and frame a jailbird for it, just like I did with Kennedy."

When Kerry read Watson's allegations, he was flabbergasted, because—as previously noted—Gary Kirstein (aka Brother-in-law) had once told him that part of his theoretical Kennedy assassination plan was to pin the murders on a "jailbird." When Kerry saw these same words used in reference to the King assassination, a red flag immediately flew up, reminding him of those long ago words of Brother-in-law about how, after they knocked off Kennedy, "next we'll get Martin Luther King." Of course, Kerry thought Kirstein was only blowing so much hot air at the time. Only now was he beginning to realize the ominous overtones connected to those words.

In an unpublished article from the period titled "Assassination Scene Heats Up," Bob Wilson wrote:

> [Robert Byron] Watson's charges were originally made in 1970, to the staff of President Nixon, and were dismissed as unfounded after an FBI investigation. Shortly thereafter, Watson was arrested for receiving a package containing heroin from Thailand in the mails.
>
> Watson and his mother, Mrs. R.W. Watson, have charged ever since then that the heroin was sent by persons unknown to them, and the narcs were then tipped off, so that Watson could be imprisoned and his charges further discredited.

Watson's story is that, in 1968, at the age of 13, he was visiting an Atlanta firm which sells archeological artifacts. (The boy was an archeology-geology buff at the time, suffering from asthma, and given to lonely and scholarly pursuits.) He claims that he overheard a group of white men discussing a plan to assassinate Rev. Martin Luther King, Jr.

Mrs. Watson insists that the boy told her of what he had heard that very day. She didn't believe him however, until after the assassination, she says, and they didn't take the story to the government until two years later, in 1970, when they spoke to some of Nixon's aides.

After the boy's heroin bust, Mrs. Watson attempted to interest other investigators, with little result. In July 1972, the boy was paroled from the Federal Youth Center in Ashland, Kentucky, and shortly re-arrested on cocaine and marijuana charges. He and his mother insist this was part of the continuing effort to frame him and thereby silence him.

Comedian-activist Dick Gregory, an ardent conspiracy student, eventually became interested in young Watson's case and, in July this year, badgered the Atlanta, Georgia, authorities into investigating the whole matter.

The investigator's again found the boy's story unconvincing and, according to the Atlanta Journal for July 30, two of the men accused by him took lie-detector tests, which they passed. While the accuracy of polygraph tests is still a matter of dispute, that seemed to close the matter.

By then, Kerry Thornley had given his

statement to the Atlanta Police Department and
began sending out Xeroxes to conspiracy
investigators.

According to Thornley, one of the men accused
by young Watson appears to be the person he
[Thornley] knew in New Orleans in the early
1960s, under a different name.

It is Thornley's belief that certain conversations
instigated by this man—seemingly abstract or
theoretical discussions of how to commit an
assassination and get away with it—were
attempts to learn if he, Thornley, could be either
(a) lured into the Dealey Plaza assassination team
or (b) framed afterwards, as a cover for the real
conspirators.

For Kerry, a fog had been long hovering over his head, and it
was due to a handful of these incidents that this fog slowly lifted
and his long buried memories of Brother-in law surfaced.

Could it have been a sort of mind control that clouded Kerry's
memory of his Brother-in-law recollections? And what had Brother-
in-law said, once upon a time, about "freak radio reception"? Had
Brother-in-law been alluding to a method of mind control known
in intelligence agency parlance as Radio Hypnotic Intracerebral
Control and Electronic Dissolution of Memory (RHIC-EDOM)?

Once Kerry opened this door to the past, the torrent of memories continued, such as one curious incident involving a typewriter
once belonging to Kerry, which he believed had been stolen by Gary
Kirstein/Brother-in-law following Memorial Day in 1961.

At the time, Kerry suspected that Brother-in-law had pur-
loined the typewriter simply because he was in need of some fast
cash. Later, Kerry speculated that the notes he compiled for
Brother-in-law while researching Nazis at the New Orleans public
library—in conjunction with this stolen typewriter—had been

orchestrated as a means to produce a manuscript, under Kerry's by-line, which could be used at a later date to trace him back to this typewriter and incriminate him in the Kennedy assassination. (Gentle reader, is your head starting to hurt?)

While doing his Nazi research for Kirstein, Kerry—in his own handwriting—had dutifully written "Hitler Was a Good Guy" on the top of each page, along with his own name. Unsuspectingly, he then turned over these "Hitler Was a Good Guy " notes to Brother-in-law, who in turn gave Kerry a few bucks for his efforts.

It should be noted that E. Howard Hunt—throughout the course of his checkered career—had a hand in the falsification of various documents and diaries, and some researchers have even speculated that it was Hunt who forged Arthur Bremer's diary, the man who shot the legs out from under George Wallace. A diary that Lee Oswald allegedly wrote possessed all the earmarks of a forgery was attributed to Hunt by certain researchers. Presumably, the intent of such forgeries was to demonstrate that the alleged authors were either psychologically unbalanced and/or politically motivated to assassinate leaders such as Kennedy or Wallace, all of this being further evidence to promote "lone nut" assassin theories. In this regard, Kerry believed that Brother-in-law had commandeered his stolen typewriter for just such a purpose, which was to be used in conjunction with the notes Kerry had gathered in the New Orleans library for Kirstein's "Hitler Was a Good Guy" book project to set Kerry up as an assassination fall guy. [12]

CHAPTER 15

Is Paranoia a Higher Form of Awareness?

"It is just that my awareness is like that of one peering at shapes in the fog. I happen to be surrounded by all the great monsters which oppress humanity—and for the moment they are much too afraid of one another to close in on me. So I am in a position to point them out, identify them, describe their general outlines—but I can seldom fill you in completely on the details of their features."

—KERRY THORNLEY, mid-70s

On account of the Robert Byron Watson revelations, Kerry became convinced that Gary Kirstein (aka Brother-in-law) had a hand in orchestrating Kennedy's assassination. This being the case, Kerry swiftly typed up a number of memos detailing his Brother-in-law conversations from years past, then randomly distributed said memos to his vast network of contacts in order to ensure that there would be some evidence left if he were suddenly fatally "silenced."

Immediately after sending out these memos, Kerry was at a party where he was given what he thought was some "funny-tasting" marijuana that made him, as he described, "uninhibited and talkative."[13] While at this party, Kerry said he was questioned intensively by a group of inquisitive individuals regarding the Kennedy assassination. A few days later, he again met one of the people from the pot party, who proceeded to pass him a pipeload of dope that,

when Kerry puffed upon it, blistered the inside of his mouth, making him suspect that certain parties were attempting to poison him.
Kerry delivered an affidavit to the Atlanta police force, dated July
25, 1975, along with the pot pipe and its contents:

> I have spoken to several people about the group
> of very nice people I met at a party at the
> Celestial Mansion on Flat Shoals Road last
> Saturday night.
>
> One person I met there who may or may not
> have been part of this group (which knew more
> about the JFK assassination re Gary Kirstein, it
> seemed, by what they said and the questions they
> asked me, than I do) was a guy who said his
> name was Jack Wolverton.
>
> He wanted a copy of the lyrics to a song I wrote
> which Dennis Rotch was singing and so I got his
> address: 1203 Euclid Ave., Apt. 2 here in Atlanta.
>
> On the night of July 22 I ran into Jack in Plaza
> Drugs.... I invited him by my house to get the
> poem, and wound up giving him five or six of my
> MOTIONS OF ADJOURNMENT poems.
>
> While we sat in the kitchen rapping, I filled up
> the enclosed pipe with "a few leftover roaches"
> and passed it to Jack. There was a long interval
> when my attention was directed elsewhere and
> Jack had the pipe.
>
> When he passed it back to me, I took a drag and
> IMMEDIATELY felt a large blister form inside my
> right check. Puzzled, I passed the pipe back to
> Jack, running my tongue over the blister. I did not
> observe carefully whether Jack actually smoked
> the pipe or merely made a pretense of doing so.
> When the pipe was returned to me, Eve, who had

been out, came in the door. I took another puff only to have yet another blister, pop up right next to the other one at the exact time the smoke made contact with the membrane inside my cheek.

Thinking it might be some sort of allergic reaction, I commented on it, and passed the pipe to Eve. She took a drag and experienced no unusual reactions.

I then went into the bathroom and examined the blisters in the mirror. They were dark red blood blisters and each was about the size of a deformed collar button.

I have had only one other experience with blisters forming instantly from any cause other than direct burns by fire, and that was in Atomic, Biological, and Chemical Warfare School ("Defense" I think they call it, not "Warfare") in the Marines. That time our instructor demonstrated the effects of mustard gas to us by placing an infinitesimal amount on each of our fingertips—the result: instant blistering.

I returned to the kitchen and commented that the blisters had formed when I had taken a drag on the pipe. Jack said: "Oh, I don't think there is any relation." Something about the certainty of his unsolicited opinion, something about the tone of voice and timing—too hasty an interjection—has caused me to become very suspicious.

Earlier I had asked Jack if he knew who those other people were at the Celestial Mansion or understood what we had been discussing. He said "no," that he had been playing music at the time on his guitar, which was true. He had been playing John Prine songs, which occupy a special place in my heart in relation to the Celestial Mansion because of a very high experience I had there in 1972 upon first discovering John Prine's music. The whole incident at the Celestial Mansion had been carefully orchestrated by people who knew a great deal about me, people I correspond with, and the JFK assassination, particularly my involvement. I was made to feel as comfortable as possible, and then I was pumped just enough to see if it was Gary Kirstein that I was naming. (Does Kenner, Louisiana, mean anything to you was one of the questions I got asked.)

On the way from Plaza to the apartment was when I asked Jack if he knew those other people. He said he did not. I then explained to him what had happened and my suspicions concerning Gary Kirstein.

Enclosed is the pipe and its contents, along with the plastic bottle the roaches were in before Jack got there, and to which he had no access. It seems to me this material should be analyzed. It was fished out of the trash by me a few days after the incident. Several important witnesses, including Ruby and Shaw died of cancer, for one thing, and some chemicals (nicotine for example) can stimulate cancer.

Shortly after Kerry delivered this affidavit, Greg Hill arrived in Atlanta to find his old pal in hysterics over the events that had recently transpired. At this time, Kerry and Greg attended a party at Cara's house that was crashed by some ski-masked bandits who stole Kerry's identification, while taking only money from the other guests present. Kerry believed that this raid was more than a random incident, and that it had been clandestinely orchestrated as a cover to intimidate him and obtain his I.D.

In a letter to Bob Shea dated November 11, 1975, Greg Hill wrote:

> I went to visit Kerry in August and besides the fact that we were all robbed by gunmen and that while we were reading a letter from Wilson and got to the word "magic," he [Wilson] or Eris or Yahweh or Santa Claus threw down a precisely timed thunderbolt (literally, and loud—the storm came a few hours later), besides all of that the visit did a lot for me in understanding Kerry's predicament and, I think, for Kerry in accepting (again) the absolute absurdity of it all.
>
> When I came to Atlanta, Kerry was in a state of fear for his life, seriously, and he has logical reasons. I'm not convinced that his life was or is in danger necessarily, but he has good reason to be concerned and it was driving him fucking nuts that nobody was willing to seriously consider that as a realistic possibility.... As it is now, I don't know what the hell is going on. Worse than that, I don't know how to help. The thing that is needed is an independent investigation of Kirstein, but I don't know how to make that happen...

Only a few years before, Kerry had considered Garrison's investigation a McCarthy-like witch-hunt, whereas now he began to suspect that Garrison might have actually been on the right track. Suddenly a string of evidence—which had once seemed but mere coincidences—were now beginning to line up, one after another, to form in his mind a conspiratorial domino row, with Kerry at center stage surrounded by a web of conspirators manipulating the movements of not only himself, but Lee Oswald, prior to the Kennedy assassination.

Bob Wilson viewed many of these so-called coincidences associated with Kerry and the JFK assassination as *synchronicities*. For those unfamiliar with Jungian psychology, synchronicities are seemingly coincidental or oddly related events that take on a greater significance, events occurring on a psychic level that transcend pure coincidence, but should not necessarily be considered part of some grand conspiracy—at least not in terms of how we normally define "conspiracy." There is a mystical component to synchronicities, as if some higher consciousness directs our lives, bringing the Thornleys and Oswalds of the world together as part of some grand, and equally mad, cosmic plan. Operation Mindfuck, indeed!

At one point, Kerry visited a hypnotist to help him uncover what had actually gone on during his service in the Marines, and if indeed the Office of Naval Intelligence (ONI) had brainwashed him to be some kind of sleeper agent. In this instance, the hypnotist was unable to discover if there was any validity to this theory, which left Kerry only more uncertain as to the world revolving around him at a dizzying pace.

Kerry's mind now became enveloped in this shadow realm, as he searched tirelessly, within and without, for a light at the end of this dark tunnel, in pursuit of the "final truth" that would make all the bad demons go away and let justice, at last, be served.

In a letter from the summer of 1975, Kerry outlined his JFK assassination conspiracy theory:

> When the Pentagon decided to wipe JFK out, they
> went to Gary [Kirstein] and contracted with him
> to do the job (according to my theory). They
> probably gave him a certain amount of money
> and provided him with whatever intelligence
> data he needed, but I doubt if they knew, or even
> wanted to know, exactly what he was doing…

Gary was more than just an intelligence operative, however. He was also a very smart crook. In addition to that, ideologically he was a textbook-type Nazi, with a very intricate understanding of how Hitler had risen to power by forging alliances between powerful people who did not trust each other, but who trusted him because he had no branch of the service, no police unit, and no bureaucracy under his direct orders.

Gary was the hustler who was right in the middle of it all. Without him the assassination would still probably have occurred. But it would not have been done so cleverly, would not have involved so many different kinds of people and organizations, and probably would have been easier to solve.

In November 1975, Kerry was visited by Discordian poet Judith Abrahms in Atlanta, as noted in a letter to Greg Hill:

> Judith Abrahms arrived for an extended, hopefully, visit the other day. I've been so involved with her staggering intellect and Babylonian sensuality lately that the 22 of November [the anniversary of Kennedy's assassination] slipped past me unawares...I've never had such a deeply intellectual and humorous friendship with a woman. Much to my surprise, I'm having a bit of difficulty adjusting to the idea that she is also an eager sexual partner. I'm more sexist than I like to think, I guess...

During this period, Kerry and Judith briefly lived together. However, their relationship ended abruptly, when Kerry started acting paranoid, accusing Judith of being somehow involved in "the

Conspiracy." Subsequently, Judith got spooked by Kerry's irrational behavior and split back to California.

■

Another revelation of Kerry's was that the JFK assassination had been orchestrated to escalate the Vietnam War. And so it was that one day in the summer of 1976—while hitchhiking north of Santa Barbara—Kerry took a load off and sat down on the road side to smoke a pipeload of tobacco. Afterwards, Kerry carelessly dumped out the smoldering ashes, then suddenly realized it was midsummer in California, where a few sparks could ignite several thousand acres of dry brushland. As Kerry furiously rubbed out the embers with a pebble, he thought about what would have happened had he actually started a wildfire.

"Hell," he said aloud, "I could burn everything in sight, admit it and tell everybody about why the Vietnam War was escalated and I'd be doing more good than harm." Later, Kerry met another vagabond on up the coast who kindled a small fire in a restricted area. Kerry ended taking the rap when several fire engines showed up and busted him and his hobo friend. Ever the opportunist, Kerry seized the moment to tell the firefighters his theories about the Vietnam War, although they didn't appear the least bit interested. Of course, the fire only covered about six square inches, as opposed to several thousand acres. For this offence, Kerry was given a $50 fine.

■

In the mid-70s, Kerry was contacted by a guy named David Bucknell, who had served (or so he claimed) with both Kerry and Oswald in the Marines. During their initial conversation, Bucknell asked Kerry if he remembered an attempt by military intelligence to recruit the three of them into some sort of spooky intelligence operation. When Kerry replied that he couldn't recall this specific incident, Bucknell proceeded to refresh Kerry's memory by describing a series of events that had transpired some two decades before.

According to Bucknell, it all began one day at El Toro base when the names Oswald, Bucknell, and Thornley were called out over the P.A. system and ordered to report to base security. When the three arrived, they were seated in a small auditorium with a number of other men. Addressing the group that day was a Marine captain and a Hispanic man in civilian clothes named "Mister B." After the recruitment lecture—which outlined a counter-espionage program targeted at Castro's Cuba—Mr. B. then interviewed the "volunteers" individually.

Kerry heard nothing more from the mysterious Mr. B., although Bucknell claimed that he and Oswald returned for further meetings. At these meetings, Bucknell was asked if he would consider teaching electronics at paramilitary operations in the jungles of South America. Bucknell was never contacted regarding this assignment. However, Oswald confided to Bucknell that he would be "defecting" to the Soviet Union on an intelligence mission in the near future. Furthermore, Bucknell told Kerry that following Oswald's arrest and subsequent murder, he "knew" that Oswald had been set up.

Bucknell became so paranoid about this whole affair that for several years afterwards he lived under a series of assumed names. According to Kerry, both he and Bucknell suspected that "Oswald may already have been an Army Intelligence agent pretending to be a Marxist at the time of Mr. B's recruitment attempt, which may have enhanced his qualifications for Mr. B's program.... At about the time all this happened, I began having vivid audio hallucinations, usually just before falling asleep."

Later, Kerry came to believe that these audio hallucinations— encountered prior to REM sleep—were induced by way of a mind control device which had been surreptitiously implanted into the base of his neck by MK-ULTRA operatives. It was through these real or imagined implants that Kerry came to believe that mind control transmissions were beamed into his brain. As Kerry explained to researcher Greg Krupey in the mid-80s: "I am implying that dreams can be produced technologically, via low-level micro-waves and that, via UHF sound projections thoughts can be planted. According to FOIA documents the CIA made a KGB agent jump out a window via UHF messages."

MK-ULTRA, for those unfamiliar with the term, was the code name for covert CIA mind control experiments started in 1953 under a program exempt from congressional oversight, involving agents and "spychiatrists" who tested radiation, drugs, electric shock, microwaves, electrode implants, and psycho-surgery on often unwitting subjects.

The ultimate goal of MK-ULTRA was to create programmed assassins a la *The Manchurian Candidate*. The CIA also tested a wide range of drugs in an attempt to find the perfect chemical compound to control minds. LSD was one such drug that deeply interested CIA spychiatrists, to the extent that in the early 50s the agency attempted to purchase the entire world supply of acid from Sandoz Laboratories in Switzerland.

That Kerry made these mind control claims is all the more curi-ous, especially when one examines related literature, namely a strange little tome published in 1967 titled *Were We Controlled?* writ-ten by journalist Arthur Ford under the pen name of "Lincoln Lawrence." Ford, through his connections with certain "intelligence agency insiders," learned of a secret CIA technology known as RHIC-EDOM, an acronym for Radio Hypnotic Intracerebral Control and Electronic Dissolution of Memory, purportedly used to program Lee Harvey Oswald to murder President Kennedy. Lawrence also suggested that Jack Ruby had been similarly mind controlled when he plugged Oswald.

In a 1975 interview, Herman Kimsey—a CIA/Army counter-intelligence agent—told researcher Hugh McDonald that "Oswald was programmed to kill, like a medium at a séance. Then the mechanism went on the blink and Oswald became a dangerous toy without direction." Three weeks after this interview, Kimsey himself died due to an apparent heart attack, not an uncommon occurrence among the ranks of those with heretical knowledge pertaining to the Kennedy assassination.

Furthermore, Guy Banister employee Jack Martin alleged that David Ferrie had hypnotically programmed Oswald to kill Kennedy. Kerry likewise suspected that Oswald had been badly brainwashed while in the Marines, and that they'd both been manipulated a la some sort of Manchurian Candidate mindfuck. Although Kerry couldn't remember specific details (after all, that is what brainwashing does) he was still quite suspicious about the whole period he'd served with Oswald in the Marines.

■

As Kerry's mid-70s paranoia intensified, likewise did his correspondence to friends and fellow Discordians. Bob Wilson, for one, was the recipient of many of these rambling discourses that wove together a vast conspiratorial web.

In one letter to Wilson, Kerry related a particularly mind-blowing acid trip he'd taken in which memories of his involvement in the assassination bubbled to the surface of his conscious mind, thus revealing his participation as an unwitting dupe in the three-ring circus of tragedy that unfolded in Dealey Plaza—all part of a mind control experiment perpetrated by the Office of Naval Intelligence (ONI).

In fact, Kerry had previously suspected ONI of monitoring his activities during the time he was writing *The Idle Warriors*, and that he and Oswald had been put under surveillance during their periods of active duty. Later, Kerry filed a Freedom of Information request with ONI to get to the bottom of all this. When ONI finally responded, they claimed to have found no reference to Kerry or Oswald in their files. In this regard, Kerry suspected that someone in ONI had either stolen or destroyed the files in question. Of course, it's kind of hard to reason with someone who's paranoid.

Although Kerry entertained a whole host of brain-boggling theories, the ONI/MK-ULTRA hypothesis remains one of the more plausible, although—like any other—it's almost impossible to nail down at this late date. In 2002, Dr. Bob Newport shared the following:

> There was a fella, and I don't remember his
> name—I think the only part of his name I ever
> heard was Gary—who came to see Greg Hill in
> the early to mid 80s, and told Greg that he [Gary]
> had been in ONI, and had known about the [LSD]
> experimentation on Kerry…. That was
> provocative and intriguing, but I never did have
> the fella's last name——I didn't hear anything
> more. And Greg didn't seem to have much more
> than what I just told you, and he never had the
> ability or the interest—I don't know which—to
> follow that any more deeper.

According to Bob Wilson, Greg Hill once told him that he thought there might have been *something* at the very core of Kerry's conspiratorial cosmology—although exactly what that something was, Greg never made clear. As Wilson recalled:

> Kerry did become clinically psychotic, but that
> doesn't mean that all of his charges were
> necessarily the result of psychosis. If he did go
> through some brain altering program while he
> was in the Marines, and he remembered part of it,
> his imagination then went off and magnified it…
>   The last time I talked to Greg Hill about Kerry
> [in the late 70s], he thought that Kerry was
> definitely off his head, but that things had

happened in New Orleans…that somehow Kerry
did get involved unintentionally with some kind
of clandestine covert operation—that he was
manipulated or maneuvered and that he was not
imagining all of it.

A lot of [Kerry's] charges were totally bonkers,
but there could be a core of truth somewhere.
And that's what Greg believed: Greg thought that
there was something to Kerry's wild charges…a
core of truth.

In a 1983 *Rolling Stone* exposé, revelations surfaced suggesting
that Atsugi Air Base—where both Kerry and Oswald were stationed—was one of two overseas outposts where the CIA conducted
MK-ULTRA drug experiments in the early 60s. This program took
place in a group of buildings at Atsugi identified as the Joint
Technical Advisory Group. This was, in reality, the CIA's Far East
base of operations.

The idea behind these experiments were to establish if drugs,
such as LSD, could be used as interrogation tools on enemy agents,
and also as a tool for agents-in-training to familiarize themselves
with LSD's effects in case they were surreptitiously dosed.

In the *Rolling Stone* article, an anonymous Marine—who had
served in the same unit at Atsugi as Oswald, and during the same
period—recounted the following:

It was pretty weird. I'm eighteen at the time, and
chasing all the whores in town, and these CIA
guys are buying my drinks and paying for the
whores and giving me a whole lot of drinks with
lots of weird drugs in them.

Pretty soon all the shadows are moving
around—we're in the bar, see—the Samurais are
everywhere, and I started to see skeletons and

things. My mind just started boiling over, going about a thousand miles a minute.

I'm sure there are going to be some little old ladies who're gonna be surprised that illegal drugs like heroin and LSD were freely used by government agents. But that's just the way it was.

While at Atsugi, Oswald was a regular habitué of the Queen Bee nightclub, which was a veritable nest of international espionage. Was it in this milieu that perhaps Lee himself was "slipped a mickey" by MK-ULTRA spychiatrists while being entertained by one of his Japanese hostesses?

If Oswald had been given acid as part of an MK-ULTRA experiment—or as part of his own undercover training—it may explain a certain "freak-out" incident that occurred while he was stationed in Taiwan. One night while Oswald was on guard duty, gunfire was heard. An officer went to investigate and discovered a trembling Oswald on the ground, sobbing and raving about certain unseen men lurking in the trees, the ones he had fired at. Was this incident on account of Oswald being dosed with acid, or due to a flashback from a previous dosing? That would certainly explain Oswald's odd behavior.

Journalist Martin Lee, coauthor of *Acid Dreams: The CIA, LSD, and the Sixties Rebellion*, uncovered a curious tale involving former New Orleans assistant district attorney Edward Gillan, who had a strange encounter with a mysterious visitor back in October 1963. The visitor in question—who showed up unannounced one afternoon—quizzed Gillan about the legality of importing a new wonder drug, LSD, into the U.S. The mysterious stranger in question claimed to be a serious student of Aldous Huxley's *The Doors of Perception*, and believed that this drug had the potential of launching a social revolution that would ultimately enlighten mankind. He also claimed he had a source for the drug, and wanted to know if it was legal to sell. (It should be noted that in 1963 the only known source for LSD was the CIA.) Gillan filed the incident away as another curiosity until he was watching TV the day after Kennedy's assassination and was blown away when he recognized that the man who had been arrested for shooting Kennedy was the very same mysterious stranger who had appeared in his office inquiring about LSD!

■

Not only is there evidence suggesting that Oswald "tripped the light fantastic," but perhaps the man he was accused of killing also dabbled in LSD experimentation, as in recent years revelations have come to light of JFK's alleged use of illicit drugs during his thousand days in office.

Several books over the last couple of decades—including *Acid Dreams* by Martin Lee and Bruce Shlain, *Flashbacks* by Timothy Leary, and *A Woman Named Jackie* by C. David Heymann—have chronicled the escapades of an adventurous spirit named Mary Pinchot, an artist and Washington socialite, whose husband was Cord Meyer, an agent of the CIA.

Ms. Pinchot became acquainted with Tim Leary during his Harvard days, requesting advice and samples of the good doctor's wares so that she could "turn on" those in "high places." Pinchot was convinced that if she could get certain prominent political leaders under the influence of acid, they would see that love is the answer to all the world's ills, then lay down their weapons, join hands with their former enemies, and go dancing off into the daisies of harmonic conversion.

Mary Pinchot, as it turns out, was yet another of Johnny-we-hardly-knew-ye's conquests, having pierced her with the mighty sword of Came-a-lot on repeated occasions while under the influence of the drugs that Mary so graciously supplied.

In the early 90s, *Mondo 2000* magazine alleged that on one occasion, Jack and Mary smoked a couple of joints, and when Mary started to spark a third, JFK was so bombed he told her he couldn't handle any more, explaining that if he got more wasted he wouldn't be able to function effectively in the result of a national emergency. Doomsday visions of his ol' buddy Nikita pushing the nuke button arose in JFK's paranoiac marijuana-muddled mind, and he wisely decided to let Mary loner the final doob in the interests of national security.

Cocaine was also among the drugs allegedly used by Kennedy, as well as the very real possibility of LSD. This is hinted at in *Flashbacks* and *Acid Dreams*, and I have no reason to doubt that on one occasion or another JFK did in fact blaze like a cosmic adventurer into the inner spaces of his mind, his psychedelic rocket ship fueled by Orange Sunshine™, landscaping New Frontiers.

Mary Pinchot-Meyer was riddled with bullets by unknown assailants and died just one short year after her boyfriend JFK had his own head blown off in Dealey Plaza.

A mind is a terrible thing to waste.

CHAPTER 16

Stan Jamison, Brother Ray, and Good Ol' Doc Stanley

"Kerry, you know, the one's whose picture was on the cover of Life *with Lee Oswald's head super-imposed upon it? Kerry had the little spider like hands and arms and narrow hips, not Oswald, just ask his wife."*

—REV. RAYMOND BROSHEARS, 1968

Sometime in 1970, Kerry, Louise Lacey, and Greg Hill began receiving dispatches from a fellow in Turlock, California, named Stan Jamison, who ran a mailing list dedicated to a wide range of topics such as growing organic sprouts, how to cure cancer via oxidation, and other alternative healing therapies.

One of Jamison's many curious contacts at this time was the Rev. Raymond Broshears (aka "Brother Ray"), who—when interviewed by Garrison's staff a couple of years earlier—had placed Kerry with Oswald and David Ferrie in New Orleans prior to the Kennedy assassination.

Afterwards, Broshears resurfaced in the Bay Area and somehow came into the possession of a device called the "Multiple Wave Oscillator" (MWO). The MWO was invented in the 1930s by a guy named Lakhovsky, and through the use of radio frequency radiation was said to produce healing therapies with effects similar in nature to Wilhelm Reich's Orgone Accumulator.

Louise, like Jamison, became intrigued by the potential healing properties of the MWO. To this end, Broshears informed Jamison that he'd be willing to hand over the MWO—that is, if Jamison wanted to pick it up at his place in Berkeley. Since Louise was in close proximity to Rev. Broshears, Jamison put the two in touch, and in turn Broshears contacted Louise.

In a letter from the period, Louise described her phone conversation with Broshears as a "mind-cracking experience," which consisted of "30 minutes of tortured insanity about his fear" of how the cops were going to bust him because he had this MWO machine, much like the same sort of persecution Wilhelm Reich received at the hands of the Feds back in the 1950s.

Shortly after their phone conversation, Louise went to Broshears' place in Berkeley to pick up the MWO machine. During their meeting, Broshears told Louise repeatedly that the MWO was "against the law and I don't break the law." Louise asked Broshears if he had tried it himself, and Brother Ray responded with an emphatic "No!," claiming he had hidden it in the back of his closet to conceal it from the omnipresent eyes of Big Brother.

Broshears opened the door of his closet to show the MWO to Louise, but refused to hand it over because he thought she'd rat him out to the Feds. Louise pointed out to Broshears that if he gave her the MWO then he wouldn't have to worry about getting busted, but Broshears was having no part of Louise's logic. Ultimately, Louise walked away from her "Brother Ray" encounter empty-handed and frustrated.

At the time of Louise's interactions with Broshears, Garrison's case against Kerry still had not been resolved, and when the topic later came up about Broshears and his MWO machine, Kerry told Louise that if she should speak with Broshears again: "Please don't try and convert him; he is far more valuable on the other side as a hostile witness!"

■

Flash forward a half-dozen years later. Stan Jamison is now sending out letters to Kerry indicating that the Secret Order of Thule (a mystical group influenced by Hitler's Third Reich) had orchestrated the JFK assassination.

Like Brother-in-law before him, Stan Jamison possessed a morbid fascination with Hitler and Nazism, and—like Brother-in-law—Jamison mentioned to Kerry certain little-known aspects of the Third Reich, such as secret S.S. pagan rituals and the occult beliefs of Hitler.

Both Brother-in-law and Jamison had also talked about secret Nazi UFOs, as well as the rumor that Nazi rocket scientists discovered free energy during World War II. Because of this, Kerry came to suspect that Jamison and Brother-In-Law were one and the same, a suspicion that motivated Kerry, in 1977, to drop in unexpectedly at Jamison's house in Turlock.

Upon arrival at Jamison's doorstep, Kerry discovered that "Not only was Jamison not the same person I had conversed with in New Orleans, but it was plain that the spine-chilling ranting in his letters was just a big put on."

Later on, Kerry heard a rumor that: "Jamison acquired his information from one Michael Stanley, then serving a prison term in California. As Lovable Ol' Doc Stanley, Michael Stanley was known to me personally as one of the heavier, darker characters of the California counter-culture. We met each other in a hip coffee house after I moved to Los Angeles about a year after John Kennedy's assassination. Although I didn't like to admit it for fear of seeming paranoid, I found Michael Stanley terrifying."

CHAPTER 17

Letters from the Edge

"Robert Anton Wilson was murdered and replaced by a double on orders from Gerald Ford."

—KERRY THORNLEY, June 1986

As Kerry's letters of the late 70s continued to arrive in the mailboxes of friends of fellow Discordians, the tone of urgency and desperation manifested itself, not only to Bob Wilson, but to all those on the business end of Kerry's mind-boggling missives.

One day, Bob got a letter from Kerry saying: "I am the most important man on the planet—I am the only one who knows all about the Kennedy assassination!" Due to this knowledge, Kerry insisted that his life was threatened by a sinister cabal of conspirators who wanted to silence him. Bob tried to calm down Kerry by rationalizing the situation, and reminding him that there was a distinct difference between "theory" and "proof." Much to Wilson's surprise, Kerry now suspected him of being involved as part of an "assassination conspiracy team" and furthermore that Bob was Kerry's CIA baby-sitter, covertly employed by the Agency to keep a watchful eye on him, although Wilson insists that he and Kerry met only once in the flesh, in Atlanta in 1967. As Bob recalled: "[Kerry] had the impression that I came to Atlanta more than once and that I had given him LSD and had removed the programming the Navy had put into him when he was in the Marines—and that I was one of his CIA handlers."

When Wilson informed Kerry that he didn't remember any of this taking place, Kerry said that was because they had brainwashed Wilson, too. Because of these suspicions, the two eventually ceased communication because—as Wilson explained in a recent interview—"It's hard to communicate with somebody when he thinks you're a diabolical mind-control agent and you're convinced that he's a little bit paranoid."

When I interviewed Wilson and Bob Newport in 2002, they addressed Kerry's mental state during this period:

> Newport: I had moved to Santa Cruz [California] in 1975, and Kerry came to see me there on one of his trips to the coast. And by that time he was completely psychotic. He was obsessed with the assassination. He would talk non-stop for hours about all of the people involved—this and that, and reasoning I couldn't follow.
>
> Wilson: This was the period when he was sending me those letters telling me that he figured out I was CIA controlled—really scaring the hell out of me.
>
> Newport: And he was bothersome to be with. I mean, he was unwashed, his self-care was gone, he wasn't eating—skinny, dirty, unkempt. His psychosis and obsessions were so incredibly intense, you could not spend very much time with him…
>
> Gorightly: You said "one of his trips." Was he just wandering around the country at that time?
>
> Newport: No. He would come to the coast and visit people. It wasn't just wandering around.
>
> Gorightly: How was he making ends meet?

Newport: Begging and stealing. He was destitute.

Gorightly: You actually think he was stealing?

Newport: I think he stole food out of garbage cans. Whether or not he robbed people? No. But stealing food? Yeah. He was destitute.

Gorightly: He did what he had to do to survive.

Newport: Yeah.

At this time, Kerry began sharing his suspicions with Greg Hill and others. A December 6, 1976, letter to Greg clearly details Kerry's extreme paranoia:

> I have seen Howard Hughes, who is still
> apparently very much alive, and his CIA double.
> I see someone I believe is Timothy Leary quite
> regularly. I have had coffee several mornings
> with someone I believe is Bob Wilson.
>   All I know for sure is that absolutely nobody
> who understands what is happening is telling me
> the truth. I am literally surrounded by the
> Intelligence Community, but after the first three
> attempts to murder me things seem to have
> cooled down and most of the spies now appear to
> be on my side...
>   The guy I think was Wilson was short, had
> wavy grey hair, a pronounced limp, and crooked
> teeth. His predisposition towards me was
> benevolent, but he seemed unfree to tell me what
> the hell was happening.
>   The guy I think is Leary says that some of the

stuff I wrote—I have been keeping a journal since the first of the year—toppled the Shanghai Four in China. I did discover that Maoist activities in Atlanta were being sponsored by Defense Industry Ruling Class Catholic (Jesuit) families who also sponsor Lester Maddox, et al.

And I did speculate that maybe Chinese Jesuits and the DuPont family had a lot of power in China (where the people refrain from unchaste behavior and wear blue uniforms) and the Chinese government did crumble a few days later.

The Nazis invented flying saucers during WWII and the assassinations and terrorism seem to have been part of an angry publicity stunt to bring to the world's attention the engine in the UFO's, which uses no fossil fuels or uranium, but relies on electromagnetic principles to generate cheap, clean energy from the ions in the air or something. Gary [Kirstein] gave me all the hints I needed to put this thing together years ago, but I did not integrate them.

See what I mean? It even gets weirder than that—at least more elaborate. But you get the idea. I'm a pawn in some stupid game of conspiracy politics.

The outfit of Nazis who murdered JFK, MLK, RFK, and Tate were working for is a defense industry security agency called Defense Industrial Security Command (DISC). Hail Eris! An incredible amount of secret society terrorism within the Intelligence Community seems to have been carried out in the name of the Discordian Society.

It is possible I have a radio in one of my tooth

fillings, installed by the C.I.A. at Atsugi, and that
I have dreams which are transmitted to me by the
Nazi Shambala. It is also possible that both the
CIA and DISC thought they had the transmitters
for me and intended to use me, each to trick the
other, in an abortive plot to overthrow the
government. If this is the case, then I would
appear to be a humanoid robot for freedom....
You don't have to believe this, but I am sincere,
and it is one of the few premises that explains
most of it.

In another letter to Greg Hill dated March 1, 1977, Kerry further illustrates his belief that Bob Wilson was a big part of the problem: "If you could get Wilson to stop lying and playing the guru for once in his life he could tell you infinitely more about it than I can..."

As Becky Glaser recalled: "A lot of the communications I got from Kerry were these incredible splats of outraged paranoia, of a very intricate variety, to the point where I couldn't follow it. It was like verbal Jackson Pollack."

In his prime, interactions with Kerry had always been a mind-expanding experience. He had a way of looking at things like no one else, so being in Kerry's presence was like a perpetual acid trip—whether one was actually tripping or not. This all seemed to change when Kerry got going on his conspiracy theories, as he would become so consumed by them that he'd tune out everything else.

From Louise Lacey's perspective, the crux of Kerry's mental problems developed when he stopping saying "NO!," which had been his personal mantra for so long. As Louise explained, Kerry was fiercely anti-authoritarian, and prior to his bouts of paranoia he had always stood up to whatever monolithic force stood in his way, continually saying "NO!" whether it was to the government, Jim Garrison, or anyone else. This was Kerry's way of dealing with people who tried to tell him what to do, and this was the simple wisdom he'd imparted to Louise many years before: Just learn to say "NO!" and people won't know how to react or what to do, and in most cases would leave you the fuck alone.

At some point, Kerry apparently quit saying "NO!" and, in essence, stopped evolving, while his friends—who, in many instances, had followed Kerry over the years—now began eclipsing him, as they continued growing, exploring, and entertaining new ideas and forms of expression.

Kerry—Louise contends—became locked in this delusory world of conspiracies, which impeded his evolution. One time, Kerry explained his struggles to her in the following manner: "It's hard to be an anarchist when your head is talking to you!"

In the depths of his paranoia, Kerry told Louise that there were two plastic radios in his head, which he couldn't stop listening to. Louise asked Kerry point blank why he simply didn't use the power of that almighty word he had taught her so many years earlier, that resounding "NO!" to tune out the noise. Kerry, looking rather sheepish, answered: "It is easier to pretend." This is not to suggest that Kerry was making up all of this stuff. What Kerry meant, in this instance, was that it was easier to pretend that his problems were someone else's responsibility. Louise thinks the reason Kerry responded in this way is because no one ever challenged him when he started rambling on about his paranoid conspiracies. So when she tried to pin him down, it put Kerry in a position he wasn't accustomed to, and resulted in a moment of clarity. This was nonetheless short-lived, as the next day he was back harping on his same old conspiratorial rants.

Bob Newport—a practicing psychiatrist—talked to Kerry about his paranoia on numerous occasions, basically telling him he was schizophrenic and that he needed to get help, but Kerry refused to accept his old friend's diagnosis, suspecting Newport—like most everyone else—of conspiring against him. No one in Kerry's circle, it seems, was free of guilt by association to this shadowy conspiracy. Greg Hill addressed this issue in a 1977 letter to Kerry:

Kerry, Brother, Friend, damn it—one thing I must make clear and that is if I think you are paranoid then I reserve the right to say it (or at least the right to form my own judgment). Fortunately, there has never been a time between us when our friendship was dependent on either one having to agree with the other. Right now I am counting on this.

IT IS NOT TRUE THAT I KNOW SOMETHING ABOUT ALL THIS THAT YOU DO NOT KNOW. (Though I reserve the right to think about it differently.)

I HAVE NOT, AM NOT AND NEVER INTEND TO LIE TO YOU OR REFUSE TO LEVEL WITH YOU.

This is level: I think that you are acting p-a-r-a-n-o-i-d as all hell. But I do not think of you as merely paranoid like a lot of others must think. After all, being correct (or not) in interpreting facts has nothing to do with being overwhelmed by outrageous circumstances and neither is the same as being in despair over what a fucked up world this is.

I don't doubt the possibility that you have been lied to and manipulated. Perhaps it is still going on, or has started again. But no way in hell is the *whole fucking planet* deceiving you. I AM NOT DECEIVING YOU. Kerry, call me mistaken, but don't call me a liar…

I don't think that this last couple of years is just between you and the conspirators.

And even given the extreme alienation of your situation, I don't think it is even just a problem of conflict between you and other human beings.

In fact, I don't think that this is even just a
conflict between you and mere reality.

It looks to me like this one is a conflict between
you and your most intimate gods. Leave the
humans alone and go deeper…

In Kerry's worldview, Operation Mindfuck had come full circle, biting him square on the derrière. As Bob Wilson ruminated in
Cosmic Trigger:

Thornley's letters to me became increasingly
denunciatory. He now believed that the
Discordian Society had been infiltrated very early
by CIA agents (probably including me) who had
used it as a cover for an assassination bureau. The
logic of this was brilliant in a surrealistic,
Kafkaesque sort of way. Try to picture a jury
keeping a straight face when examining a
conspiracy that worshipped the Goddess of
Confusion, honored Emperor Norton as a saint,
had a Holy Book called "How I Found Goddess
and What I Did to Her After I Found Her," and
featured personnel who called themselves
Malaclypse the Younger, Ho Chih Zen, Mordecai
the Foul, Lady L, F.A.B., Fang the Unwashed,
Harold Lord Randomfactor, Onrak the
Backwards, et al….

Thanks to Kerry (as well as conspiracy researcher Mae
Brussell) Bob Wilson gained the reputation as some sort of CIA
super-spook, as legend grew that both he and compatriot Timothy
Leary were Illuminati ringleaders who had masterminded the
Kennedy assassination parade. Of course, Wilson found such non-
sense outlandish and somewhat hilarious, as it was surrealistically

reminiscent of just the type of conspiratorial hoax that he and Kerry had promulgated throughout the late 60s and early 70s. As Bob related: "Mae Brussell claimed I was an agent of the Rockefeller Conspiracy, and I confessed in a magazine called *Conspiracy Digest* that David Rockefeller came around every two weeks with gold bars to keep me well stocked...I thought this would help improve my credit rating, but unfortunately no one seemed to believe it, but Mae."

Kerry—before becoming paranoid himself—very eloquently, and on many occasions addressed the subject of paranoia, often parodying those groups and individuals who had created elaborate conspiracy theories which mirrored their own muddled minds.

Later, Kerry became like the very people he'd parodied—such as Garrison, for instance, who seemed to accept many a half-baked theory, as long as it fit his worldview, which oddly enough included Kerry as a principal player in the crime of the century. As writer Bob Black once said to Kerry: "You used to satirize conspiracy theories; now you believe in them." To that observation, Kerry solemnly agreed.

■

In the mid-70s, Kerry's family got together to celebrate Christmas once at his parents' place in Palos Verdes, California. During the holiday, Kerry's brothers attempted an intervention. Dick was the first to take Kerry aside, and explained to him that he, as well, had once suffered delusions, and had seriously thought that his own personal choices in 1967 had caused the Six Day War. Kerry—feeling he'd found a conspiratorial soul-mate in his younger brother—frantically replied: "Then you know exactly what I'm talking about! I feel like my actions have similar effects and I cannot ignore that!"

Unfortunately, instead of helping Kerry, Dick felt himself being sucked back into the same delusory miasma that he had pulled himself out of several years before. So, instead of easing Kerry out of his own delusional funk, Dick felt himself slipping back into his previous paranoia. To protect his own tenuous foothold on sanity, he backed off. As Dick recalled:

> Toward the end of the visit, Kerry said he'd send me a bunch of his spiral bound tablets to read and was convinced they would change my mind. A week or so later they arrived in a box to my Carson City home. I read them and then sat down to write what I hoped would be a loving, brother-to-brother letter. I told him how much I loved and admired him and how I'd always looked up to him. I told him how much I appreciated his love and respect for me. But, I also told him I thought he was delusional. Within days, Kerry fired back a post card which read: "You're just another goddamned lawyer!"

During this Christmas reunion, Dick had a brief phone conversation with Camden Benares, who had always been able to maintain a connection with Kerry. Camden told Dick that he simply tried to listen to Kerry without judgment. He also joked about being perceived by Kerry, at times, as a member of one conspiracy or another. Of course, this was nothing out of the ordinary, as Kerry suspected many of his old friends as being threads in some vast conspiratorial web, all interconnected spiders spinning strands for their Illuminati Masters on high.

Tom Thornley also tried to intervene during this Christmas reunion, albeit without success, as Kerry started going on about the many-headed conspiratorial beast lurking in the shadows. To illustrate his point, Kerry suggested that if he and Tom walked down any crowded city street, he'd realize that everyone knew Kerry. So the two set up an experiment, but unfortunately Kerry was wearing an orange sailor hat with the brim pulled down, and was carrying a purse. Naturally, Tom attributed the attention Kerry drew to his appearance to the purse and sailor hat ensemble. Kerry later described the results of the experiment as "inconclusive."

■

Another incident that attributed to Kerry's psychological deterioration was the murder (or supposed murder) of his ex-girlfriend, Jessica Luck. Kerry first learned of Jessica's murder sometime in 1974, courtesy of R.C. Tuttles, who was Kerry's supervisor at the Georgia Nuts and Bolts Company, where he was then working. Tuttles was another of those whom Kerry suspected of being an intelligence agent whose primary mission was to keep an eye on him and uncover Kerry's knowledge of the Kennedy assassination.

Through Tuttles, Kerry became convinced that Jessica Luck was murdered while being filmed in a pornographic "snuff" movie, and that her murder was related to Kerry's introducing her to Gary Kirstein in 1961. This, in turn, led her to the movie makers and murderers—who in association with Kirstein—eliminated Jessica as a means of silencing her as a potential witness to those conversations of the early 60s involving Kerry, Kirstein, and Slim Brooks. Among the ranks of these movie makers/murderers, Kerry counted Bob Wilson and Bob Shea. In a December 6, 1976, letter to Greg Hill, Kerry wrote: "I accused Shea and Wilson of murdering Jessica last Easter, when both of them got strange with me in their correspondence and refused to co-operate with my attempts to find Jessica."

As previously noted, conspiracy researcher Mae Brussell implicated Bob Wilson and Tim Leary in CIA mind control activities, which, oddly enough, seemed to dovetail with some of Kerry's crazier notions. When a mouthpiece of the Symbionese Liberation Army—the Bay Area Research Collective—concluded that Wilson was Leary's CIA "baby-sitter," all Bob could do was laugh at the absurdity of it all. A week later, when he received a bomb threat, the humor started wearing thin.

Soon after, Operation Mindfuck reached critical mass on

October 3, 1976, when Wilson's teenage daughter, Luna, was murdered at a Berkeley clothing store where she was employed, beaten to death by burglars. Given this heartbreaking development, Wilson found himself in no mood for Kerry's continual stream of paranoid diatribes, which Wilson now found considerably more disturbing, given his recent tragedy.

As earlier noted—throughout the 60s and early 70s—the collective consciousness of Bob and Kerry was, in many respects, on a parallel track. When they first started corresponding in the mid-60s, both were blown away by how much their thinking philosophically corresponded. In a letter to this author in the early 90s, Kerry reminisced about how Wilson, for awhile, even became his personal mentor, turning him on to a whole host of individualist anarchist thinkers, such as Proudhon, Warren, Tucker, Spooner, Borsodi, Labadie, etc., all of whom influenced Kerry to a great degree.

In turn, Kerry no doubt influenced Wilson, as their interactions usually fed on one another, producing many of the great Discordian scriptures, and if it weren't for the collective influence of Kerry and Greg Hill, *Illuminatus*, as we know it, would have never been written.

When Kerry and Wilson got into their Bavarian Illuminati Mindfuck phase their heads were also synchronously tuned to the concept of how political paranoia can run completely amok, becoming in essence whatever one wants their conspiratorial madness to become—that is, if they're willing to dispel critical reasoning and jump on the rickety bandwagon of the paranoids.

And even though their thinking was strikingly similar for a certain space in time, it did diverge in respect to Kerry's lifelong tendency to take to an extreme whatever current hobbyhorse he was then riding—this well before he lost his hold on simple sanity. Kerry was always an extremist, even when his head was screwed on relatively straight, as he had a habit of totally embracing whatever new passion caught his ever-changing fancy, be it libertarianism, Zenarchy, Kerista, or the dreaded Bavarian Illuminati. Into these diverse pursuits Kerry would wholeheartedly and haphazardly hurl himself for six months, or a year or whatever, then move on to another something or another, taking it as far as he could before becoming captivated by something else, that would, in turn, lead him in a new and illuminating direction.

But after Kerry went over the paranoid edge, this all fell by the wayside, as his head got stuck on one sheet of monotonous music that played the same tired tune over and again for many years. Somewhere—between Florida and California—Kerry lost his critical-thinking faculties in regards to how paranoia can get *way* out of hand; this is the point where Bob and Kerry's respective paths parted ways and started moving in opposite directions: Wilson toward Skeptical Illumination and Kerry into Evangelical Paranoia.

■

By January 1977, Kerry's paranoia had escalated to the nth degree, as chronicled in a letter sent to the House Select Committee on Assassinations in which he recounted a series of events which happened at a "Atlanta Friends' meeting," a group of Quakers who provided ministry and group counseling sessions.

Kerry—who at this time had become quite distressed by what he viewed as his unwitting participation in the Kennedy assassination—sought counsel through this group, which, in due time, he came to believe had been infiltrated by the intelligence community, and in particular one member, Mary Jo Padgett.

Mary Jo Padgett, Kerry surmised, was:

> an extremely high-level intelligence community
> dirty work organizer for elements of the Southern
> Rim (military-industrial complex) of the ruling
> class, including very probably the Dupont family.
> I believe these elements have been conducting a
> virtual reign of terror in this area for some years,
> not to mention corruption of the various levels of

government, and that they must have been involved rather deeply in the assassinations of John F. Kennedy and Martin Luther King, Jr....

I believe that Mary Jo Padgett may have conspired in the apparent murder of Robert Anton Wilson's daughter and that Tom Kenworthy probably knows something about this. I believe that R.C. Suttles of Georgia Nut and Bolt knows something about Mary Jo Padgett's ties to the government of China...

I'm rather strongly convinced that the Illuminatus character, Atlanta Hope, is based substantially on Mary Jo Padgett....

My major concern during these Meetings for Suffering was getting information about Jessica Luck, former lover of mine and a key witness to my charges linking "Kirstein" to Carlos Marcello. I was expecting to put into motion wheels that would bring me news of Jessica's welfare, since I was told by R.C. Suttles at Georgia Nut and Bolt that she was murdered in a "snuff movie," which he claimed to have seen.

To this day I do not know how or where Jessica Luck is.

In other words, my chosen place of worship is so infiltrated by the intelligence community that I cannot get even minimal support from it as an organization.

■

Kerry later came to believe (as did Bob Wilson, though in a somewhat different context) that Operation Mindfuck had swung open the doors of some spooky psychic realm—a realm with a sometimes twisted sense of humor—ostensibly inviting in a whole host of mad gods and hobgoblins, no doubt encouraged by the chaotic forces invoked by Eris.

As Greg Hill told an interviewer during this period: "Ravenhurst [Thornley] has recently been in a state of extreme discord. We were talking about Eris and confusion and he said, 'You know, if I had realized that all of this was going to come *true*, I would have chosen Venus.'"

During Kerry's visits with friends in the Bay Area, a pattern often developed. At first, he'd appear to be all right, but after drinking a beer or two or smoking a doob, something would once again trigger those waves of paranoia. As Louise Lacey recalled:

> If you gave him a joint, or a beer, he would just take off—babble, babble, babble, babble—you couldn't even get him to listen—that was the important thing. So I never gave him a joint anymore—that was sad (laughs)...
>
> [Kerry] always had a drama about drugs. Like the first time he took acid. I remember we were driving down the freeway in L.A.—you know, this was in the 60s—and he was telling me about taking acid and he said a red dragon came out of his mouth, and I thought: "Wow, that's never happened to anyone else I've heard from!"

In later years, Louise occasionally saw Kerry at Greg Hill's place, and though Kerry seldom drank, Greg was perpetually imbibing, and thus would offer Kerry whatever he was having, inevitably setting the wheels in motion for another of Kerry's conspiratorial rants. So, when Greg would pass a highball Kerry's way, Louise—well aware of the consequences of an intoxicated Thornley—would tell Greg, under her breath, "No, no—don't give him any," because she knew what would happen—that the drugs or alcohol would unleash this "drama" from the core of Kerry's being. And once the alcohol had taken hold, off he would once again go, going on and on and on, not even looking at anyone, just talking to the wall, or a potted plant, because he'd get so wound up in his conspiratorial cosmology.

Meanwhile, Louise and Greg would carry on with their own conversation.

Another friend, Becky Glaser, had always considered Kerry an "intellectual wild man." But oddly enough—when he got deep into his conspiracy raps—his wildness of old would disappear and, in fact, Kerry would become downright rational-sounding in his presentation of this paranoid worldview. As Becky explained it, Kerry "had a rationally constructed paranoid universe that the rest of us didn't participate in…. I'd sit back and look at the structure that Kerry lived in, this universe that he inhabited alone, and it always made me wonder if my paradigm was correct."

But what Becky had originally found so captivating about Kerry was missing from this paranoid universe. So, in essence, when Kerry got off on his conspiracy raps, all the vibrant energy that had infused his being in years past instantly disappeared, and with it his famous puckish sense of humor.

In fact, Kerry had no sense of humor about his "conspiracy" whatsoever. Becky found that she couldn't joke with him at all about it, or she would be suspected of being a party to "the Conspiracy." Conversely—when Kerry wasn't in this conspiratorial mindset—his sense of humor returned.

During one stay with Louise Lacey, it got to the point where she couldn't leave Kerry alone in her house for fear he would do something detrimental to himself or the surrounding environs. One time—when Louise wasn't around—Kerry left a pan on the stove that almost caused a fire. Fortunately, Louise arrived home in time to avert disaster. After turning off the stove, she ran downstairs to find Kerry, who was totally oblivious to what'd happened. As this incident caused some measure of concern, Louise asked Kerry how he thought they should handle this situation, as it was becoming apparent that it was dangerous to leave him alone. Kerry's answer to this dilemma was that he and Louise should be together at all times during his stay with her, so that is exactly what he did, accompanying Louise whenever she went out. At night—as he lay in bed—the voices would start calling out. During this time, Louise remembers Kerry yelling aloud: "Leave me alone—I've got to get some sleep!"

Throughout the late 70s, Kerry's friends and family reached out to help him, but for the most part their efforts seemed to be misunderstood, as detailed in a March 1977 letter to Greg Hill in San Francisco:

> My charming ex, Cara, called my folks and told them I am crazy and she was thinking about having me committed and asked them if they could pay the hospital bills. (Cara has consistently refused to discuss the details of what I've been dealing with but hesitates not at all when it comes to passing judgment on my responses.) The ultimate result of all this was that my parents sent me a hundred bucks to come out and visit them. (They do not think I'm crazy, but then out here I'm not so far having to put up with the same shit I was dealing with back there.)
>
> I was accompanied all the way to the West Coast on the bus by four people who were, I think, with military intelligence. But I have already got all the essential information on the people in Atlanta who were hassling me into the hands of the Committee on Assassinations. I think their main trip was to make sure I came to the Coast as I said I intended, and didn't double back for D.C., and also to get their hands on the set of filing cards I had compiled and upon which

my set of rough notes for the Committee were
based (which I ditched successfully). One thing
Wilson was very right about: they are stupid.

My ticket is good all the way up to San
Francisco, so I will be up to see you probably next
week sometime for a visit of from a few days to a
couple of weeks—during which I plan to go
punch Wilson in the nose or something equally
satisfactory. This will be an orientation visit, then
in late spring or early summer I figure on coming
up there to live.

Right now I have exactly what I need. A room
in my folks' house. Access to a typewriter. All I
can eat. Spending money. So I plan to make the
most of it. An opportunity to get my shit
together—the half of it which I didn't get together
by living on the street in Atlanta in the middle of
the winter.

Kerry later wrote about his stay with his parents:

The Bum could tell his parents were already
getting uptight. A few days ago, just after his
arrival from Atlanta, they were extending him a
virtual blank check on reality.

Then it was "we know you need a rest" and
"help yourself to the food" and "whenever you
need money, just ask."

But they were still Depression Generation and he
was still of the Psychedelic Generation, and it was
only a few days before the old conflicts began
grinding beneath the surface…. It had been a
welcome rest and now the Bum was uncomfortable
enough to know it was time to move on…

Soon after, Kerry relocated to a renovated chicken coop in Sunland, California, a close distance to Camden Benares' pad. The chicken coop in question had been fixed up—cleaned up and washed out—by its owner, who was letting Kerry live there "rent-free" during his stay. At this time, Camden's buddy John Carr had a chance to meet Kerry, and had this to say about their historic chicken coop conference:

> We sat around, smoked a few joints and talked—- it was pretty disjointed, and he looked pretty wild, he looked like the kind of homeless late 60s victim you find in the street—he had that thousand-yard stare.
>
> I had heard all the stories about Kerry, I knew what a fantastic friend of Camden's he'd been for so many years, and Camden really mourned that…. When Kerry left Camp Meeker the whole thing sorta fell apart—Kerry got into the Garrison thing, and into the Oswald thing—and it got crazier and crazier.
>
> And Camden thought Kerry was just a wonderful writer—he always tried to encourage Kerry to go into mainstream writing—that was his whole idea: Kerry needed to be a writer. Go out and write and get away from his obsessions and write some good fiction and he'd be okay. That was his theory on how to make Kerry better. He tried to encourage him as much as he could, but by then it was hopeless—he knew he was just a paranoid schiz.
>
> From then on he'd hear from him every couple of months, every six months, maybe get a postcard, and that was about it, and Camden felt really bad about that—I mean, he didn't feel like

he could do anything, because Kerry was *(pshew!)*
walking his own line…. It was certainly
discouraging, you don't like to see a good friend
descend into that level. You know, it was just the
way it was, depressing.

Another friend Kerry suspected of being in on "the
Conspiracy" was old Marine pal Bud Simco. At Atsugi Air Base in
Japan, Simco had been the squadron S&C (Secret and Confidential)
File Clerk, and because of this security clearance Kerry later came
to suspect that Simco was keeping tabs on him. These suspicions led
to a falling out between Kerry and Bud in the early 70s, although
according to Bud this falling out was mainly one-sided, the result
of Kerry's belief that he was a spy.

However—in the late 70s, while living in San Francisco—Bud
returned home to his apartment one afternoon to discover someone
had spread rose petals all along the path to his door. On the door
was a note from Kerry, informing Bud that he was in town and
would be back later to visit. As Simco recalled:

> He did return later on and we did visit for a few
> hours. This was during a period when Kerry took
> a vow of silence, and would communicate only
> by writing in a notebook. Actually, we had quite a
> nice visit. He said at the time that he was over
> thinking I was some kind of agent sent to spy on
> him, and said his vow of silence was helping him
> sort things out. His written comments were lucid
> and intelligent. Although he wondered why I was
> not enthusiastic about his response to what his
> plans were, when he said, essentially, he would
> support himself by begging in the park.

CHAPTER 18

Black Helicopters Over Tampa

"The insane *are the overt psychotics—the people in mental institutions, or the people who are likely to wind up there if they aren't very careful, or very lucky. The* sane *are the repressed psychotics—the people who are deeply threatened by crazy thinking, and whom therefore indirectly or directly maintain our rigid system of psychological discrimination. The* outsane *are the inverse psychotics—the people who know how to make psychosis work for them.... Enlightening never strikes the same place twice."*

—KERRY THORNLEY, circa late 60s

One can only theorize as to the primary cause of Kerry's psychological problems. I suspect that several factors led to his paranoia, and key among them was the Garrison investigation. As Kerry's friend (and famed Kennedy assassination researcher) David Lifton explained in 2002:

> You're dealing with a New Orleans version of a five and dime Salem Witch Hunt [the Garrison investigation]—and poor Kerry got his mind warped by this thing and bent out of shape and instead of being the critically reasoning person I knew him to be, he ended being a paranoid schiz. And these idiots who think Clay Shaw was guilty,

and Garrison was a person who came down from Mount Olympus with the solution of the Kennedy assassination, are off their rocker.

One thing I have that nobody else has…I have the tapes of Kerry and me discussing the situation in real time as it was happening. Because, I said, "Kerry, this is very unusual—let's tape these conversations." And he said, "Fine." So I have several hours of tapes, which I've never transcribed…I remember one remark, he said: "You know, I don't believe in God—there could be a God…. But if there is a God, he'd have to be such a son of a bitch to do this to me." [laughs] So at the time he was perfectly rational, he had a black sense of humor, he was delightfully cynical, and he didn't believe any of this stuff [conspiracy theories]. He believed he was the victim of an idiot prosecutor who couldn't reason his way out of a paper bag, who had the philosophy of a statist. And, you know, Kerry was a libertarian. So he was very upset about that, and I felt very guilty, having gotten him involved in something that had such a bad ending.

Kerry once described the defining moment which led to his paranoia as having occurred in Tampa during the course of Garrison's investigation, when several helicopters buzzed his house for over ten minutes, scaring the bejesus out of him and fueling his paranoia ever the more.

Kerry believed Garrison was behind this helicopter house-buzzing, and that the Jolly Green Giant had used his Florida law enforcement contacts to orchestrate this aerial harassment. Curiously enough, Cara Thornley has no memory of this incident, although it is entirely possible she have may have been out of the house when it occurred. Of course, it's also possible that the entire incident was pure delusion.

If this helicopter incident was the key factor that drove him over the edge, it was not simply a matter of Kerry immediately snapping. What I believe happened to Kerry was a gradual disintegration, which reached its nadir in the mid-70s when he believed that nearly everyone he ever knew was part of "the Conspiracy."

Others suspected that an ill-fated love affair greatly contributed to Kerry's subsequent mental snap. Kerry described it as an "eight-year-long, off-again-on-again, affair/friendship/rivalry/ego-game/karmic unraveling." The "affair" in question was with Grace Caplinger, who Kerry had been one time writing a book about, *Can Grace Come Out And Play?* In a confessional letter from late 1969, Kerry addressed the matter:

> For an opinionated sonofabitch like me, learning things and finding out you are wrong are inseparable—so it has been, since education, painful. I learned, for example, that the sort of polygamy I always advocated is precarious at best—since, I at least, cannot ordinarily, to my own surprise, really love (in the full sense of a life-time devotion) two different women to the degree each needs and deserves, not at the same time. And any conflict between them just tears me apart.
>
> Put on top of this that most if not all else there is to it—or was—is that we happen also to be each others' ego trips, and the whole thing becomes as difficult to integrate as a queer spade in Mississippi…

When I shared the above letter with Grace Caplinger (now Grace Zabriskie) in early 2003, this was her reply:

I have no idea where this long affair thing comes
from. Kerry and I and my then husband, Rob,
had an intense friendship, which graduated, or
from another point of view disintegrated into
more of a friendship between me and Kerry. The
friendship was centered around an intense shared
love for and fascination with the philosophy of
Ayn Rand. We were all in our early twenties. This
friendship was briefly interrupted by an incident
one evening while Rob was away. I was not
happy with Rob, and Kerry was on the outs with
his then girlfriend, Jessica [Luck]. The incident
consisted of several hours of Kerry ranting about
how excluding sexuality from our friendship was
"irrational"…worst thing one student of
Objectivism could possibly say to another, I
guess, and then perhaps four and a half minutes
in bed before I asked him to leave. More
haranguing about irrationality on the way out, as
I remember, and that was it. That was the affair.
There was no further sexual aspect to the
friendship that eventually resumed, and
continued until…I'm not sure. I think Kerry left
New Orleans. Within a year or so I moved to
Atlanta, and Kerry and I corresponded for years.
He asked me at one point to send him all his
letters as he was trying to construct a timeline, for
Garrison, of what he'd been doing during those
years. I sent him all the letters. He wrote
sporadically after that, and I stopped ever writing
back after he informed me that he believed that 1)
I was involved somehow in some conspiracy…to
do what I wasn't ever quite clear on, and 2) that I
was involved somehow in "snuff films." Maybe

because I was an actor in films by then. I don't
know…I lost hope that I could make him see
reason in these matters, and I stopped imagining
that we could ever be friends again.

From Kerry's frame of reference, his affair with Grace lasted
a decade, although according to Grace the sexual aspect of their relationship was only four minutes in duration. It's my suspicion that
the first seeds of Kerry's psychosis began to manifest in the latter
half of the 60s, and one way it did was through this fixation on
Grace and what Kerry perceived as the termination of their love
affair. At some point, Kerry's relationship with Grace became
magnified in his mind, and grew to be much more than, in reality,
it ever was.

There were a couple of episodes which transpired in the late
60s—related by Bud Simco and Dick Thornley—when Kerry acted
irrationally, and totally out of character, perhaps portending to a
mental problem then beginning to surface.

One such incident occurred in mid 1967 with some of Kerry's
Kerista friends during a discussion of an upcoming swing party, and
whether or not the party was going to be "clothing optional."
Apparently this issue became a big deal with Kerry, who railed
against the whole clothing-optional idea, and in fact became rather
vocal, alienating many of his Kerista friends in the process. This
position, Dick noted, flew in the face of everything his big brother
had stood for. Instead of being open and flexible, Kerry suddenly
solidified into the reverse mirror image of all he'd resisted for so
long: that of a narrow-minded and controlling individual.

Around the same time, Kerry blew up at Bud Simco. As Bud
recalled:

Kerry had made arrangements to interview a Zen
monk in a religious retreat near Los Angeles. He
asked if I wanted to come along. I agreed. On the

day of the scheduled interview—I believe on a
Sunday—I arrived early at Kerry's house in
Watts. The four of us proceeded in Kerry's
Volkswagen. Kerry and I were accompanied by
our wives. We had only been on the road for a
few minutes—it was still early—and Bob Dylan's
song "Mr. Tambourine Man" started to play on
the radio. Kerry said something like, "You know,
he's singing about an acid pusher." I disagreed,
and said that I thought the song's title
made reference to the acid experience itself, and
not to the person who provided the LSD. My
response was matter-of-fact—not confrontational.
I thought this would have been obvious to
anyone, although I didn't say so.

Kerry became angry and emotional, yelling,
"CHRIST, CAN'T I HAVE AN OPINION ABOUT
ANYTHING?" Whereupon he immediately
turned the car around and drove directly back to
his house. I was surprised. I didn't perceive the
reason for his anger. Of course Kerry had an
opinion—about everything, and I had never
known him to be hesitant in expressing an
opinion about anything. My wife was also
surprised at his unexpected outburst—over
nothing at all; neither of us understood Kerry's
behavior. After his outburst, Cara said something
like, "Kerry, what's wrong? Bud's your friend!"
But Kerry, still angry, returned to his house,
where my car was parked, and my wife and I
returned to Long Beach.

Presumably these incidents laid the groundwork for an unset-
tled mind that went off its hinges in the mid-70s when Kerry's

"Brother-in-law" memories were triggered while visiting Greg Hill in New York. (Now, whether Kerry's "Brother-in-Law" memories were delusions—that's another issue.)

Another aspect of psychotic breaks is that they often result from stressful situations, such as when a person is placed in a position where he or she has to take on greater responsibility. Kerry, in the early 70s, was attempting the eternal balancing act of being a free spirit/artist while at the same time taking on the responsibility of fatherhood. This situation, among others, may have played a part in his breakdown.

■

As Kerry delved ever deeper into his own conspiracies, an increasingly bizarre picture began to emerge. Initially, in the mid-70s—when these sinister figures first starting flitting in the shadows—Kerry came to the conclusion that he'd been "wired" (or implanted with a mind control device) during his service in the Marines. Later, Kerry came to believe that this insidious mind zap had started much earlier, perhaps even before birth, and that he was a product, of what he termed, a "German breeding experiment"; an experiment that presumably used both him and Oswald as guinea pigs.

In time, Kerry even came to suspect his own parents were Axis spies who had cut a deal with Nazi Occultists conducting these eugenics experiments, the ultimate purpose of which was to create a Manchurian candidate. However, Kerry claimed he became "what they call a mutant, because I didn't turn out to be a racist.... I wasn't turning out to be the good Nazi they hoped I would be."

As Kerry told *SteamShovel Press* editor Kenn Thomas in a 1991 interview:

> It's been indicated to me...that I am the son of
> Admiral Donitz[14], and this is one of the reasons
> I've been getting all this attention over the

years…and they refer to Oswald as my "brother," and your brother is someone who comes from a breeding experiment. I've heard him referred to many times in Cant Language as my brother…

I thought it all started when I met Oswald in the Marines, but the more I've investigated, the more I've tried to piece it together, the more I've realized it had to start earlier than that.... They weed people out in the breeding experiments. They pick two of them, and they kill one of them…they take two of them, and they observe them for a number of years, then they get rid of one of them, and that's what I think they were doing with me and Oswald.

While Kerry occasionally addressed his alleged mind control in a lighthearted and/or Zen-like manner, I don't believe that his mind control revelations were total put-ons, although at times Kerry probably felt that all the metaphysical jokes he'd played on others over the years had come back to bite him.

Kerry once admitted that—in some surreal way or another—he owed everything he'd become to the ominous specter of mind control—and this wasn't necessarily a bad thing, either. For good or ill, this arcane path that Kerry had been led down (or which he *believed* he'd been led down) had made him, in essence, all that he was. And had not these malevolent behind-the-scenes machinations transpired, Kerry quite obviously would never have written *The Idle Warriors* and *Oswald* and gone on to lead such a colorful, though complicated, life. So, in this respect, mind control had been a blessing in disguise. Or, as Kerry explained in the *SteamShovel Press* interview:

Kerry: I harbored the conceit, up until I discovered I was a mind control subject, that I was a particularly independent thinker. And so it came to me rather hard that I owed much of my thinking and much of my independence, or what looked to me like my independence [to mind control], which was actually not independence at all.... I'd probably have become an Elder in the Mormon Church if I hadn't become a mind control subject—it probably would have been the most perfectly boring life you would imagine."

Kenn Thomas: So you've been saved by mind control?

Kerry: [laughs] Yeah, right...not that I think it's a nice thing—it's a hideous thing for your identity to be stolen from you.

Of course, some would suggest that Kerry feigned mind control victimization and/or mental illness to muddy the waters so that he could conceal his role in the Kennedy assassination dance party. As Jonathan Vankin wrote in *Conspiracies, Coverups and Crimes*:

Nonetheless, I still wonder if it's all a put-on. Is Thornley's intricately conspiratorial autobiography an elaborate mind-game he plays with himself and anyone who'll join in. Or is he really an intelligence agent, with a macabre cover story for his role in the John F. Kennedy conspiracy? Or could the story be true? Is Kerry Thornley a helpless pawn in a game beyond anyone's comprehension, who somehow figured out what has been happening to him? (p. 5-6).

Kerry's Little Five Points friend Beth Lavoie found Kerry to be enigmatic as well:

THE PRANKSTER AND THE CONSPIRACY

> When I first met [Kerry] you couldn't tell
> whether he was crazy—or if he was crazy like a
> fox? Did he burn his brain out with all that acid?
> Is he just wanting you to think that he's crazy?
> [laughs] And that was a part of the thing that was
> fun. Whether he was crazy or not, he was a very
> intelligent person, and just had a very unique
> sense of humor and way of expressing himself....
> It was just fun to be around him, because he kept
> you guessing.

■

The key question in unraveling what transpired in New Orleans prior to the Kennedy Assassination is this: Were Kerry's meetings with "Brother-in-law" and Slim Brooks nothing more than confabulations?

David Lifton contends that all of Kerry's post-Garrison investigation memories should be discounted because they were the product of unbalanced mind. And although Lifton considers Thornley's *Dreadlock Recollections*—Kerry's retelling of his Brother-in-law meetings in New Orleans during the early 60s—pure confabulation (and Garrison's investigation a monumental crock of horsewater) he just the same believes that Oswald was an intelligence agent who got sucked into a Kennedy assassination conspiracy. (In fact, Lifton is currently working on a book on this same theme.)

One of the few people who could have verified Kerry's mythic meetings with Brother-in-law was Greg Hill, who met both Gary Kirstein and Slim Brooks while in New Orleans. But, alas, this confirmation will not be forthcoming, as Greg has shed the mortal coil.

When I asked Grace (Caplinger) Zabriskie if she'd met Brother-in-law or Slim Brooks in New Orleans, she replied:

I met Slim several times, didn't really feel I knew him. All the things Kerry writes about Slim don't tally with anything I was privy to in him. All I ever saw was the laconic, sort of "country" affect he cultivated…. I THINK I may have heard about Brother-in-Law back then, but it's possible I only heard about him later, in letters from Kerry. You know, though, it's also a fact that the mention of Brother-in-Law gives me a dark feeling, the kind it's hard to imagine I got without ever setting eyes on him. It's possible we were introduced at the Bourbon House, or somewhere around the Quarter.

While Kerry might have actually met an individual named "Brother-in-law" who made all kinds of curious statements—which included a theoretical plot to kill Kennedy—it may have been Kerry's own paranoid worldview that took what Brother-in-law told him and blew it out of proportion, turning it into a conspiratorial cosmology.

With that being said, I don't entirely rule out the possibility that Brother-in-law may have been E. Howard Hunt, because if anyone could pull off a Brother-in-law-type impersonation, it would have been the enigmatic Mr. Hunt, who was a renowned master of disguise, as well as one of the spookiest apparitions in espionage history.

So if Hunt was Brother-in-law, then who exactly was Slim Brooks? Kerry later speculated that Slim Brooks was, in reality, a fellow named Jerry Milton Brooks, a former Minuteman and employee of Guy Banister. Furthermore, Kerry suspected that Slim acted as navigational advisor for the Bay of Pigs invasion, and had been assigned to keep an eye on Kerry at the behest of the intelligence community.

CHAPTER 19

Discordian Interlude #23

"Before I was a Discordian, when I entered my room only to be reminded by its disarray that it was a mess, I felt a sense of defeat. These days when that happens I just say, 'Hail Eris!'—our customary salute to any embodiment of chaos—and then I cheerfully carry on, secure in the knowledge that the constellations look no better."

—KERRY THORNLEY

On November 23, 1976—which just so happens to be a holy Discordian Holiday, both due to the mystical manifestation of the number 23 and because it's Harpo Marx's birthday—a young Englishman named Kenneth Campbell premiered a ten-hour stage production of *Illuminatus* at the Science-Fiction Theatre in Liverpool. In true Discordian fashion, the production consisted of five plays of five acts each, with each act 23 minutes in length. As Bob Wilson wrote in *Cosmic Trigger:*

> Ken Campbell's adaptation was totally faithful to this nihilistic spirit and contained long unexpurgated speeches from the novel explaining at sometimes tedious length just why everything the government does is always done wrong. The audiences didn't mind this pedantic lecturing because it was well integrated into a kaleidoscope of humor, suspense, and plenty of sex (more simulated blow jobs than any drama in history, I believe) (p. 224).

Campbell flew the Wilson/Shea duo across the pond for the London production, which was attended by none other than Queen Elizabeth. For HM's benefit, Wilson made a cameo appearance: "The cast dared me to do a walk-on role during the National Theatre run. I agreed and became an extra in the Black Mass, where I was upstaged by the goat, who kept sneezing. Nonetheless, there I was, bare-ass naked, chanting 'Do what thou wilt shall be the whole of the law' under the patronage of Elizabeth II, Queen of England, and I will never stop wondering how much of that was programmed by [Aleister] Crowley before I was even born."

The following year, a Discordian reunion of sorts took place that included Bob and Arlen Wilson, Louise Lacey, Greg Hill, and Bob and Rita Newport, among several other friends of the Wilsons who traveled to Seattle to take in an *Illuminatus* stage production.

'Twas a chilly night in Seattle, so someone (who shall remain nameless) produced enough MDMA for one and all to imbibe (ingested between the second and third acts) which in due time took the chill from the bones of the assembled Discordians—and cranked up the glow surrounding their collected auras—as they sat enraptured, entranced by the spectacle which unfolded.

The MDMA notwithstanding, Louise Lacey recalls the *Illuminatus* stage production as a "sublime experience." As usual, laughter was a common theme. On the plane to Seattle, the group laughed all the way there, and in Seattle they laughed all through the stage play, laughed the rest of the night, and laughed all the way back home.

■

Greg Hill often described himself as a "transcendental atheist" who started the Discordian Movement as an atheistic joke. However— during the course of his Discordian adventures—he found that his interactions with Eris had affected him profoundly. As Hill explained to Margot Adler in the late 70s:

Eris is an authentic goddess. Furthermore, she is an old one. In the beginning I saw myself as a cosmic clown. I characterized myself as Malaclypse the Younger. But if you do this type of thing well enough, it starts to work. In due time the polarities between atheism and theism became absurd. The engagement was transcendent. And when you transcend one, you have to transcend the other. I started out with the idea that all gods are an illusion. By the end I had learned that it's up to you to decide whether gods exist, and if you take a goddess of confusion seriously, it will send you through as profound and valid a metaphysical trip as taking a god like Yahweh seriously. The trips will be different, but they will both be transcendental. Eris is a valid goddess in so far as gods are valid; the gods are valid when we choose them to be (p. 335).

The beauty of Discordianism is that each "Pope" chooses his or her own path of discovery. As Greg Hill was a self-proclaimed "transcendental atheist" and Bob Wilson conversely referred to himself as a "transcendental agnostic," Kerry, upon occasion, dubbed himself a "transcendental paranoid." So, as you can see, Discordianism is a madness of one's own making: a do-it-yourself religion that can go off in any direction.

Discordianism in time found a whole host of imitators, or rightly, a slew of whacked out "spoof religions" that followed in its wake, such as the Church of the SubGenius, which is quick to acknowledge the collective influence of Malaclypse the Younger and Omar Khayyam Ravenhurst. Among other spiritual heirs of Thornley and Hill, the Cacophony Society of California can certainly be counted, and, if one wants to extrapolate further, the Burning Man Festival, which takes place each year at the Black Rock Desert in Nevada, certainly owes a nod to the Goddess of Confusion, in addition to Kerry's early involvement in neo-paganism.

Certain ideas and catch phrases in the *Principia Discordia* have served as "in-jokes" within the neo-pagan scene since its emergence in the early 70s. Often, if there is an accident during a Wiccan ceremony, a participant will proclaim, "Hail Eris. All Hail Discordia." Bob Wilson—a frequent dabbler in paganism—described in *Drawing Down the Moon* the differences and similarities between neo-pagans and Discordians this way:

> Much of the Pagan movement started out as jokes, and gradually, as people found out they were getting something out of it, they became serious. Discordianism has a built-in check against getting too serious. The sacred scriptures are so absurd—as soon as you consult the scriptures again, you start laughing.... You take any of these ideas far enough and they reveal the absurdity of all ideas. They show that ideas are only tools and that no idea should be sacrosanct. Thus, Discordianism is a necessary balance. It's a fail-safe system. It remains a joke and provides perspective. It's a satire on human intelligence and is based on the idea that whatever your map of reality, it's ninety percent your own creation. People should accept this and be proud of their own artistry. Discordianism can't be dogmatic. The whole language would have to change for people to lose track that it was all a joke to begin with. It would take a thousand years (p. 333).

In one of his final interviews, Kerry had this to say about his involvement in neo-paganism:

My influence on the occult has been exaggerated.
I've never quite understood why it's like this, but
there is a book called *Drawing Down the Moon* that
credits me with founding the neo-pagan
movement in the United States of America. I got
into neo-paganism in 1966, I guess it was—very
briefly, and then I took an acid trip that was just a
terrible bummer; and the next day we went down
to the beach, and there were some guys with us
with a skull on a post, sitting around beating
drums, and it made me go on a complete
bummer about paganism for years afterwards.

Kerry should be remembered not only as the forefather of
Discordianism, and a major influence on neo-paganism, but also as
a key player in the history of independent zines. In the mid-70s,
Kerry came up with "wall newspapers," a concept which consisted
of making Xerox copies of one-page rants and distributing them in
the streets of Little Five Points, Atlanta, usually posting half a dozen
copies at key points about town, then using word of mouth to
spread interest in his offbeat publishing empire. It was this method
that finally allowed Kerry to reach a larger audience as the zine
movement soon became a global phenomenon.

The "Zine Revolution"—as it has now become known—
really started gathering steam in the late 80s with the proliferation
of Kinko's, not to mention the abuse of office copying machines after
hours by clandestine zinesters. With these available resources at
hand, independent publishing suddenly became affordable to a dis-
sident subculture of punks, political activists, body modifiers/tat-
too artists, conspiracy theorists, religious cranks, pagans, anarchists,
Discordians, psychedelic enthusiasts, and a zillion and one other
alienated oddballs, who—within the burgeoning subculture—

were given an outlet.

Kerry was at the forefront of this movement. In early 1986—using his "wall newspaper" method of publishing—Kerry came out with the first issue of *Kultcha*, a broadside focusing on "art, sex, and religion." Other wall newspapers Kerry self-published in years to come were *The Decadent Worker*—Little Five Points' version of a Hollywood gossip column—and *Cactus Flower Gazette*, Kerry's collected notes for a Zen anarchism ideology.

As Kerry wrote about distributing his publications in the streets of Little Five Points (L5P):

> I like to think that over two-and-a-half years of
> such activity has raised the vibes in my
> immediate surroundings considerably. Beyond
> the satisfaction of refuting a few of the lies the
> intelligence community spreads to counter my
> attempts to bring to light data about my belatedly
> discovered involvement in the JFK murder and
> such related matters as the premeditated
> escalation of the Indochina war and German
> breeding experiments right here in the U.S., there
> is no other profit involved.

Kerry posted notices about his wall newspapers in such seminal zines as *FactSheet 5* and *Fnord Generation*, which in turn brought in even more subscribers to his one-page letter-sized missives. As always, Kerry wasn't in it to turn a profit, but as a means of communicating his unique vision. For a dollar he would send you half a dozen or so wall newspapers. If you didn't have any money, he'd give you some anyway. Either way, it didn't really matter much to Kerry, because he was "working long hours washing dishes and many issues wind up being reprinted, and I also get lots of interesting mail art and zines in return."

One of the main attractions for those who became involved in the zine revolution (present company included) was that it was a means to meet like-minded folks and trade your own publication for those of others, a self-proliferating process that brought whole networks of artists and publishers together—many of whom ultimately progressed to the Internet, turning their zine efforts into webpages, newsgroups, message boards, and e-mail lists.

During those halcyon days of the late 60s and early 70s, Kerry oversaw a vast network of Discordian co-conspirators. Today similar interactions happen on a daily basis with Internet newsgroups. Discordianism now has a sizeable presence on the Net and continues to thrive in its many unusual forms, more than 40 years after its genesis.

As previously noted, the first edition of the *Principia Discordia*—consisting of a mere five copies—was published in 1965. It was not until 1969 and 1970—with the second, third, and fourth editions—that a significant number of copies were finally printed. Finally, in 1979, *Loompanics*—an alternative book publisher in Washington State—finally brought the book into wider distribution, as it started appearing outside of California.

Lastly, because of companies like Steve Jackson Games, the *Principia Discordia* is now widely available in North America through a vast number of commercial outlets, including many comic book stores. Given the fact that the *Principia Discordia* has always been an underground publication that Thornley and Hill never intended to be copyrighted, from its very inception it was placed in the public domain, thus allowing anyone to publish it in whole or part. Now, with the advent of the Internet, the *Principia Discordia* is available for one and all to enjoy, free of charge, as any simple web search will reveal.

Shortly before his death, Kerry had the opportunity to finally see what this Internet hubbub was about. In the company of friend and co-conspirator Sondra London, he visited a cabal of cyber-savvy Discordians who unveiled the website that London had constructed for him, as well other Discordian sites, not to mention the Internet version of *Principia Discordia*. An impromptu Discordian chat room was set up, with Kerry entertaining questions in his one and only live chat session.

The Goddess was pleased.

CHAPTER 20

Zen and the Art of Dishwashing

"To be called a lunatic is a compliment to anyone who recognizes a better position than the one taken by allegedly rational human beings. Therefore, if there cannot be lunacy for all, there should at least be equality for lunatics. To those who are accused of being on the periphery of the lunatic fringe, all things are possible. It is on the outer periphery of the lunatic fringe, beyond lunacy, where the cosmic mystery is unfolding."

—CAMDEN BENARES

From the late 70s onwards, Kerry supported himself by operating a circuit from Florida to Atlanta—including the sacred streets of Little Five Points—selling his "wall newspapers" or whatever else could earn him a few bucks. Among other endeavors, Kerry sold flowers and buttons with slogans. Then, at one point, he said to hell with work altogether and made his home for a while in a storm drain.

As conspiracy researcher Jonathan Vankin has noted, it was Kerry's peripatetic wanderings—and his reliance on menial jobs (as opposed to white-collar employment[15])—that first raised the eyebrows of certain assassination researchers, who wondered why someone with such a keen intellect had seldom ascended beyond a blue-collar existence.

Many of these researchers suspected that Kerry was an intelligence community asset, and that the reason he never stayed too long in any one place—and worked at a variety of seemingly dead-end jobs—was due to his clandestine employment as a secret agent, where the ability to pack up and leave at a moment's notice is a highly valued asset. With that being said, if Kerry had been an intelligence agent, he was probably the most unconventional spook who ever lived. Or, as Becky Glaser told me: "Can you imagine trying to involve Kerry in a plot to assassinate the president of the United States? No spook in their right mind would find Kerry the least bit reliable, 'cause he was a loose cannon as a human being—even before he went nuts."

■

In the early 80s, Kerry donned yet another Discordian persona, that of the Reverend Jesse Sump, and forthwith published his own set of irreverent Gospels entitled: "THE KID WAS PERFECT! Or the Gospel of Jesus According to Fred the Publican as revealed by the Goddess Eris Discordia in an act of Divine Embellishment to Reverend Jesse Sump, Ancient Abbreviated Calif. Of California and Pastor Present of the Church of the Anarchist Avatar and First Commercial Evangelical Erisian Orthodox Church of the SubGenius."

Under the persona of the Honorable Rev. Sump, Kerry penned one of his most cutting social commentaries in the form of a letter to a certain Rev. Stanley in Atlanta who preached that gays were the scourge of the earth:

Reverend Charles Stanley   12 February 1986
First Baptist Church
Atlanta, Georgia

Dear Reverend Stanley:
    As one who has long insisted motor vehicles are God's punishment for political apathy I was struck by your assertion that AIDS is God's penalty for homosexuality. Since the Bible

explicitly forbids cigarette smoking, lung cancer is divine retribution for that sin. Therefore it follows that common colds are caused by invoking God's displeasure in living too far from the warm climate of the Holy Land. Medical science will forever be in your debt for revealing that the true cause of poor health is going against God's manifest natural system of law and order.

I need your help, though, in figuring out what sins some of the other diseases—such as muscular dystrophy, infantile paralysis and bubonic plague—were intended to cure. I suggest you preach a sermon on this in the near future called "God's Wonderful Biological Warfare Campaign Against Sin," which I will attend and take notes.

For I am in exceptionally good health and I wish to convince all my sick friends that if, like me, they were without sin they could insult the suffering and less fortunate in the same smug self-assurance that you and I do without fear of being smitten by small pox.

Yours for casting that first infected stone

Reverend Jesse Sump
First Evangelical and Unrepentant
Church of No Faith (Discordian)

■

Throughout the early 80s, Kerry was living off and on in Tampa with his then girlfriend, Paula Petty. However, much of his time was spent hitchhiking Florida's southeast coast, living the life of an illuminated hobo. As Kerry wrote in 1984:

> So my general plan is about the same each day; I
> just begin slowly wending my way toward Stock
> Island, with the possibility that I will hitch all the
> way to Marathon Key or Miami or somewhere;
> usually before I get beyond the south end of
> Stock Island, I'm in shape for the day—with
> enough to eat and etc., and without a cent to
> spare. I either find money or food or someone
> gives me something or what have you....
>
> I went on down into downtown Key West,
> where the weather was exceedingly drunk. Sat on
> the Duval St. jetty and drank beer and rum and
> ignored one of the most beautiful sunsets you can
> imagine—with a bunch of pirates and other
> bums.
>
> 'Twasn't long before I crashed on my favorite
> balcony of a house somebody was going to build
> once and then [they] thought better of it. I woke
> up early because roosters were crowing and I'd
> gone to bed early. Being too drunk for much else.
>
> This morning before breakfast I found three
> beers. So I'm wasted away in Key West again
> over a steaming cup of coffee....
>
> Reality always requires certain unpleasant
> adjustments, no matter where you find yourself
> stationed in the class structure. The knack is to
> follow the Tao and know where to find lost
> money and abandoned goods. Other than that, it
> is simply a matter of a certain patient attitude
> which is usually soon rewarded. Anyway,
> yesterday I got a guy stoned who showed me
> where to get work heading shrimp—in case I

decide to become upwardly mobile.

I'm halfway up the island again on U.S. 1. Whenever I can't think of anything else to do, I go north. This is Saturday, 28 January 1984. It is still rather early in the morning. I look forward to what I think is probably going to be one of the more interesting days of my unmilitary career.

I found a wallet with $8 in it, belonging to James Murphy in Davie, FLA. I sent it back to him with $2 worth of postage stamps in exchange for $2 of the $8, and a note of explanation.

So it's been that kind of day. I applied for a job as a dishwasher at Wag's. They were very nice, but said I'd have to shave off my beard....

I'm feeling ambitious. I'm thinking of getting a job and climbing my way up into Key West society, of getting a bicycle and then using my wages as capital to become an entrepreneur. I could wind up like Art—making things to sell to tourists and living on my own island. I could dine with my dates at Rooftop Café and look down on the streets I left behind. A swashbuckling Key West entrepreneur. I could build boats in glass bottles. Or design planters of driftwood. Or hustle grass. Or write my own calypso songs and print them up as posters for boutiques.

I saw my mysterious friend, Roy who is parading Duval with a squirt gun these days, acting slightly psychotic, and I got picked up by a transvestite, only to be ditched in a couple of minutes. So, since I was going to crash anyway, I went to bed...

Although an avowed hitchhiker, Kerry once borrowed his girl-friend Paula's car, which in turn led to his arrest in Tampa for driving without a license. Thereafter, Kerry conformed with the rest of society and got a driver's license. This development, it so happened, was in contradiction to what Kerry had stated in a flyer reproduced in Wilson's *Cosmic Trigger*—the one about using only his thumbprint for identification. This, in turn, caused certain conspiracy theorists to suspect that Kerry was impersonating himself!

Except for a VW van—which he and Cara had for a short time in the late 60s—Kerry never owned a car, which was probably a good thing. As Louise Lacey noted, Kerry "knew his limitations," which meant he had no business driving. During those years, Kerry had enough trouble simply surviving, let alone navigating a couple tons of steel. Because of this, Kerry became the consummate hitch-hiker, which certainly had its benefits, as it introduced him to a steady string of new acquaintances with whom he could share his life's stories.

A letter to Greg Hill from the mid-80s further illustrates Kerry's vagabond nature, as well as the incredible network of connections he maintained:

> I will be ambling out to Tampa in the latter half of
> June, visiting Elayne in New Jersey, a delightful
> psych student in Boston named Sean Hugh—
> maybe Arthur Hlavarty in Durham on the way—
> Bob McDonald in Virginia—some Oklahoma
> Libertarian, possibly the SubGenii, certainly
> Semaj the Elder in Davenport, et al. No telling
> how long it will take me to reach California, but
> I'll try to send you a postcard of advance
> warning…I'll probably come back to Tampa at
> least another year. Paula says that's okay if I work
> full time until Christmas, to which I've no
> objection. Next winter after that I'll probably go

to Miami and find work long enough to get my own home until spring. Unless, somewhere along the line, I should find a publisher for one of my books—in which case all plans will be up for rethinking.

By the late 80s, Kerry had become a major player in the Church of SubGenius, a spoof religion influenced to a great degree by its predecessor, Discordianism. Ever the sexual exhibitionist, Kerry once sent a photo of himself nude, fucking a chair, to Rev. Ivan Stang's SubGenius mag *Stark Fist of Removal*. Stang, of course, published it, albeit with Kerry's dick blacked out. As Stang later noted: "Kerry had love in his heart for all things, even chairs."

■

The early 90s found Kerry actively engaged in the art of dishwashing, as he explained in the *SteamShovel Press* interview: "I made a Zen discipline out of washing dishes. I sat there and tried to concentrate on washing the dishes, and thinking about nothing else as I was washing the dishes, and I took as much pride in being a dishwasher as I take in being a writer."

Back in December 1989, Frank Reiss opened A Capella Books in Little Five Points. Not long after, he encountered an "odd-seeming character"—with intense eyes and a long beard—posting curious-looking leaflets around town. Frank was a little surprised when this fellow came into his store and inquired about a rare title: *What Is Communist Anarchism?* Frank conducted a book search and found a copy, which happened to be relatively expensive.

As it turns out, this "odd-seeming character" went ahead and paid for the book, although it was evident he wasn't comfortable spending that much money. As time went by—and Frank began to learn more about the L5P scene—he discovered that this guy, Kerry Thornley, was a legend around town with a reputation as a "wild man." Still, it wasn't until a couple years later, with the publication of *The Idle Warriors* and *Zenarchy*, that Frank approached Kerry, although somewhat timidly, and asked him if he'd be interested in doing a book signing. Much to Frank's surprise, he found this alleged madman "disarmingly charming." Without reservation, Kerry told Frank he'd love to do a signing, as he wasn't at all adverse to the prospect of self-promotion. (Even anarchists need to pay the rent!)

Soon after, Kerry approached Frank about working at A Capella. Frank was reluctant to hire Kerry, given his kooky reputation. At some point, though, Frank found himself needing extra help, so he gave Kerry a job. Kerry eventually asked Frank if he could live in the back of the store, in the furnace room, which Frank considered a completely uninhabitable space. In fact, the idea of someone wanting to live back there seemed bizarre to Frank, although he agreed to rent Kerry the room.

In short order, Kerry was able to transform what Frank considered a "really gross space" into somewhat habitable quarters. Kerry constructed a bed that was elevated off the ground on some sort of makeshift structure, and designed a space for all his files and papers, which were quite extensive, taking up most of the room, and arranged in a surprisingly orderly fashion, given the fact that Kerry was a card-carrying Discordian.

"What struck me was how much order he brought to this little space," Frank remembered. Although Kerry was primarily a vagabond throughout the latter part of his life, it is noteworthy that he'd been able to maintain this collection of papers, as if he felt, and rightly so, that he would one day leave behind a literary legacy.

One of Kerry's frequent visitors to A Capella was John Paccasassi, who recounted the following:

> Kerry had two stray cats that he adopted that
> lived back there. They had apparently found a
> good supply of mice to eat, so that's where the

cats use to live. And one time I was looking for
Kerry, and I went behind the bookstore, and one
of his cats had scooped up a mouse in her paw,
thrown it up in the air and caught it in her
mouth. I wish I'd had a video camera. It was
something straight out of the National
Geographic Explorer. It was beautiful!

In time, Kerry's collection of cats expanded to a total of 13. To accommodate them, he constructed an elaborate "cat condo" on the back end of the building, adjacent to his room, a huge contraption—built out of scrap lumber and whatever else he could rummage—which allowed the cats to skitter freely in and out of his room, crawling all around, up rickety ladders and through tunnels, an amusement park for the feline crowd, which the health department eventually made Kerry tear down.

According to Frank Reiss, Kerry was a hardworking and energetic employee, although there was one drawback, that being the steady string of visitors, namely Kerry's circle of homeless friends who just wanted to have a place to hang out.

L5P, at this time, was a haven for transient kids in search of an alternative lifestyle. These kids invariably gravitated to Kerry, who was the living embodiment of someone dancing to the beat of his own drummer. Initially these kids became attracted to Kerry on account of his semi-celebrity status, then decided to stick around when they discovered he possessed a kind heart and took an sincere interest in their welfare, especially the attractive young girls, who would often visit Kerry back in his furnace room. This group of young girls surrounding Kerry became known as "the Thornleyettes."

Unfortunately, some of this crowd surrounding Kerry occasionally stirred up trouble, such as one guy who ended up hitting on one of A Capella's female employees, which in turn led to an altercation where said employee shot Kerry's friend in the butt!

During his off time, Kerry could often be found selling his books and assorted bric-a-brac at a stand in front of A Capella, where he spoke to passersby about his life following the Kennedy assassination, of being under CIA surveillance, and how the KGB had given him a disease after he'd been seduced by a comely Russian agent.

Eventually, Kerry came to believe that nearly every woman he'd ever slept with was in on "the conspiracy." At one time, Kerry claimed a squadron of Nazi women had been sent to L5P—direct from the Fatherland and equipped with thick accents—with the express purpose of having intercourse with him to breed a chapter of the Future Fuehrers of America. Kerry never indicated whether he took these real or imagined goose-stepping seductresses up on their carnal offer, but knowing his fondness for the fairer sex, I'm sure Kerry was tempted.

■

As Frank Reiss became more aware of the conspiratorial legends surrounding Kerry, he began to hear tales that everywhere Kerry had worked around L5P, mysterious strangers in dark suits would show up. Frank never took any of these stories seriously until one Christmas when he treated all of the A Capella employees to dinner at the Star Bar in L5P.

Sometime during the course of festivities, the bartender came over and passed around drinks to everyone, compliments of a gentleman seated at another table. In due course, Frank's wife, Cynthia, went over and thanked the fellow—a conservative-appearing middle-aged man—and invited him over to their table. After exchanging pleasantries, the fellow informed the group that he was a veterinarian, and spoke with what Frank considered to be an obviously phony Scottish accent.

As the evening wore on, the man with the phony Scottish accent engaged those at Frank's table in conversation about one topic or another. However—after Kerry left—the conversation wound up being exclusively about him. As Frank recalled:

> It was so strange…clearly this guy wasn't who he said he was, and one way or another the conversation got around to Kerry and Oswald and all this other stuff…and that wasn't the only time…
>
> Within a couple of months of this incident, my wife and I were out for dinner in the neighborhood, and again—this has never happened before to us, and it has never happened since—we're sitting in a restaurant, and once again the waiter comes up and says, "This couple over here wants to buy ya'all a bottle of wine," and we accept and we invite them over to the table, and this time it's this young couple…. And we start talking about everything in the world and before it's all over, we start talking about Kerry Thornley, and him working for me and what I knew about him…. And those two incidents—whenever I end up talking to anybody about Kerry Thornley…there's something there…that stuff just wasn't out of the blue, and I told Kerry about it and it didn't faze him at all. He said, "Oh yeah, that stuff happens all the time—they're all over the place…"
>
> [These incidents] fit the same description as what I had heard from other people who knew Kerry before me and would say: "Oh yeah, when [Kerry] used to work at The Pub there were always these men in dark suits."

■

Chris Wilhoite—a wandering minstrel who made his way to L5P in the early 90s—remembered how he first became acquainted with Kerry:

> I had just read the *Illuminatus* trilogy and was pondering what was what when I noticed the pages of a novel about Oswald and JFK on the telephone poles in L5P. The last page had the name Kerry Thornley on it. Synchronicity #1. Around the same time, I noticed an unusual/ enigmatic/ groovy looking fellow in tie-died cotton who occasionally strolled through the park with the smile of a Buddha, and somehow I knew there was something special about him. One night, I was playing one of my songs on acoustic guitar in the park and this Buddhaesque being stopped and listened and paid me a compliment. I still didn't catch his name. A friend had told me more about the mysterious author of the JFK sheets and said he'd written a book called *Zenarchy*, a name that appealed deeply to me, but I still didn't match the person with the name.
>
> Then, one day a friend told me that Kerry Thornley had, in the course of one day, been called by Oliver Stone to be a consultant for the JFK film, [shortly afterward] had dual kidney failure and his landlady flipped a mental cog and kicked everybody out of the boarding house where he lived. So, Kerry needed a place to stay. I immediately volunteered space in my duplex. My friend told me to talk to Kerry, he was in front of A Capella books, signing and selling his work. Who did I see in front of the store, but the groovy

Buddha I had noticed before! I invited him to
crash at my pad, and this became the beginning
of a long and fruitful friendship.

Another close friend of Kerry's during this period was John
Paccasassi, who Kerry once described as "this squat Latino with
black curls and horn-rimmed sunglasses." If the two weren't busy
discussing assassination conspiracy theories—or working on a
sequel to the *Principia Discordia*—they could be found getting
stoned and watching old movies together. John and Kerry also
shared an interest in the history of the Third Reich, and the Nazi
breeding experiments. In fact, Paccasassi believed he'd been part of
the same type of breeding experiments as Kerry. There were other
times, though, when John and Kerry didn't quite see eye to eye:

> One thing that Kerry use to get into, that I'd find
> upsetting, was every now and then he'd go off on
> this tear about how the Vietnam War was his fault
> because Brother-in-law asked him: "If we were to
> have a shooting war, should we have a shooting
> war in Vietnam or in Cuba?" And Kerry said,
> "Probably Vietnam." And these were just idle
> words, Kerry was probably having a few beers,
> and he was probably feeling a little bit loose—he
> probably didn't take it that seriously—and then
> years later he's beatin' himself with chains over
> this shit. And that really bothered me. And I'd
> say, "You can believe that if you want to but it's
> BULLSHIT and I don't want to hear it!" I mean
> that really used to upset me. 'Cause he had no
> right to be tormenting himself with that. The man
> was in absolute fucking agony over it.

Like a lot of Kerry's friends, Paccasassi was not immune to

being considered part of "the conspiracy," although John didn't let Kerry's paranoia interfere with their friendship. "I had to make a decision not to take personal offense at any of this. That was basically a condition of having Kerry as a friend was that I had to make a decision that if he accuses me of being a member of the Ecuadorian secret police or some shit like that I wasn't going to take it personally."

Fortunately, Kerry would never dwell too long on such negative trips, as the next day you might find him displaying an almost childlike wonderment, such as this incident Paccasassi once observed: "I remember seeing him walking through L5P, and finding a grasshopper and putting it on his finger, and just continuing to walk through L5P with this grasshopper on his finger, and it just had a real Zen quality to it."

■

In 1991, Kerry experienced kidney failure, from which he recovered somewhat swiftly. Later that year, Kerry's publisher at IllumiNet Press, Ron Bonds, phoned him with some seemingly good news: "Oliver Stone is looking for you!" Kerry—who didn't have a clue as to who the hell Stone was—soon after was on an all-expense-paid trip to California to meet the famed director, who was then researching his movie *JFK*.

When Kerry arrived in L.A., he was met at the airport by his old friend David Lifton, who hadn't seen Kerry for a number of years. The two spent several hours together, which included a tape-recorded interview at the home of a friend of Lifton's who was a licensed therapist. After the interview, she told Lifton: "I hope you realize you are dealing with a classic schizophrenic."

Afterwards, Lifton dropped Kerry off at Oliver Stone's offices in Santa Monica, where in short order he was asked the $64,000 question: Was Kerry absolutely sure he hadn't met with Oswald in 1963? Of course, Kerry again denied having seen Oswald after their

Marine service together. As this obviously wasn't what Stone wanted to hear, Kerry's visit with the director was short.

Soon after his meeting with Stone, Kerry made an appearance on the TV tabloid magazine show *A Current Affair*, an event that had been arranged, in part, by controversial author Sondra London, then in collaboration with Kerry on a project about his involvement in the Kennedy assassination, *Confession to a Conspiracy*.[16]

Broadcast on February 25, 1992, *A Current Affair* presented the piece as "the end of one man's 28-year vow of silence" which couldn't have been farther from the truth, as Kerry had been going on about his unwitting participation in the Kennedy assassination since the mid-70s.

In the lead-in, anchor Maureen O'Boyle went on to say that "Thornley testified to the Warren Commission, but like their secret files, his lips have been sealed...until today, Steve Dunleavy was the first man since Earl Warren to hear Thornley's bombshell story!"

Of course, this lead-in was riddled with as many inaccuracies as the Warren Report itself. The piece to follow depicted Kerry as part of a conspiracy, which—in the words of reporter Steve Dunleavy—"used the exotic background of New Orleans as his headquarters for a deranged plot to assassinate John F. Kennedy." The most controversial part of the interview came when Kerry uttered these inflammatory lines: "I wanted to shoot him. I wanted to assassinate him very much...I wanted him dead. I would have shot him myself. I would have stood there with a rifle and pulled the trigger if I would have had the chance."

What wasn't pointed out to the audience is that Kerry's "confession" described his feelings toward Kennedy in the early 60s. And although Kerry made a pastime during that period of mouthing off about killing Kennedy, in reality he was never a violent man, so all this talk about shooting JFK seemed so much bluster and folderol. Unfortunately, these comments about shooting Kennedy deeply affected certain members of Kerry's family, who were aghast that he'd speak out in such a manner.

Over all, Kerry felt the *Current Affair* interview went well in that it provided a forum for his message. Unfortunately—when he went to cash the check for his appearance—it bounced!

When Greg Hill saw the *Current Affair* episode, he was dismayed. In his opinion, the producers had not indicated that Kerry was, or had been, mentally ill. Afterwards, Greg asked Kerry about his appearance on the program, and why he said he'd plotted Kennedy's assassination, since this claim wasn't true. Kerry replied: "I want people to know that the official version is incorrect" and he explained to Greg that the reason he was extending this hyperbole (of his role in the assassination) was as a means to illuminate the masses. Hail Eris, of course.

■

Although he had mellowed (somewhat) over the years, Kerry still possessed a mischievous nature, as evidenced during opening night of a play at Seven Stages Theater in L5P, which occurred in the mid-90s.

As the story goes, there was a certain actor who had become disgruntled, apparently because he didn't land a part in the production. Somehow Kerry got involved and convinced the guy to go into the theater on opening night with a bucket full of ketchup and, during the course of the play, throw it onstage in protest. This resulted in the disgruntled actor getting punched in the nose by the director, after which a small riot erupted.

Meanwhile, Kerry stood in the wings, laughing his fool head off.

Chris Wilhoite bore witness to any number of Kerry's surrealist pranks, such as one that occurred on Halloween morning in 1993:

I was living in a VW camper van behind a
restaurant in L5P. I had just had breakfast and
was standing at the corner across from the park,
when Kerry comes walking from the far end of
the square, wearing a white cloak with a hood
and carrying a sign reading "World Will End
SOON. Get your tickets NOW!" As he passed
down the street, snowflakes (unseasonal for Oct.
31 in Atlanta) began to fall right behind Kerry,
and as he passed across my field of vision, the
snow came in like a curtain drawn by Kerry. My
friend Wolf, standing directly behind me said:
"Yep, hell just froze over!"

One day Kerry and Chris were hanging out in front of the
Tête-à-Tête Café, with a wooden box full of copies of *The Principia
Discordia* and *Zenarchy*, which Kerry was selling/giving away.
(Buyer: "How much?" Kerry: "How much do you have?" Buyer: "A
quarter." Kerry: "That's plenty!") On Kerry's wooden box was a
sign that said: *Principia Discordia*—much funnier than the Bible!

At one point, a Christian zealot happened by, noticed Kerry's
sign and started shouting, "Much funnier than the Bible? The Bible's
not funny!" In response, a local zealous Marxist who was seated
behind Kerry and Chris jumped up and started shouting down the
Christian. Kerry, smiling, closed his box and walked away, with
Chris following after, exclaiming: "Hail Eris! All Hail Discordia!"

In 1994—prior to Super Bowl XXVIII in Atlanta—Kerry and a
handful of L5P colleagues hatched a plot that became infamous in
the annals of Super Sunday goofs. The prank in question revolved
around some posters that Kerry and his conspirators hung throughout the greater Atlanta area that read: "Boycott the illegal weapons
amnesty program: Don't bring your illegal weapons to the Super
Bowl in exchange for tickets!"

Of course, there was no amnesty program; this was just a ruse that Kerry and his cohorts cooked up with the intended reverse effect of getting a bunch of bone-headed people to show up with their illegal weapons and try to turn them in for Super Bowl tickets. This, in turn, led to several arrests on Super Bowl Sunday.

Goddess Eris had struck again.

■

In the early 90s, the L5P business association rallied together in a campaign to "clean up" the town. Apparently, the business association wanted to make L5P a "yuppie-friendly" community, meanwhile keeping the image of bohemia alive without actually having any of those bothersome bohemians around to clutter up the streets.

Granted, there were problems in the neighborhood that needed to be addressed, such as some aggressive panhandling and a very visible homeless problem. According to Kerry's friend and L5P habitué, Beth Lavoie, these were just a couple of the problems the business association were attempting to deal with, but the way they went about cleaning up L5P was "fascist and illegal—a violation of people's rights."

Along with the homeless and panhandling problems, Beth felt that the business association targeted anyone who was considered a nuisance, such as street venders who sold trinkets without licenses, kids playing hacky sack, drummers, or anybody else who didn't fit the preferred profile of the upwardly mobile consumer. In essence, the business association was trying to get rid of the L5P street scene, which was the very reason the town had such a colorful history.

Kerry was one of the most vocal spokesmen against the business association, and was instrumental in helping to organize the local street people against it. One of Kerry's main areas of contention was an off-duty cop named McFarlane that the business association had hired to police the streets. Officer McFarlane, allegedly, had a reputation of abuse and some people claimed that he'd actually attacked them. Kerry hated McFarlane and made no bones about it.

For a short period of time, Frank Reiss served as president of the business association, which in turn led to arguments between him and Kerry over what the association was trying to do, and in particular the much-loathed Officer McFarlane, whom Kerry considered a thug. As Frank recalled:

> [Kerry and I] had spirited debates—this is the way we'd interact on neighborhood issues.... And he would get real worked up, and I would be defensive—it would be a confrontation to some extent. And then eventually it would all just turn into a big joke and he'd write something really funny about it, and distribute it. And then I started thinking: "Maybe he just does all of this for entertainment."

Ultimately, the business association was successful in removing the "bad elements" from the streets. But with it most of the local color also was removed, and L5P has now become but another yuppie haven, and the kids who used to hang out in the streets—and saw Kerry as a something of a hero—had all moved on.

CHAPTER 21

The Fallen Idols of Discord

"Life is not a problem to be solved, but a mystery to be lived."

—GREG HILL, from his notebook, date unknown

Kerry Thornley and Greg Hill could be considered tragic figures, both gifted and at the same time haunted by certain demons, perhaps invoked by Goddess Eris. For Kerry, the demons were howling in his head of a vast conspiracy; how and why they got there, one can only surmise. Greg's demons, however, were largely self-induced, brought on by that oldest evil of them all, alcohol. As previously noted, Greg fell victim to bouts of severe depression, as illustrated in a letter to Kerry from the mid 70s:

> Last time I was in complete despair (on the Russian River) the only reason I did not commit suicide is because my death would not solve the injustice that I was perceiving. It would solve the pain but would not solve the injustice. Strangely, the despair was even deeper than the pain. Same thing happened the other time I hit those depths—around age 20. It was not injustice that overwhelmed me that time but my sheer damn inability to know anything with any deep level of certainty. When despair is deep enough, even death is pointless.
>
> Now I live without knowledge and I live without justice. I don't know why—I just live it. So be it.

The injustice of which Greg spoke was that true love had never given him a fair shake, and that the love of his life had been sabotaged by a vindictive ex-husband. Greg's subsequent descent into alcoholism was an attempt to ease the pain, a pain that never left him, but could only be deadened, to a certain extent, by self-medication.

Like Greg, Camden Benares also suffered severe bouts of depression, although Camden was always able to snap out of these biochemical funks and eventually get back on his feet again.

One such episode occurred in the late 80s, when Camden's wife June found him curled up in a ball in their garage, suffering a nervous breakdown. Seeing no other alternative, she committed Camden to the Veterans Hospital in Los Angeles, where he spent five months.

True to his nature, Camden ended up editing the VA Hospital newspaper, and by the time he left was even running the therapy sessions and driving the shrink there crazy, who couldn't wait to sign him out!

■

In March 1993, Kerry had a relapse with his kidney problems and thereafter began dialysis three times a week. Due to this turn of events, Kerry was forced to quit his job as a Zen Buddhist dishwasher at the Mexican restaurant, Tapatio's, and become, as he termed it, "an anarchist ward of the state."

Having practiced the anarchist ethic all his life, Kerry made a point of never accepting government-sponsored handouts such as Social Security or welfare. Instead, he sold things on the streets like his $1 "wall newspapers" or buttons or flowers. Unfortunately this all changed with his kidney ailment, and he had to go on disability.

Kerry, through all his struggles, was able to retain a sense of humor, which indicates that even at the worst of times he had some perspective as to his place in the universe, however whacked-out it may have been. As Bob Wilson observed: "Thornley is the only clinical case, in my experience, that managed to keep his sense of humor. He lost his sense of humor off and on—but he always seemed to get it back again.... He felt he was above it [the conspiracy], and in some curious way, he could laugh at it."

For the record, Kerry was never institutionalized, which attests to the fact that his paranoias never got to the point where he wasn't able to care for himself. Even during the roughest times— when he was on the edge of madness, teetering over some conspiratorial abyss—Kerry still had that beatific gleam in his eye.

One explanation for Kerry's paranoid schizophrenia may have been related to genetic predisposition and triggered by subsequent LSD experimentation. Similar psychological disturbances were experienced in the late 60s by Kerry's youngest brother, Dick, at which time he displayed paranoid schizophrenic symptoms. This was most likely induced, Dick now suspects, by a combination of extensive LSD use and overall emotional instability.

During this period, Dick discovered double-meanings in newspaper headlines, overheard conversations, and even in the flight of seagulls. Although quite similar to John Nash's story in *A Beautiful Mind*, it never got to the point where Dick imagined people hiding in the shadows, waving guns and threatening him with personal bodily harm. For a while, though, Dick's parents were concerned enough that they considered committing him to UCLA's rehab unit.

Ultimately, Dick was able pull himself out of his paranoia by laying off the drugs and ignoring those "private" meanings he found in flying seagulls and overheard conversations. (Kerry—at the height of his own paranoia—experienced similar double meanings and eventually came to believe that intelligence agents were using what he called "Cant Language" to communicate surreptitiously to him. In return, Kerry developed his own Cant Language to communicate back to these envisioned intelligence community spooks, although, in all probability, this was one long internal dialogue between Kerry and his unbalanced brain.)

In *A Beautiful Mind*, John Nash was besieged by visual hallucinations in the form of enemy agents on clandestine missions for
some super-secret shadowy government agency. (Sound familiar?)
In contrast to what is presented in the movie, Nash's real-life delusions came exclusively in the form of auditory hallucinations,
which is the most common manifestation of schizophrenia. Auditory
hallucinations such as these were experienced by Dick Thornley during his own brief bout with psychosis, although never to the extent
of the beautiful madness that enveloped John Nash.

Kerry, as well, was besieged by audio hallucinations. Like
Nash, he felt, upon occasion, that aliens were communicating to
him. Furthermore, Kerry suspected that he'd been implanted with
a mind-control device while serving in the Marines, and it was
because of this surreptitious inter-cranial device that he experienced
auditory hallucinations, just prior to falling to sleep, while in the
hypnogogic state.

Nash, as has been well documented, was one of the most original minds of his generation. As a 20-year-old Princeton grad student, he made a stunning breakthrough in the field of Game
Theory. His thesis on the dynamics of human conflict thereafter rev-
olutionized economics and eventually earned him the Nobel Prize.

As mentioned earlier, Game Theory was the guiding philosophy behind "Operation Mindfuck," perhaps the most infamous of
all Discordian pranks. Another Discordian connection with Nash
comes in the form of the mysterious number 23, which, incredibly
enough, was Nash's favorite prime number! After going off the deep
end, Nash spent endless hours exploring variations of the number
23 in his pursuit to achieve a method to receive messages from
heaven. Don't ask me how this was all supposed to work, but the
gist of Nash's theory revolved around what he termed "probability coincidence," which sounds a hell of a lot like "synchronicity"
to me. (The popular definition of synchronicity is "meaningful coincidence.") So by fate or dumb luck, Nash somehow stumbled upon
several key Discordian themes, on or around the same time that the

Discordian Society was first being hatched by Kerry Thornley and Greg Hill.

It was at the height of his career that Nash suffered his psychotic break, when—as a 30-year-old MIT professor—he interrupted a lecture to announce that he was on the cover of the latest issue of *Life* magazine, disguised as the pope. Nash went on to assert that foreign governments were communicating with him through *The New York Times*, which sounds similar to Kerry's "Cant Language." Nash thereafter turned down a prestigious post at the University of Chicago because, as he said, he was about to become "the Emperor of Antarctica." (Shades of Emperor Norton!)

"Madness can be an escape," Nash once said. "If things are not so good, you maybe want to imagine something better. In madness, I thought I was the most important person in the world." Such delusions of grandeur are not unique to the world of the schizophrenic. Kerry fell prey to similar delusions, envisioning himself a key chess piece in a worldwide conspiracy.

Bob Newport worked as a psychiatrist for most of his professional life. This is his take on Kerry's mental problems:

> You have to look at two things: One, Kerry got into LSD quite heavily in the late 60s and that was certainly a factor in it, though I don't think that was causative....
>
> Secondly, Kerry's father was an alcoholic and he was a rigid, judgmental, angry kind of guy. And he was Mormon, and Kerry grew up experiencing his judgments, his rigidity and anger…and watching his hypocrisy, as he was an alcoholic, and drank Cokes, coffee, smoked cigarettes, and the rest of it, which gave Kerry, in my opinion, an erratic relationship with his father and authority....
>
> That's what pushed him into his anti-

establishmentarianism. And then when Garrison
attacked him, I believe he was driven by the need
to defend himself against his father's abuse—
another kind of it. And because he had been so
caught up in psychedelics, and his mind was
working at hyper-speed because of that, he was
driven into this incredible obsession for years and
years.

Throughout these years, Newport tried to help his old friend,
but eventually became frustrated and gave up because Kerry
wouldn't accept his help. Kerry felt he didn't need it. However,
Kerry ultimately received treatment for his mental illness in the
early 90s while in the hospital for his kidney problems. At this time,
Kerry's primary care physician referred him to a psychiatrist who
diagnosed Kerry as paranoid schizophrenic, and prescribed anti-
psychotic meds that helped quiet the implants in his head, real or
imagined.

Such as it was, Kerry viewed the whole psychoanalytical establishment as a product of Nazism and an outgrowth of the eugenics
movement, which dovetailed into his conspiracy theories regarding
German breeding experiments. However, Kerry was a surprisingly
practical guy at times, who would take care of himself if he had reason to believe something would be beneficial to his well being. Just
the same, Kerry (being Kerry) rejected his psychiatrist's diagnosis
of paranoid schizophrenia, telling her: "How can you make that
diagnosis when you haven't even read the Warren Report!?"

CHAPTER 22

Where Have All the Discordians Gone? (The Passage of Omar and Mal-2)

"And so it is that we, as men, do not exist until we do; and then it is that we play with our world of existent things, and order and disorder them, and so it shall be that Non-existence shall take us back. From Existence, and that nameless Spirituality shall return to Void, like a tired child home from a very wild circus."

—MALACLYPSE THE YOUNGER, *Principia Discordia*

Leading up to the 1996 Summer Olympics, many Atlanta locals lost their housing due to rent hikes put in effect by landlords trying to capitalize on the event. Among the displaced were Kerry and his roommate, Chris Wilhoite, as well as Chris's girlfriend, Beth Lavoie. And so it was that Kerry, Chris, Beth, and several others ended up camping out in the woods for a few weeks. Under normal conditions Kerry would have loved this primitive lifestyle, but unfortunately he was too sick to enjoy it, and it was probably due to the summer heat and exposure to the elements that his kidney condition worsened, landing him in the hospital. Beth Lavoie remembered:

> I told him I would watch over his [13] cats.... And they're running around out in the woods, and I'm trying to keep track of them. Oh my God, it was stressful! Because he cared so much about them, ya know, and when I went to the hospital he was

gonna ask [about them]. So I started keeping a
notebook with all the cats' names in it—and some
of them looked alike! And only he could tell the
difference, and I'd tell him: "Well, I think I've
seen so and so" [laughs].

In late 1998, Kerry moved to a cottage on a defunct three-acre farm in southeast Atlanta, at an artists' colony called the Mill House. It was here that he spent his final days in the company his beloved cats.

The rare disorder from which Kerry suffered—Wegner's granulomatosis—eventually progressed into a whole host of maladies that included chronic renal failure, congestive heart failure, endocarditis, difficulty urinating and defecating, and bilateral conjunctivitis. On top of all that, Kerry suffered from dry, cracked skin, which exhibited itself in open sores all over his emaciated body.

At one point, Kerry's brother Dick offered to investigate the prospects of donating one of his kidneys. Kerry, though touched by the gesture, refused, telling Dick: "I know how important it is to have *both* your kidneys."

In his final interview—conducted by Sondra London in late 1998—Kerry attributed his rapidly declining health to a flea infestation passed on to him by his cats. Kerry believed that these fleas had burrowed into his body and were living under his skin, causing his health to deteriorate further.

When Kerry shared this theoretical diagnosis with his primary care physician, he was told he was getting himself all worked up about nothing, and his doctor prescribed Thorazine to treat his anxiety. Kerry refused the Thorazine, and insisted on a second opinion.

Over time, Kerry received several opinions, none of which he agreed with. One doctor said he had a case of the chiggers, another said it was an allergy, while a third diagnosed Kerry's condition as scabies.

Ultimately, Kerry felt he was getting the runaround, and that his skin problems were never adequately treated. In the Sondra London interview, Kerry told her that the fleas had already done irreparable damage and that he felt his days were numbered.

Although Kerry had come a long way in moderating many of his past obsessions, this theory about fleas inside his body obviously sounds farfetched. The tone of his voice—as recorded in London's interview—does indeed sound somewhat paranoid, as if Kerry had latched onto this notion about fleas and it became an obsession in the same manner Kerry had embraced other seemingly far-out theories over the years.

Just before Thanksgiving 1998, Kerry was rushed to Atlanta's Crawford Long Hospital for emergency bladder surgery, and while awaiting dialysis went into cardiac arrest at 12:30 a.m. on November 28. Resuscitation efforts proved unsuccessful and he was pronounced dead at approximately 1:15 that morning.

Whether by design or sheer folly, the curious number of 23 people attended a service for Kerry at a crematorium in Cobb County on November 29. A second memorial service was held at Shambhala Center in Atlanta on the Fifth of December, and so the 23 enigma lives on, accompanied of course by the ever-present Law of Fives.

At the Shambhala Center memorial service, longtime friend Barbara Joye delivered one of the more memorable lines of the evening: "Kerry had the best sense of humor of any paranoid schizophrenic I ever knew."

Shortly after his memorial service, brothers Tom and Dick—along with Kerry's son Kreg—scattered Kerry's ashes at Dillon Beach in northern California. The Thornley trio climbed out on a rock they thought was located in the surf, but just as the ashes were being scattered, a good-sized wave appeared and splashed only Tom, drenching him quite thoroughly. Tom (half jokingly) figured this was Kerry's parting shot, as there had always been a bit of a friction between the two Thornley brothers.

Hail Eris, no doubt.

■

Helen Thornley was devastated by her son's death. A little more than a year after Kerry's passing—on December 2, 1999—she died at the age of 86 while receiving hospice care at the home of her son, Dick. The cause listed on Helen's death certificate was congestive heart failure. "But," according to Dick "it would be more accurate to say she died of failure to thrive." Kerry's father, Kenneth, had passed away four years earlier, on November 7, 1995, at the age of 83. The cause of death was pneumonia, a complication of prostate cancer.

As for the rest of the Thornley clan, they continue to prosper. Cara Thornley is director of the Atlanta Shambhala Center, located in Decatur, which offers free meditation classes and "other educational, artistic, and cultural courses in both a Buddhist and a nonsectarian form." Kerry once claimed that the reason Cara became a Buddhist was so she could find a way to deal with him. Through it all, Cara was the rock in Kerry's life. After their separation, she never stopped caring for and loving him, and was probably the person most responsible for his survival throughout the 70s, when his paranoia was at its worst.

Kerry's son Kreg owns and operates Thunder Bubble Pictures, an Atlanta-based indie filmmaking company that makes "unique shorts for film festivals, local screenings, and our own general amusement." Kreg has done work for both Comedy Central and Nickelodeon and his influences range from Man Ray to Mike Myers. When not doing freelance film work, Kreg's also a part-time web designer, and has performed with Atlanta bands such as Lawn Chair Frontier and 20 lb. Test. More information about Kreg can be found at Kregthornley.com/company.htm.

Kerry's brother Tom is a successful general contractor in the Napa, California, area. As for younger brother Dick, he lives in Carson City, Nevada, and since 1981 has been doing contract legal research out of his home, meanwhile raising five sons with his wife.

■

Gregory H. Hill, known to the world as Malaclypse the Younger, passed away on July 20, 2000. Louise Lacey wrote an obit for Greg, excerpted here:

> Mr. Hill was an avid researcher of an impressively wide range of subjects, a man of many dimensions with a complex personality revealing different aspects of himself to his friends. He was also a passionate man, passionate in his suffering, passionate in his reaction to the alienation he felt from his culture, and passionate in his pursuit of information and knowledge.

In a memorial to Greg, Bob Newport wrote:

> Alcohol, tobacco (and marijuana) remain cultural favorites, and they wreak their havoc on our bodies. Greg died of esophageal cancer, which has been referred to as "the signature cancer" of the alcoholic and smoker. Not only do drinking and smoking ruin our bodies, they have limited effectiveness in eliminating pain. They are great initially and in the short term, but once the intoxication wears off and physiological addiction sets in, their anesthetic value fails considerably. Greg lived with disappointment for many years; he institutionalized unhappiness. He was grouchy much of the time, with only an occasional twinkle in his eye, but oh what a twinkle. Bright enough to dispel the curses of greyface. Loud enough to attract the attention of the wedding party to his own golden apple rolling across the stage. When he put it on paper,

we all laughed and nodded wisely; when he
brought it out in conversation we awakened to
the absurdities of everyday life.

Although esophageal cancer was listed as the chief cause of
Greg's demise, it could be argued that he died of a broken heart due
to his breakup in the early 70s with ex-wife Jeanetta. After this marriage, Greg gradually moved away from his creative side and pursued a career as a bank clerk, eventually ending up as a top
manager for Bank of America. As Discordian synchronicity would
have it, Greg worked 23 years for B of A.

From the late 70s onward, Bob Wilson heard less from Greg
Hill every year, until it got to the point where Greg became a recluse,
withdrawing from many of his old friends who had made up the
Discordian network. According to Wilson: "I sent Greg an e-mail [in
the mid-90s] and he wrote back, 'I'm too busy for e-mail today'...I
didn't hear anything from him until my wife [Arlen] died. He sent
an orchid, with no return address, so I couldn't send him a thank-
you card. Figure that out...I can't...Maybe he was such a hopeless
alcoholic, he didn't want to be bothered by the outside world."

Throughout the 80s, Greg climbed the rungs of the B of A hierarchy. Early in the history of computer word processing—before the
advent of software programs such as Microsoft Word—Greg played
a pivotal role in developing B of A's word processing department,
all the while a functioning alcoholic, devoting himself to work by
day, then coming home at night and drinking. In those years, Greg
seldom left home, except for going to work. One of the few things
that he did that was at all creative during these years was to put out
a computer nerd newsletter called *Golden Gate Word Processing
Xchange.*

Greg also had a hand in developing one of the first computer
solitaire games, the likes of which so many workers now goof off
with when their boss is looking the other way. This achievement,
I'm sure, is one that Greg would be infinitely proud of, playing—
as he has—such a instrumental role in undermining corporate

American culture.

All hail Discordia!

■

Louise Lacey lives in the Bay Area working on a number of projects, including a recently released book that combines affordable California house hunting and California history, which is available at Findacaliforniahome.com.

In addition, she operates two other websites at Growingnative.com and Healthresearchinstitute.com, the first dedicated to growing native Californian plants, the second where Louise shares her knowledge of hemorrhoids, among other health-related matters.

While in her early twenties, Louise cut her teeth as an editor at Novel Books in Chicago, along the way editing Kerry's first book, *Oswald*. The mid-60s found her relocated in the Bay Area as research director for *Ramparts*, the cutting edge political/activist magazine of its day. Among other endeavors, Louise played a major role in the Earth People's Park project, not to mention interacting with the Who's Who of the Discordian Society. She also called bullshit on Timothy Leary once, but that's another story…

During the 70s, Louise published a "feminist periodical" called *Woman's Choice*, as well as penning her classic tome on natural birth control, *Lunaception: A Feminine Odyssey into Fertility and Contraception*, published in 1975. She is planning to update and reprint it in 2003.

While all of this was going on, Louise discovered that she was a power-place dowser, that ancient art of tuning into earth energies. (Hail Eris!) The 80s found her holding down a number of diverse jobs, such as a researcher on a drug treatment program study and writing software user manuals in Silicon Valley.

In the mid-90s, Louise suffered a stroke. You would never suspect it, looking at her today, as she continues to thrive. To keep the windows of her perception adequately squeegeed, Louise takes an annual trek to the mountains to drop LSD.

■

Becky Glaser—now living in the hills near Santa Cruz—stays busy racing endurance horses and, above all, being a mom, which apparently takes up most of her time and makes her parents quite happy to see their free-spirited daughter settled down. Little do they suspect!

■

One of the most beloved figures to emerge from Kerry's colorful circle of friends was Camden Benares. Benares—who died of a massive heart attack in 1999—was someone who seemingly did it all throughout the course of his life, working a myriad of jobs, such as disc jockey, tech writer for the aviation industry, theater manager, alternative press editor, freelance writer, coffeehouse comic, lyrics writer, psychodrama actor, sexual liberation spokesman, Zen lecturer, and meditation teacher.

In the early 80s, Benares worked on the first wave of electronic video games and interactive toys at the Santa Monica Electronic Toy Think Tank and was also involved in the very early days of computer technology, when he worked for the Berkeley Computer Company back in the early 70s.

In Europe, Benares is still considered one of the top authorities on Zen, and his books have been published in German, Dutch, and several other languages. He wrote a total of three books in his Zen series, the second of which was *A Handful of Zen*. His final book, *Riding Buddha's Bicycle,* was finished shortly before he died, and remains unpublished at this date.

Among other predilections, Benares had a fondness for dressing up for parties, and one of his favorite costumes was that of a

Roman Catholic cleric. Sporting a trimmed beard, Benares really looked like an honest-to-god cleric, and played it off perfectly, as anyone who didn't know him thought he was the real deal.

On one occasion—dressed in his cleric clothes—Benares talked his wife June into accompanying him to a party dressed as a nun, where they spent the entire evening holding hands and groping. After the party, Camden and June—still bedecked in their godly accoutrements—visited a Denny's in West L.A., where they made out. As would be expected, people began freaking out upon witnessing this unholy spectacle, as in between sacrilegious smooches Camden gave blessings and benedictions to the stunned Denny's patrons.

■

Allen (Bud) Simco currently resides in San Diego, where he pursues many interests including music, writing, painting, and photography. Check out his website at Alsimco.home.att.net to get a glimpse of this multi-faceted man.

■

Dr. Robert Newport can be found in Los Angeles, where he relocated after retiring from his psychiatry practice. Bob currently devotes himself to his new passion, painting. Among other activities, he's on the advisory board of the number one cryonics firm in the world, ALCOR Life Extension, and is a trained and practiced ALCOR cryonics technician—which means he actually knows how to freeze people! Bob also has plans to put together a collection of his Discordian Archives on the Internet. Look for it sometime in the near future at Cyberspacechapeljoyous.com.

■

Robert Anton Wilson has more than 33 books to his credit, publishes a newsletter called *Trajectories*, maintains a website at RAWilson.com, and interacts with a large number of enlightened humans (or soon-to-be enlightened humans) each day over the Internet with an e-mail list dedicated to all things Discordian. He has made both a comedy record (*Secrets of Power*), and a punk rock record (*The Chocolate Biscuit Conspiracy*).

Your present author strongly suggests that the curious reader lay their hands on Wilson's *Cosmic Trigger* to find out more about this remarkable man fnord.

■

Grace (Caplinger) Zabriskie, whose father owned the famous French Quarter gay bar, Café Lafitte in Exile, was among a circle of Kerry's New Orleans friends in the early 60s. At one point, Kerry began work on a novel about Grace called *Can Grace Come Out and Play?* It was Grace's sister, Lane Caplinger, who, with Greg Hill, ran off copies of the first edition of the *Principia Discordia* on the office copying machine, when she worked as a secretary for Jim Garrison.

Rumor has it that Grace—well known in the French Quarter as an aspiring poet—was the subject of Bob Dylan's "Like A Rolling Stone," and the lines "You used to be so amused/ At Napoleon in rags and the language that he used" were a reference to Kerry. (It should be noted that Kerry was the favorite waiter of Leander Perez, a powerful New Orleans political boss. Perez—somewhere along the line—dubbed Kerry "Napoleon.")

In the early 70s, Grace appeared in several movies in the Atlanta area in addition to performing in the theater. Her first major movie role was in *Norma Rae* in 1979, and since then she has worked in more than 40 films, among them *Fried Green Tomatoes*, *Drugstore Cowboy* and *Even Cowgirls Get the Blues*. Perhaps her most memorable role was as Laura Palmer's mother, Sara, in David Lynch's *Twin Peaks* television series.

In recent years, Grace has also made a name for herself as a visual artist. Her functional art is on display at the L.A. gallery ArtHaus, a sampling of which can be found at Arthaus.com.

■

The person most responsible for reviving Kerry's career was Ron Bonds of IllumiNet Press. Before starting IllumiNet, Ron—a devotee of the fun and strange alike—ran a record label called EOD (Elvis on Drugs), and was also responsible for starting a spoof religion in the early 80s known far and wide as the Church of Beaver Cleaver. In 1990, Ron decided to try his hand at the publishing biz, and the first book released by IllumiNet was Kerry's *The Idle Warriors*. A couple of years later, IllumiNet published *Zenarchy*, and a new edition of the *Principia Discordia* was being readied for publication just prior to Ron's untimely death in the spring of 2001.[17]

According to Kerry—and others I have talked to—Ron was afraid to publish *Dreadlock Recollections* for fear that it would be hazardous to his health.

■

For a couple of years, I tried emailing Sondra London—otherwise known as "the Erisian Elestria" in certain sectors of the Discordian subculture—although she never responded to my overtures. Somehow I got the impression that Ms. London felt I was competition as a chronicler of the Kerry Thornley legacy, and did not care to share the mantle. After all, it was London who declared—at Kerry's memorial service—that she was his true love and the one chosen to carry on this legacy.

Perhaps Sondra's reluctance to enter into any type of dialogue with your present author was because she considered me part of the—insert creepy organ music here—"conspiracy!" I say this because, at Kerry's memorial service, Ms. London was overheard to say: "Now I realize what Kerry was talking about. Since he died, they're after me too!"[18]

Eventually, though, I was able to contact Sondra with the intent of purchasing a series of videotaped interviews she conducted with Kerry during the period the two were collaborating on *Confessions of a Conspiracy to Assassinate JFK*. (Funny how the prospect of commerce can open up the lines of communication!)

To learn more about the controversial Sondra London, you can navigate to Sondralondon.com, a seemingly odd mixture of post-9/11 patriotism and serial killer groupie-ism, in addition to a fair amount of Kerry Thornley-related material.

Hail, Eris—to the extreme!

Synchronicities a-Plenty!

"When we see repetitious patterns or excessive familiarity (that defies ordinary probability), we call that synchronicity. Quantum scientists call this the 'law of affinity' whereby like attracts like. In other words, you will attract a similar."

—PETER MOON, *The Montauk Pulse*

In the initial stages of researching this book I received a cryptic e-mail from a fellow named Robert Newport informing me of the solemn news of Greg Hill's passing in July 2000.

Since I had no idea who this Newport fellow was, I responded to his e-mail, informing him that I happened to be writing a book about Kerry Thornley, and was wondering if he had known Kerry as well. To this, the mysterious Mr. Newport replied in the affirmative. In fact, Newport informed me that he'd been close friends with Kerry in high school, and had also been a founding member of The Discordian Society.

To this day, it remains a mystery as to why and how Newport knew to contact me. Granted, I helped distribute one of Kerry's final interviews on the Internet and participated in a radio broadcast about Kerry soon after his death, but how Newport knew to contact me at a private e-mail address (not the address I display on my website), remains a mystery. When I later brought this up, Newport himself was unclear as to how he came to contact me. One can only write it off to the mad influence of Goddess Eris.

Similar synchronicities continued to unfold in their own mystifying way, as throughout the course of events Goddess seemed to hover over my reeling head, assisting me in each new step along this crazy path of discovery, which I'd haphazardly stumbled upon. Hail Eris!

Along the way I had the good fortune to interview Robert Anton Wilson, a legendary figure in Discordian/Illuminati lore. Mr. Wilson was the ultimate gentleman, allowing myself and co-conspirator Greg Bishop into his humble abode, and even pouring us a sip of scotch before opening up about his memories of Kerry.

The term "renaissance man" is bandied about far too often these days, but Wilson certainly lives up to that title. Being in the company of the man was likened unto hobnobbing with a genuine Buddha, albeit of the Bavarian Illuminati variety. Also in attendance that magical eve was the aforementioned Dr. Bob Newport, who brought a sampling of his Discordian archives.

During the visit, Newport suggested that I seek out other anomalous Kerry contactees, namely Louise Lacey and Bill Stephens, two humans I had never before heard of. Both Louise and Bill were of immeasurable help in unraveling the mysterious enigma of Kerry Wendell Thornley, and I am eternally grateful to Newport for all his contacts.

And so it was that each new contact led to another, and one door led to several others, and on and on. Things kept falling into my lap by the grace of some gone chick who rules the cosmos in a very chaotic fashion.

■

On Christmas Eve of 2001, my wife and I visited Louise Lacey in the Bay Area. As in the case of all Discordians I've had the good fortune to meet, Louise is another kindly spirit who has evidently been enlightened—in some form or manner—by her interactions with such noble spirits as Mord, Omar, and Mal-2. Previously, Louise sent me a box of rare Discordian archives which included many yellowing letters composed by Kerry, classic correspondence with other Operation Mindfuck conspirators, and a slew of rare Discordian artifacts.

We spent three hours with Louise that day, pouring through her voluminous files in search of articles and Discordian-related correspondence, not to mention some photos she'd taken in the mid-80s of Kerry in her front yard in Berkeley holding a harmonica and looking hobo-holy. Although we discovered several cool Kerry photos from bygone days, the ones with the harmonica were nowhere to be found, as if Eris herself had plucked them from our space-time continuum and deposited them Goddess knows where. Crazy bitch!

At one point in our visit, Louise recounted the time she'd done some research work—on the history of the first drum—for Mickey Hart of the Grateful Dead. During the course of conducting her research at the Berkeley UC Anthropology Library, Louise employed a method of dowsing to assist her in locating pertinent passages related to the history of the drum. She used this method of literary dowsing to save herself endless hours of pouring through multiple shelves dedicated to drum history. (It should be noted that Louise is a somewhat famous figure in the world of dowsing, especially "Power Place Dowsing.") Anyway, Louise demonstrated what she had done at the Berkeley UC Anthropology Library way back when, by running her hands over her own bookshelf, then stopping at a place on the bookshelf where her intuition told her to.

Such as it was, we didn't find the Kerry-with-the-harmonica photo that afternoon, but Louise promised she would continue to seek it. As fickle fate would have it, Louise e-mailed me soon after with the following astounding revelation: "You know where I found the two photos of Kerry? At that place on the bookshelf where my hand ended up when I was telling the story about how I found the piece of information for Hart by dowsing!"

And so it was that synchronicity had struck again, as it did many times throughout the course of my research on the irrepressible Bull Goose of Limbo.

Hail Eris! All hail Discordia!

NOTES

1   *The Idle Warriors* was set aside for almost thirty years until 1991 when Ron Bonds at IllumiNet Press—a publishing house famous for providing a forum for subjects which inhabit the marginal fringe—finally published it.

2   Sometime after writing this, I was granted Discordian Popehood by none other than Lady L., F.A.B. when she presented me with an original Discordian Pope card that had once passed through the very hands of Malaclypse the Younger. When I confided to Lady L. that I wasn't sure if I was ready to accept such an important responsibility as Discordian Popehood, her reply was, in typical Discordian fashion: "You are ready when you say you are." In due time, I did accept this blessed honor, after of course deciding what my Discordian Pope name would be: "The Wrong Reverend Houdini Kundalini, of the Church of Unwavering Indifference." This name pleased Lady L.

3   In the early 1970s, Gordon Novel was involved with Watergate conspirator Charles Colson in a plan to erase portions of President Nixon's Watergate tapes.

4   In 1965, Raymond Broshears was investigated by the Secret Service for having made a threat on President Lyndon Johnson's life, and was briefly taken into custody in November of that year. Under interrogation, Broshears claimed he'd made the threat in order to be placed under protective custody, where he would be safe from unspecified "harassment." Broshears later escaped prosecution by basing his defense on mental illness, which probably wasn't too far from the truth. In 1975, Broshears surfaced once again in the investigation of an assassination attempt on President Gerald Ford in San Francisco.

5   When asked about the possibility that Kerry learned photo engraving from his father, Kerry's brother Dick had this to say: "No, it would be absurd to suggest Kerry learned any part of Dad's trade, or even that he had access to his shop. Tom and I both worked for Dad as delivery boys, at times, but I think I'm the only one who had any idea of how the process even worked. Kerry was exceedingly bright and very artistic. If he really wanted to learn how to doctor photos, etc., I'm sure he could have figured it out on his own."

6   Although John Spencer denied that Shaw and Thornley ever met, in later years Kerry claimed that he *had* met Shaw at Spencer's apartment when he went to retrieve the *Idle Warriors* manuscript he had loaned to Spencer over one weekend.

7   Camden Benares' Discordian alter ego was Felix Pendragon. Felix, as the legend goes, always carried a pen, and in that pen was a joint. So, when somebody asked Camden who Felix Pendragon was, he'd take out the pen, remove the joint, and "drag on" it. (At one time or another, Camden was also known in Discordian circles as the Count of Fives.)

8   PURSE and PUTZ were terms coined by Robert Anton Wilson.

9   The "Playboy Forum" letter hoax appeared in the April 1969 issue of *Playboy*.

10 Another synchronicity connecting The John Dillinger Died For You Society and the Kennedy assassination comes in the form of Guy Banister, who—while with the F.B.I.—participated in the killing of Dillinger at the Biograph Theater. This incident turned Banister into a star agent within the ranks of the bureau, and because of this J. Edgar Hoover promoted him to Special Agent in Charge of the Chicago Office.

11 Following a two-year trial, Clay Shaw was acquitted of all charges, although Garrison claimed governmental interference kept him from effectively prosecuting the case. Afterwards, Shaw retired to his home in New Orleans a "broken man" having depleted his entire fortune in the long legal battle, and was deeply anguished over the disclosure, by Garrison, of his homosexuality. He died of cancer in 1974.

12 E. Howard Hunt once falsified memos for the Nixon administration, which stated that President Kennedy had ordered the assassination of South Vietnamese President Diem—accusations that were patently false and intended to paint a picture of Kennedy as a war-mongering hawk. On the contrary, Kennedy had planned to pull completely out of Vietnam just prior to his death, and many now believe that one of the primary reasons that he was killed was his opposition to the wishes of the Military Industrial Complex.

13 When Louise Lacey read this line, she laughed: "Kerry was *always* uninhibited and talkative."

14 Legend has it that Admiral Donitz was the "secret fuehrer," as documented in the book *Donitz: The Last Fuhrer* by Peter Renfield. In this regard, stories of secret Nazi outposts in Antarctica abounded, including tales of Nazi flying saucers levitating in and out of the Hollow Earth. Many of these rumors suggested that Hitler was alive and well, but maybe in reality it was Admiral Donitz fulfilling the aforementioned role of secret fuehrer in the frozen remoteness of Antarctica.

[15] The exception to Kerry's blue-collar employment record was his stint as managing editor of *The Innovator* in the mid 60s.

[16] As of this writing, *Confession to a Conspiracy* can be found on the Internet at http://www.sondralondon.com/tales/thornley. *Confession to a Conspiracy* is, for the most part, a slight re-working of the manuscript *Dreadlock Recollections*, which Kerry began circulating in the mid-80s.

[17] The official cause of Ron Bonds' death was food poisoning, although conspiracy researcher Kenn Thomas—in a soon-to-be-released revised edition of his book *The Octopus*—speculates that the deaths of Bonds and *Octopus* co-author Jim Keith may have been the result of a conspiracy.

[18] A reliable source informed me that Kerry thought Sondra London was "crazy." To this, I responded: "That's the pot calling the kettle cracked!"

SOURCES

PRIMARY SOURCES

Lady L, F.A.B.'s Discordian archives, provided courtesy of Louise Lacey.

The Rev. Hypocrates Magoun's Discordian archives, provided courtesy of Dr. Robert Newport.

Gregory Hill's archives, courtesy of Dr. Robert Newport.

House Select Committee on Assassination Files, obtained through FOIA request.

New Orleans Grand Jury Testimony of Kerry Thornley for the Garrison Investigation.

"Memoranda concerning my knowledge of Kerry Thornley's association with Lee Harvey Oswald" by Buddy Allen Simco, dated October 17, 1978.

Kerry Thornley's affidavits, correspondence and other writings, dated mid-60s through the early 90s and acquired through various sources, including the aforementioned Discordian archives of Louise Lacey, Bob Newport, and Gregory Hill.

Correspondence between Kerry Thornley and the author, compiled throughout the 1990s.

INTERVIEWS

Sylvia Bortin, February 4, 2003

John F. Carr, May 20, 2002

Becky Glaser, February 27, 2002

Louise Lacey, August 13, September 24, and December 19, 2001; July 28, 2002; January 2, 2003.

Beth Lavoie, February 5, 2003

David Lifton, May 29, 2002

Bob Newport, July 9, 2001; April 4, 2002

John Paccasassi, March 4 and 8, 2003

Frank Reiss, December 12, 2002

Allen (Bud) Simco, February 12 and 17, 2003

Bill Stephens, August 29, 2001

Dick Thornley, e-mail correspondence and phone interviews, beginning December 21, 2001, through Spring 2003

Christopher Wilhoite, e-mail correspondence, February 2003

Robert Anton Wilson, July 9, 2001; February 5, 2003

Grace Zabriskie, e-mail correspondence, March through May 2003

OTHER SOURCES

Adler, Margot, *Drawing Down the Moon; Witches, Druids, Goddess-Worshippers, and Other Pagans in America Today* (Penguin Books, 1986).

Benares, Camden, *Zen Without Zen Masters* (New Falcon Publications, 1990).

Biles, Joe G., *In History's Shadow: Lee Harvey Oswald, Kerry Thornley and the Garrison Investigation* (Writer's Club Press, 2002).

Canfield, Michael L. and Alan J. Weberman, *Coup d'Etat in America: The CIA and the Assassination of John F. Kennedy* (Third Press, 1975).

Epstein, Edward Jay, *Counterplot* (Viking Press, 1969).

Fensterwald Jr., Bernard, *Assassination of JFK by Coincidence or Conspiracy?* (Zebra Books, 1977).

Haslam, Edward T., *Mary, Ferrie and The Monkey Virus: The Story of an Underground Medical Laboratory* (Wordsworth Communications 1995).

Keith, Jim, *Mass Control: Engineering Human Consciousness* (IllumiNet Press, 1999).

Klatch, Rebecca E., *A Generation Divided: The New Left, The New Right, and the 1960's* (University of California Press, Berkeley, 1999).

Lincoln, Lawrence, *Were We Controlled?* (University Books, Inc., 1967).

Malaclypse the Younger, *Principia Discordia* (Loomponics Unlimited).

Marchetti, Victor and John D. Marks, *The CIA and the Cult Of Intelligence* (Alfred A. Knopf, 1974).

Popkin, Peter , *The Second Oswald* (Avon Books, 1966).

Thornley, Kerry, "Is Paranoia a Form Of Awareness?" from *Secret and Suppressed*, edited by Jim Keith (Feral House, 1993).

Thornley, Kerry, *Oswald* (New Classics House, 1965).

Thornley, Kerry, *Zenarchy* (IllumiNet Press, 1991).

Thornley, Kerry, *Idle Warriors* (IllumiNet Press, 1991).

Wilgus, Neal, *The Illuminoids: Secret Societies & Political Paranoia* (Sun Publishing, 1978).

Wilson, Robert Anton, *Cosmic Trigger Volume One: The Final Secret of the Illuminati* (New Falcon Publications, 1993).

Wilson, Robert Anton with Miriam Joan Hill, *Everything Is Under Control: Conspiracies, Cults, and Coverups* (Harper Collins, 1998).

Wilson, Robert Anton and Robert Shea, *The Illuminatus* trilogy (Dell, 1975).

Vankin, Jonathan, *Conspiracies, Cover-ups and Crimes: Political Manipulation and Mind Control in America* (Paragon House, 1991).

WEBSITES

"Inside The Garrison Investigation"—The Thomas Bethell Diary
http://mcadams.posc.mu.edu/bethell1.htm

"Adventures in Propinquity: The Case of Jim Garrison" by Joe B. Giles
http://www.wf.net/~biles/jfk/

"Confession to a Conspiracy" by Kerry Thornley
http://www.sondralondon.com/tales/thornley/

"From Underground to Internet: The *Principia Discordia*"
http://husky1.stmarys.ca/~discord/intro.htm

History Matters Archives-Kerry Thornley
http://history-matters.com/archive/jfk/garr/
grandjury/Thornley/ html/Thornley_0001a.htm

Jim Garrison's New Orleans Photo Gallery
http://www.jfk-online.com/jgphotosmisc.html

False Witness: Aptly Titled by Jim Eugenio and Bill Davy
http://www.webcom.com/ctka/pr599-lambert.html

Principia Discordia
http://mindcontrolforums.com/hambone/body.html

Small Lies, Big Lies and Outright Whoppers
http://mcadams.posc.mu.edu/jimlie.htm

ACKNOWLEDGMENTS

Thanks to:

Bob Newport for being the catalyst who helped launch this mad quest. Without his aid and abetment, who knows what would have become of it all.

Bob Wilson for initiating me as a high priest of the Bavarian Illuminati.

Louise Lacey for her generosity, good humor, and support. Thanks for dinner, too!

Allen Simco for dishwashing recollections delivered over a tapped line.

Dick Thornley for providing innumerable pieces of the puzzle.

Grace Zabriskie for her straightforward responses, and to her daughter, Marion, for sharing the past.

Bill Stephens and Sylvia Bortin for a glimpse of Kerry as a teenager.

My wife, Heather, for her editorial input.

Greg Bishop for recording a conversation that was abducted by the Office of Information Awareness and analyzed by Naval Intelligence before the tape finally ended up in my mailbox several months after it was sent!

Becky Glaser for memories of banana peels and urban revolution.

John F. Carr for his "pot and plot" memories of Camden Benares.

Tim Cridland for some photos of Kerry in L5P.

Kenn Thomas of *SteamShovel Press* for so many things that I've already forgotten half of them.

Rev. Ivan Stang of the Church of the SubGenius for a photo of Kerry with a chair.

Greg Krupey for sharing his yellowing Thorneylean correspondence of yore.

Kevin Belford for a dub of the *Current Affair* videotape.

Frank Reiss for his tales of MIBs haunting the finer eateries of L5P.

Barbara Joye, Chris Wilhoite, Beth Lavoie, and John Paccasassi for further L5P memories.

Tom Reisinger of *Soldier of Fortune* magazine for helping me with some background checks.

For those of you I've forgotten, a self-inflicted lash with a wet noodle is now being administered. (Actually, it feels kinda good...)

A Partial List of Discordian Conspirators

(in alphabetical disorder)

Judith Abrahms: (Discordian name withheld)

Camden Benares: Felix Pendragon, the Count of Fives

Slim Brooks: Keeper of the Submarine Keys

Gregory Hill: Malaclypse the Younger, Ignotum P. Ignotious, Rev. Dr. Occupant, Professor Iggy, Mad Malik, Mal-2

Stan Jamison: Coman Ra – Lt. Colonel, Commanding 1st Intergalactic Confederacy Advance Detail—Planet Shan

Alan Kishbaugh: The Earl of Nines

Louise Lacey: Lady L., F.A.B.

Roger Lovin: Fang the Unwashed

Bob McElroy: Mungo

Thomas Patrick McNamara: Thomas the Gnostic, Rev. Pope Thomas the First

Bob Newport: Rev. Hypocrates Magoun

Onrak the Backwards (real name unknown)

John Paccasassi: San Juan Bautista

Tim Wheeler: Harold Lord Randomfactor

Bob and Yvonne Shea: Josh the Dill and Bonnie Buns

Kerry Thornley: Omar Khayyam Ravenhurst, Ho Chi Zen, the
    Bull Goose of Limbo, Rev. Jesse Sump

Robert Anton Wilson: Mordecai Malignatus, Mordecai the Foul

Barbara Reid: The Goddess Eris

Images

Thornley's senior class picture, 1957.

Greg Hill's senior class picture, 1959.

The cover of Apocalypse: A Trade Journal for Doom Prophets, published by Greg Hill and Kerry Thornley in 1960.
(Courtesy of the Rt. Rev. Dr. Hypocrates Magoun M.D.)

(Courtesy of the Rt. Rev. Dr. Hypocrates Magoun M.D.)

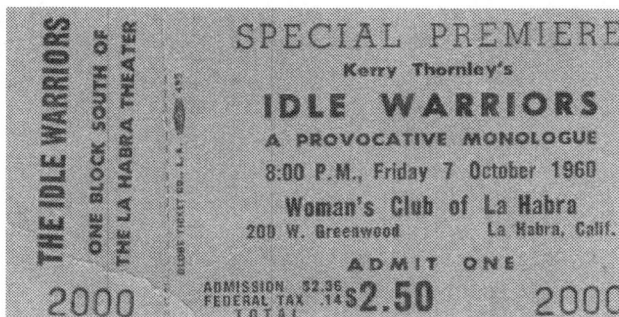

SPECIAL PREMIERE

Kerry Thornley's

IDLE WARRIORS

A PROVOCATIVE MONOLOGUE

8:00 P.M., Friday 7 October 1960

Woman's Club of La Habra
200 W. Greenwood   La Habra, Calif.

ADMIT ONE

ADMISSION $2.36
FEDERAL TAX .14 $2.50
TOTAL

2000   2000

THE IDLE WARRIORS

ONE BLOCK SOUTH OF
THE LA HABRA THEATER

Of this photo, published in *Open City* magazine, Harold Weisberg had the following to say: "A flower in the mouth of Kerry Thornley is as appropriate as the word 'love' in the mouth of a whore!"

Greg Hill, a few weeks before he died. At the time he told Louise Lacey: "I am a dead man walking." (Courtesy of Rt. Rev. Dr. Hypocrates Magoun M.D.)

Sacred Chao
(Courtesy of the Rt. Rev. Dr. Hypocrates Magoun M.D.)

Discordian propaganda distributed by Bob Wilson circa late 60s/early 70s.
(Courtesy of the Rt. Rev. Dr. Hypocrates Magoun, M.D.)

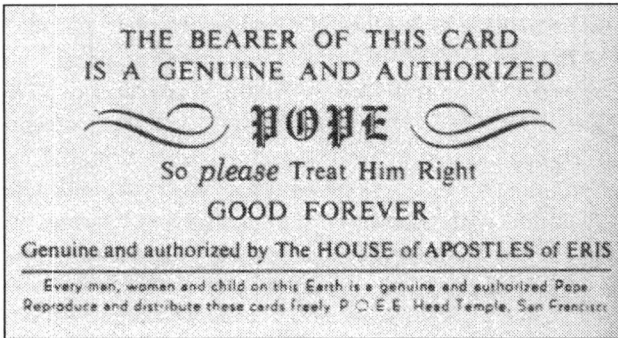

THE BEARER OF THIS CARD
IS A GENUINE AND AUTHORIZED

POPE

So *please* Treat Him Right

GOOD FOREVER

Genuine and authorized by The HOUSE of APOSTLES of ERIS

Every man, woman and child on this Earth is a genuine and authorized Pope
Reproduce and distribute these cards freely P.O.E.E. Head Temple, San Francisco

A Discordian membership card circulated by Hill and Thornley.
(Courtesy of the Rt. Rev. Dr. Hypocrates Magoun, M.D.)

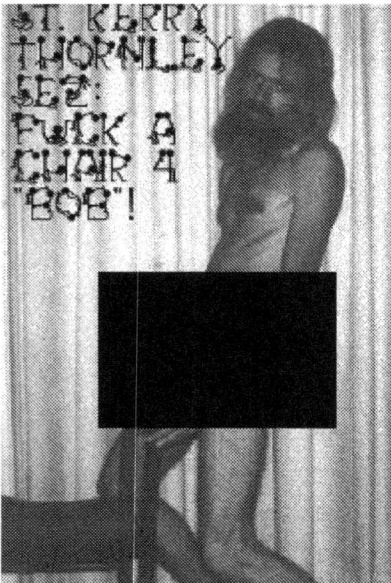

"Kerry had a love in his heart for all
things, even chairs." (From the collection
of Rev. Ivan Stang.)

Kerry in Little Five Points during the
summer of 1992.
(Photo courtesy of Tim Cridland.)

Robert Anton Wilson, 1978.
(Courtesy of Robert Anton Wilson.
All rights reversed.)

Photo of Louise Lacey by Faith Echtermeyer.
(Courtesy of Louise Lacey.)

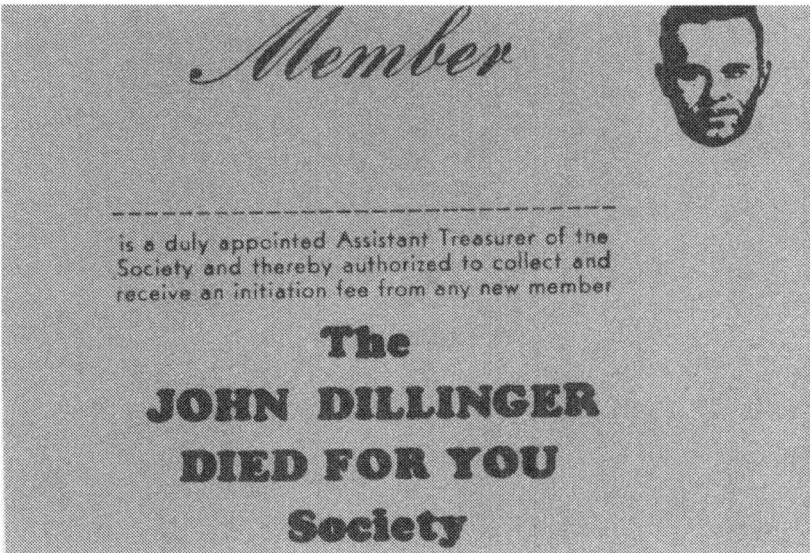

Membership card for the John Dillinger Died for You Society.
(Courtesy of the Rt. Rev. Dr. Hypocrates Magoun, M.D.)

THE PRANKSTER AND THE CONSPIRACY

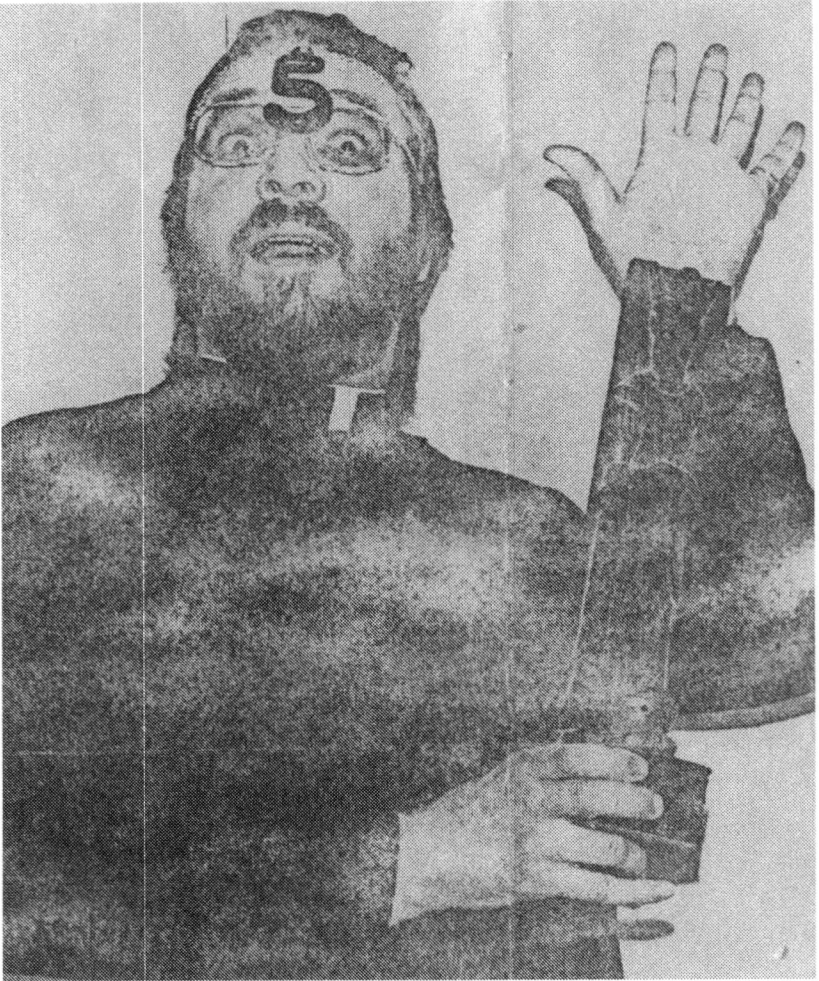

Camden Benares, The Count of Fives.
(Courtesy of the Rt. Rev. Dr. Hypocrates Magoun, M.D.)

THE PRANKSTER AND THE CONSPIRACY

Discordian propaganda distributed by Greg Hill in 1975.
(Courtesy of the Rt. Rev. Dr. Hypocrates Magoun, M.D.)

A Greg Hill collage.
(Courtesy of the Rt. Rev. Dr. Hypocrates Magoun M.D.)

www.ingramcontent.com/pod-product-compliance
Lightning Source LLC
Chambersburg PA
CBHW031945080426
42735CB00007B/268